FAITH AND KNOWLEDGE

A Critical Inquiry

Paul Giurlanda, F.S.C.

UNIVERSITY
PRESS OF
AMERICA

LANHAM • NEW YORK • LONDON

Copyright © 1987 by

Paul Giurlanda, F.S.C.

University Press of America,® Inc.

4720 Boston Way
Lanham, MD 20706

3 Henrietta Street
London WC2E 8LU England

British Cataloging in Publication Information Available

Library of Congress Cataloging in Publication Data

Giurlanda, Paul, 1946-
  Faith and knowledge.

  Bibliography: p.
  1. Faith and reason.   2. Gadamer, Hans Georg,
1900-   .   I. Title.
BT50.G45   1987   231'.042   86-26627
ISBN 0-8191-5759-7 (alk. paper)
ISBN 0-8191-5760-0 (pbk. : alk. paper)

In memory of

Ann Giurlanda

TABLE OF CONTENTS

Author's Preface

Many years ago, in the city of Detroit, at St. Juliana's Grammar School, conducted by the Servite Sisters, a boy was required to memorize a short prayer from the Baltimore Catechism known as the "Act of Faith." At the time the prayer disturbed him with its odd circularity. He thought it puzzling, even dishonest, to believe things, including the existence and trustworthiness of God, on the word of that same God, "who could neither deceive nor be deceived." This book might be regarded as a dialogue between a man and that boy.

To speak somewhat more prosaically, I would like to acknowledge that this manuscript was written as a doctoral dissertation at the Graduate Theological Union in Berkeley, and has, as one might expect, many godparents. The problematic of the book began to emerge during concurrent seminars, one by Robert N. Bellah and the other by David Stagaman, SJ. In both, rather improbably, Hans-Georg Gadamer was central. I wish to thank David Stagaman for his willingness to tell me things I needed to hear when I didn't want to hear them; to Betty Over, Registrar of the GTU, for her legendary unfailing kindness; to Norman Cook, FSC, and the Brothers of the San Francisco District of the Christian Brothers for the financial and emotional support necessary to complete this project; and to Timothy McCarthy, FSC, head of the Religious Studies Department at St. Mary's College of California, for his understanding and help. None of these people should be blamed for the remaining weaknesses of this study.

Paul Giurlanda, FSC
St. Mary's College of California
Moraga

Preface to Faith and Knowledge
by Paul Giurlanda

by
Robert N. Bellah

Paul Giurlanda has written a book with the paradoxical thesis that faith is the non-foundational foundation of our common life. "Non-foundational" is here used in the technical sense which denies that there is any scientifically certain basis for life or even for scientific inquiry itself. "Foundation" is here used in the common sense that faith is the indispensable basis for any common endeavor, even that of science itself. Far from being an expression of modern irrationalism this position has been argued with increasing sophistication in philosophy generally and the philosophy of science in particular as Giurlanda shows in Chapter 1. But Giurlanda's particular contribution is to link this fascinating development within philosophy to issues in contemporary theology. This he does largely with the help of Hans-Georg Gadamer, whose importance for the argument is such that originally Giurlanda gave his book the sub-title of "A Gadamerian Inquiry."

This book can be recommended for its exposition of Gadamer's often dense and difficult thought, particularly if Gadamer is as important to all the current problems in the human studies (both social sciences and humanities) as I believe. But it is much more than that. It clarifies and extends the Gadamerian analysis by applying it extensively to the Christian community, something Gadamer himself has never done. And most important of all, through this application to Christianity Giurlanda makes the general point that faith, knowledge, and community are so inextricablly interconnected that no one of these three can be understood without the other two. The implication, which only reinforces a growing conviction of my own, is that theology, philosophy and sociology are much more inextricably related than we have for a long time thought. Habits of the Heart, which is certainly sociological, has been called at the same time public philosophy and even public sociology. Though the connection may not seem obvious, this book it seems to me gives the justification for such simultaneous attributions to a single work.

This is not the place to attempt an exposition of Giurlanda's central argument, especially since his Introduction does such a good job in that regard. Rather in this brief preface I would like to call attention particularly to Chapter 4 on scripture, in many ways a pivotal chapter in the book. It is certainly true that not all theological works need a major scriptural reference, though some current trends in theology would think the burden of proof would rest in the question why not. But Giurlanda's concern for the central disclosive events of Christian history that are at once the basis of Christian faith, knowledge, and community, makes an extensive treatment of scripture indispensable. In a chapter that is modest and claims little originality the exegesis is remarkably fresh and compelling. This it seems to me is due to the frame of reference in which it is undertaken. Because of the questions he asks Giurlanda's exegesis is scholarly without being archaeological, concerned witht he authority of the text for the community without a hint of inerrantism. Chapter 6 on tradition, though necessarily more diffuse because of its submject matter, has much the same freshness for the same reason.

Giurlanda's modest use of Tracy and Hauerwas in the last chapter should not cause us to over look the fact that the argument, though consonant with many authorities, is his own- a signally helpful effort in the recovery of a vital understanding of faith, knowledge, and community. It deserves a wide and attentive audience.

Introduction: A View of the Terrain

Faith, we are told, seeks to understand. What *we* seek to understand, however, is faith itself, or rather, the faith of the followers of Jesus. The word was not created by them, of course. In the Greek of early Christian times, there was already something called *pistis*, trust in the word of a witness. One had *faith* because one had not seen for oneself. But Christians did place the act of believing a messenger's "good news" in the center of their existence. Stated baldly, the Christian claim that one not only *can* but *should* base one's fate on the bare word of a person speaking in the market place has always seemed outrageous to some. How can one be expected to change one's life on such flimsy grounds? Would one not do better to seek for knowledge, or at least to guide oneself by one's own carefully considered opinion?

But this statement of the issue is already a sort of interpretation, an interpretation from the point of view of a skeptical observer. From the point of view of the early witnesses and those who received their message, however, the situation was quite different. Flesh and blood the early preachers surely were, but the message they carried was not. It was the very word of God. Thus, while it would certainly be absurd to entrust one's life to Paul or Peter, or James or John, it would be the worst kind of absurdity not to entrust oneself to God, once God had decided to give a word of hope. That faith is in some sense certain (paradoxical as this may sound), because it is based on the testimony of the only God, has been the unbroken teaching of the Christian tradition for two thousand years.

But if Christians have insisted for all this time on the centrality of faith, they have not been unaware of the doubt which seems to be its inevitable counterpart. The fairly modern notion of "motives for faith" seems to have some ancestry in Paul's passionate plea to the Galatians: "Did you experience so many things in vain?--if it really is in vain. Does

1

he who supplies the Spirit to you and works miracles among you do so by works of the law, or by hearing with faith?" (3:4,5). One could imagine Moses saying something similar to the Jews after the Exodus. Here, without losing its paradoxical quality, faith is seen as the precondition for the experience of new life. While there are no real grounds for faith, faith is easily enough shown as itself the ground for salvation. Though this is a theme which can be found through the New Testament, in the Pauline letters, in the magnificent passages of the Johannine literature, and in the synoptics, perhaps it is enough for the moment to point to the dominical saying in Mark: "All things are possible to him who believes." (9:23).

An emphasis on the seeming absurdity of faith has been especially strong in the Protestant tradition, and since Barth's rediscovery of Kierkegaard, has gained added vigor. But, of course, the stronger the emphasis on the scandal of faith, the greater is the corresponding problem of doubt. The Catholic tradition, meanwhile, while not denying the fact of faith's graced character, has nevertheless attempted to show that faith is at least not an irrational posture. While no one can be logically argued into faith, one can be shown that faith is not *opposed* to logic and to reason. Catholic attempts to do natural theology often seem, however, either to prove the unproveable, or, by the very gap between proof and faith to leave us hanging in mid-air.

There are at least two presuppositions which keep both Protestants and Catholics from understanding more fully what faith is. The first is that for both, faith must be carefully distinguished from knowledge. It seems self- evident to all that, if faith is to be seen as the gift which the New Testament insists it is, it must be carefully distinguished from what we can achieve "on our own", as it were, i.e., knowledge of the world. The second is that for both, faith is an act in the life of a single individual. Again, it seems self- evident that the most important thing about faith is that it is the graced yet free decision of some individual to believe in the revelation of God on the ground of God's trustworthiness. Both of these presuppositions seem well-attested in the New Testament and in the tradition. Nevertheless, these notions require examination. At worst, they can make faith seem like an unintelligible, absurd, and isolated event in the life of a person, having little to do with what went before, and directing what goes after only in an external way.

We need an account of faith, knowledge and community which will show their essential interrelationship, and yet preserve the gratuity of faith. Such an account would also help to confront the strident demand of modernity that all beliefs present themselves before the bar of reason. If we can develop an account of faith which shows that the kind of knowledge which we regard as "hard" or "certain" or "rigorous" is itself only intelligible against the background of a community of knowledge in which we already have implicit faith, we may begin to see that some of the dichotomies which have been giving us trouble will dissolve. Knowledge at its core may wind up having much more in common with faith, grace and community history than we previously thought. But if we are not going to collapse the Christian revelation into a general account of "human nature", we will have to show that Christian revelation is *both* unique *and* representative of humankind at its best.

What we suggest, then, is to see faith as the *way of being* of a community, characterizing and constituting not just Christian community, but any community. Thus modernity's characteristic preoccupation--the attempt to found all knowledge through a method of doubt and experiment open in principle to any rational mind--must itself be subjected to critique. Our first task, then, will be to show that foundationalism (or "objectivism") is itself problematic, and that there are viable alternatives to a notion of truth which equates it with what can be established by technique. If we can show that this is true for human community in general, we will be able to see why the forms of foundationalism which have arisen with modernity in the Christian community (in Catholicism, the stress on individual, infallible dogmas; in Protestantism, the emphasis on inerrant truths contained in the scriptures) are actually *opposed* to the deepest springs of the Christian religion. Such a ground-clearing enterprise

3

would have to demonstrate that the critique of foundationalism is not only a live option in the world of contemporary philosophy, but, more than that, is something about which several otherwise diverse currents of thought can agree. If we can show, for example, that philosophers of science (like Michael Polanyi, Thomas Kuhn, Stephen Toulmin) are in increasing revolt against the positivistic and mechanistic world view represented by LaPlace; if we can show that moral philosophers like Alasdair MacIntyre can argue quite convincingly against the prevailing emotivist notions of moralists; and if we can show that these two otherwise diverse schools of scholarship point to the necessity of a community of shared values and perceptions underlying all critical inquiry, then we will have gone a ways toward validating our central thesis. We will have shown, in other words, that faith, knowledge and community are best understood together.

We can, however, do more than this. Philosophers like those mentioned above are basically writing in an Anglo-American cultural context. We wish to argue, however, that the thought of Martin Heidegger, his critique of present- at-hand knowledge, his recognition of the pre-understanding behind any inquiry, and his insistence on the centrality of language, are vitally important for our inquiry, and that the work of Hans-Georg Gadamer, Heidegger's student, will be our best guide along the path thus opened up. In other words, our basic philosophical problematic will be provided for by Gadamer's Truth and Method. More than anyone else, we will contend, Gadamer has shown how faith, knowledge and community interpenetrate, even though he does not use those words.

What Gadamer will show us, we claim, is the need to retrieve the ancient tradition of practical wisdom, what Aristotle called *phronesis* and what Aquinas referred to as the intellectual virtue of *prudentia*.

Though *prudentia* has remained alive in Western culture, as Gadamer shows, partially through the tradition of rhetoric, it has been increasingly sundered from the intellectual life.

Aristotle's brilliant phenomenology of prudence in the <u>Ethics</u> and the <u>Politics</u> was linked with an elevation of "contemplation" to the highest rank of knowledge. The precise interrelation of *phronesis* and *theoria* in Aristotle is not completely clear, and it is not even clear what *exactly* theoria is. But it is clear that Western culture has turned theoria into scientific knowledge, "objective," certain fact, and has forgotten prudence. Once the facts are known, what need for deliberation? Prudence, connoisseurship, and human judgment seem to be outmoded. Of the three classical forms of knowledge: *theoria, techne*, and *praxis*, the first has been increasingly collapsed into the second, and the third regarded as a necessary evil soon to be eliminated when computers are better programmed.

Against the contemporary elevation of technology to the center of the stage, we will argue, with Gadamer, for a *communal context of knowing.* Technologism is another example of a human temptation to seek an exactitude and certainty which are not human, and not possible. It is at this point that we will have to do with an objection from the left wing. The emphasis on the interrelationship among faith, knowledge and community can be seen as a retrieval of a liberating truth about being human, a truth which frees us from the tyranny of machine intelligence controlling our lives, a happy return to quality after the reign of quantity. The danger, of course, is that we will hand ourselves over to uncritical romanticism, and that an uncritical romanticism may hand us over to something much worse. Not for nothing, say the critics, were the ages of faith also ages of witch-burning and intolerance. Any attempt to heal the divisions in the human psyche between fact and value, faith and knowledge, individual and community, is going to have to deal with the Enlightenment critique of tradition. The heavy emphasis on the "social construction of reality" (in Peter Berger's phrase) is open to the charge that a community and its speech may be corrupt and oppressive. Marx and Freud and Nietzsche have shown how the knowledge which is handed on by the tradition of the community may actually be a cover-up for domination of one class by another. Without objective verifiability apart from human approval, apart from the word of authority, how can we be sure that we are not being deluded?

5

This question goes to the heart of our project. It is comparatively easy to decry the dehumanizing effects on society of technologism, the sundering of fact from value, and so forth. But unless we deal with the *reasons* why so many would prefer the dehumanizing future of science to a community of traditional values, we will be engaging in cheap nostalgia. When the Enlightenment thinkers turned their backs on tradition, supernaturalism and religious faith, they did so because a century of "religious" warfare had thoroughly discredited, in their eyes at least, the religious beliefs for which both sides had fought. Since Christians killed each other in the name of belief, it seemed that the only solution would be to give up beliefs which couldn't be empirically proven, or at least not to impose one's "over-beliefs" on others. Beliefs which failed the test of empirical proof had to be given up. Doubt, rather than trust, had to be the order of the day, if human beings were to survive.

The remarkable successes of "the scientific method" (or what was perceived to be the scientific method) only made the revolt against tradition all the more prestigious. Faith increasingly looked like the heavy hand of the past. At its worst, it concealed oppression. At its best, it was a brake on progress, which increasingly was linked with methodical doubt, science, and movements for social justice. Is it possible to argue for tradition and faith without bad faith?

Precisely because of our heavy emphasis on the communal context of knowing, we must deal with the criticism that a community and its speech may be corrupt, and that the only way out of this dilemma is some sort of objective criterion of verifiability, whether formal or material. Such a criterion, if it could be found, would enable us to critique the tradition, holding on to what is valuable and discarding what is not. It seems to be the prerequisite for progress. Without it, there is no Archimedean point, and the world remains unmoved. For us there is no Archimedean point, whether in the heavens or on the earth, no criterion with which to judge the tradition from outside the tradition. Obviously, this contention needs something more than assertion. Perhaps the classic debate here

6

remains that between Jurgen Habermas, an important representative of the Frankfurt school of sociology of knowledge, and Gadamer. The debate between Gadamer and Habermas is a debate about *doubt* which will help us clarify the nature of *faith*. Siding with Gadamer, we will claim that any critique of the past, of one's own tradition, presupposes a number of things, among them being a trust that the community has the capacity to be an honest and receptive audience.

There are, in other words, already values and principles to appeal to in the argument, or there would be no argument. The revulsion, for example, felt by the Enlightenment against the spectacle of Christians killing each other in the name of Christ, is revolting precisely because of the nature of Christ's gentle teaching. The irony is only visible to those who believe that fraternal love rather than, say, holy war, is of the essence of religion. Similarly, doubt can only show up *as* doubt against the context of something taken for granted as obvious, i.e., taken on faith. Far from being provable by scientific method, what is "obvious" in a community is usually *so* obvious that it doesn't come up for questioning, but rather remains as the horizon of questions.

What will emerge from our discussion of the inter-relationship of faith, knowledge, and community, we hope, is the conviction that *any* community, to be a community at all, is possessed of an unspoken mutual giving-over, a basic trust, the alternative being a kind of chaos below the level of the brutes. We will claim, then, that faith can helpfully be seen not simply as the possession of an individual in relationship to other individuals or to the ground of being, but rather, as the communal possession of any group, from chess club to the United Nations. Faith is the very *fact* of a community. But there are surely differences among communities, different kinds and degrees of faith, and so faith is also helpfully seen as the *style* of a community. In other words, faith not only *constitutes* a community, it also *characterizes* each one in its own way.

If this anthropology of the group, sketchy as it is, nevertheless provides us with a plausible account of the relationships between our three key concepts, then perhaps we are enabled to reach the explicitly theological part of our project. If faith constitutes and characterizes human community--any human community--then what can be said of the kind of faith which constitutes the community of the followers of Jesus of Nazareth?

In order to deal with the question of *Christian* faith and *Christian* community, we must make the leap from the implicit faith which grounds all community to the explicitation of that faith which marks religious community. The question of faith which arises every day for individuals and communities is the question of faith vs. despair, suicide vs. life, going on vs. refusal to go on. In all probability, a crisis of confidence in a group of chess players in their club is not what we are talking about, because such a crisis would probably not reveal the hidden presuppositions of mutual trust. Of course, it *could* do that, but the odds are that a community which explicitly and self-consciously uses religious language will be necessary for the question of faith to arise in the horizon of human beings. The question of faith, as we are calling it, is not the question of whether this or that aspect of my life may be trusted, or whether this or that project may be continued. It is rather the hidden question of whether *anything* may be trusted at all, whether *any* project may profitably be continued.

It may seem odd to raise the issue of religious community vs. a community which is not religious, since historically all cultures and all languages contain religious concepts. It is certainly not the case, as far as we can tell, that communities start off without religious language and then proceed to develop it; as far as we can tell, religious language is co-eval with language. Nevertheless, the possibility of a truly non-religious culture arises, perhaps for the first time, in our own age, and it must be dealt with honestly, even if we tend to regard it on our part as (almost literally) a contradiction in terms.

We claim, then, that religious language serves the function within a community of dealing with the question of *whether* and *how* we should go on, not just today, but for all the tomorrows we can concretely imagine; our stance, as it were, toward going on itself.

But, as has often been commented upon, there is no such thing as "religious language" in general. There is only Christian language, Buddhist language, Jewish language. The language of the Christian community centers around the memory of the death and resurrection of Jesus, but also includes the story of Jesus' life, his teachings and his friends, as well as a rich tradition accumulated over the span of the centuries. It is a story, chiefly, about the way the man Jesus faced his death, with fear and trembling but also with courage and trust, and about how what happened after his death can give us the courage to deal with our own fears and our own selfishness in the face of mystery and death. It is a memory which will be discovered in the way Christians talk, how they act, and how they talk about how they act. It is part of their social reality, the style and fabric of their lives. It is the memory which forms the tradition and the conversation which they not only *have* but *are*.

In order to develop a theologically sensitive account of the way in which the Christian community interprets the Jesus story, the Jesus tradition, and in so doing constitutes itself as the people of the Jesus tradition-- Christians--we will continue to make use of the insights of Gadamer, especially his seminal concept of *openness*. Gadamer, however, has not written explicitly on theological issues. We will have to call upon a theologian who has taken some of Gadamer's basic insights and applied them to the task of illuminating Christian theology. Such a theologian, whose debt to Gadamer is obvious and freely acknowledged, is David Tracy. In his discussion of the *classic*, Tracy will help us to see just *how* faith is revealed in the Christian community. Tracy's interest, however, is almost exclusively in formal issues. In his own terms, he is a foundational theologian. Since what we are doing here is basically foundational theology, he should be of special help to us. Still, the thrust of our argument leads to us very much

9

to the concrete. So we must not be content with stating formal principles. What we must do is to find people who are engaging in the theological enterprise from a perspective congruent with ours. And by theological enterprise we mean not the enterprise of providing philosophical descriptions or justifications, but the enterprise of actually making use of the Christian tradition to illuminate the issues confronting the Christian community.

And so we want to find a theologian, a dialogue partner, who is actually doing the kind of theology for which we are calling. A theologian who answers this description is Stanley Hauerwas. We will claim that one can gather from Hauerwas' essays on moral issues facing the Christian community something like the notion of faith which we are advocating. Put simply: by setting Tracy and Hauerwas in some kind of dialogue with each other, we can continue to correct and flesh out our own developing understanding of faith as the foundation and style of a particular community, in our case, the Christian community.

The last sentence reveals a problem which is a major concern of Tracy and, to a lesser extent, of Hauerwas. The concern is, how does one relate the particularity of Christian commitments to those of other communities? Without "objective" truth, is each community's affirmation to be regarded as equally valid, or worse, arbitrary? To an extent this problem will be dealt with in our discussion of Gadamer and Habermas, but as we face the concrete issues of life in this community, we must ask again what distinguishes "Christian" faith from all other forms of explicit religious faith. What we wish to say is that in Christianity, the implicit faith of *all* communities is clearly unveiled in the life and death of Jesus. Dialogue with other religious communities is possible and fruitful because we all finally face the mystery together as people who are only human, grasped by the mystery but never grasping it. At the heart of the project of this paper is, one hopes, a profound humility, literally a closeness to the earth, and to its people.

What we are moving toward in this analysis, then, may be stated in a tentative way as follows: truth is hidden in the language and practice of a community; the truth revealed and yet concealed (through sinfulness) in the community of Jesus is the truth about faith. In its continuing play with the memory of Jesus (in worship, in preaching, in word and deed), the community discovers itself as a place where faith is unveiled, where the courage to go on is celebrated and affirmed, and where the way to go on is shown. The community discovers itself as a place were faith works itself out in a hope and love which are the hope and love of Jesus. The story of Jesus, then, as played out in the community, brings us again and again to where we always in some sense already are: to the place of mystery--unexplainable, uncontrollable, but freeing and inspiriting. Theology in this account is not then a science of timeless and inerrant truths universally valid, but what Edward Farley has called theology/*habitus*--a kind of practical wisdom which helps the community to understand how the memory of Jesus needs to be applied at each new, unpredictable stage in the journey of the community. For, as Gadamer insists, it is only in the *application* that we know what something means. The meaning of the life of Jesus is discovered anew, then, each time it casts light on the path in front of us.

Chapter One
Foundationalism: Attacks and Alternatives

The purpose of this chapter is to give a critique of the account of knowledge called variously foundationalism, objectivism, absolutism, etc. It is an account which, as we have already suggested, has proven unhelpful, or even harmful to a rich understanding of faith, the subject of our inquiry. Along with describing objectivism and its inadequacies, we will offer several alternatives to it from several different schools of thought. The alternative which we will develop as our own, and that of Heidegger and Gadamer, is rooted in a tradition which in many ways is ancient, looking at times to Aristotle, to Augustine, and to Kierkegaard as forebears, and including the many different kinds of thinkers labelled "existentialists." In this chapter, however, we will deliberately exclude from our purview writers clearly associated with existentialism. We do this to show that the attack on objectivism can be mounted *apart from* the continental thinkers whom we will follow, and is therefore not the narrow position of an isolated group fleeing irresponsibly from the demands of a scientific culture.

Of course, if we could call up philosophers of science, preferably men who have actually practiced science, as defenders of our case, so much the better. And this is precisely what we can do. By employing the thought of philosophers of science like Stephen Toulmin and Michael Polanyi, or the chief critic of computer intelligence today, Hubert Dreyfus, we will not be accused of skirting the hard questions. If foundationalism does not work in physics, then, *a fortiori*, it is bankrupt in the human sciences. Our practice in this chapter, then, will be to go from somewhat conservative attacks on foundationalism (Toulmin) through those which are willing to take the argument further (Polanyi, Dreyfus). Finally, we will conclude the discussion with a look at Alasdair MacIntyre, an ethician, who will deal with the questions only implied in the work of the other men.

I. Stephen Toulmin: Intelligence as Evolutionary

It is important to understand that foundationalism is a *response to a problem*, a problem as old as human thought. It is the skeptical or cynical position that the conversation is rigged right from the start; that those who are richer or stronger or more skilled in argumentation, or more forceful in personality are the ones who will always triumph. Thus what happens in every conversation is that the powerful impose their will on the weak. Stephen Toulmin makes this point quite well in <u>Human Understanding</u>:

> If the testimony of the senses referred--as Heraclitus had insisted--only to particular moments and places, we needed some more permanent theoretical principles to adjudicate between the contradictions in their evidence. If the same mutability and contingency undercut the basis of language also--as Cratylus next inferred--we needed, in addition, some more enduring criteria to guarantee the accepted meanings of words. And if 'justice' were not to be merely a name for 'the will of the politically stronger'--as Thrasymachus argued in Plato's <u>Republic</u>--philosophers must show social and political disagreements could be resolved by appeal to general principles rather than by resort to naked power.[1]

In order to meet the objection of skeptics that conversation was inherently corrupt, philosophers had to search for a something beyond the situation, i.e., beyond the testimony of the senses, beyond the contingency of language and beyond influence by the strength of the powerful. The need, in other words, was for an impartial forum, a judge who could not be suborned. Toulmin's analysis here remains helpful:

> From early on, however, all the philosophical theories proposed as solutions to this problem began to develop in a single direction. The need for an impartial forum and procedures was understood as

13

calling for a single, unchanging, and uniquely authoritative system of ideas and beliefs. The prime exemplar of such a universal and authoritative system was found in the new abstract networks of logic and geometry. In this way, 'objectivity,' in the sense of impartiality, became equated with the 'objectivity' of timeless truths; the rational merits of an intellectual position were identified with its logical coherence; and the philosopher's measure of a man's rationality become his ability to recognise, without further argument, the validity of the axioms, formal entailments, and logical necessities on which the claims of the authoritative system depended.[2]

Thus, to *save* the conversation, we must go *outside* the conversation. The "direction" as Toulmin calls it, takes a variety of forms in the history of philosophy, but the appeal remains the same: upon this, at last, we must all agree. But this solution has some odd results. For one thing, the conversation is effectively ended, even more devastatingly than by the suspicion that the talk is rigged.

Another difficulty is that different schools of thought wind up with different universal principles--the famous "scandal of philosophy." In the face of less-than-universal acceptance of what are supposed to be universal principles, the suspicion arises that power and manipulation are once again at work in the conversation. Skepticism is back.

But there is still another objection, the most telling. In his discussion of "absolutism" (foundationalism) Toulmin uses Gottlob Frege, the 19th century German mathematician and philosopher as the classic example of what he means by the term. Frege was adamant about removing from the realm of philosophy any concern about psychology, sociology and history.

For his purposes it was beside the point to ask how men's actual use of number-conceptions had developed historically, or what differences anthropologists had found between the methods of

14

counting and figuring used in different cultures; such factual studies merely chronicled the changing meanings of number-words in our historical gropings towards fully adequate or 'pure' number-conceptions. A rationally based arithmetic, by contrast, must concern itself with the ideal and final system of number-concepts, and this will provide a unique intellectual standard, or template, for judging all men's earlier and cruder proto-arithmetical creations.[3]

Frege's program is important to consider because it is such a good example of foundationalism, but more importantly, because it has been highly influential on later philosophers like Bertrand Russell and the logical positivists. The "genetic fallacy" (explaining concepts by their historical origins) and the "psychological fallacy" (explaining concepts by their source in the personality of the scholar who comes up with them) were all exposed as gross mistakes. And yet, as we have suggested, Frege's program for science and philosophy is so clear that it makes it easy to raise a difficulty: "By analyzing our standards of rational judgment in abstract terms, we avoid . . . the immediate problem of historical *relativism*; but we do so only at the price of replacing it by a problem of historical *relevance*."[4] The better you get at analyzing reality in terms removed from the projects and concerns of human beings, the more clearly does the question arise: so what? One could, of course, retreat into the position that philosophy (most notably in the area of pure logic) is simply an *aesthetic* exercise with no importance for the rest of life, but few would want to so divorce philosophy from the search for truth.

Toulmin's rejection of objectivism puts him back into Plato's quandry: in the absence of absolute truth, what alternative is there but sheer, chaotic relativism? In Toulmin's own analysis he used Collingwood, the British historian and philosopher, as counterpoint, on the relativist side, to Frege. But the alternative to objectivism need not be the belief that all statements are basically arbitrary, or that conceptual change is basically irrational, *caused* rather than argued for. At this point, Toulmin must move from attacking with equal fervor both objectivism and its adversary, and make a constructive proposal: How *do* we get out of the dilemma?

The legal metaphor is helpful for Toulmin, as it has been for other philosophers of knowledge, for the common-law tradition represents an ongoing non-absolutist yet decisive application of knowledge: "Rationality, we shall argue, has its own 'courts' in which all clear-headed men with suitable experience are qualified to act as judges or jurors."[5] Thus, when pressed, Toulmin's appeal is to "a decent respect for the opinions of mankind," as that classic 18th century document, the Declaration of Independence, would have it. But rationality does not operate in as disinterested a way as this metaphor might suggest. For one thing, it operates by means of different "jurisdictions" (to continue the legal metaphor), each of which has its traditions, goals and procedures. These jurisdictions correspond to what we could call intellectual disciplines. Thus, science is an intellectual discipline with a variety of subfields, such as physics, astronomy, biology, etc. By what process, however, does rationality operate in its various disciplines? On what basis, in other words, do people make their judgments as the judges and jurors Toulmin claims them to be?

This is an important question, one which Thomas Kuhn brought to prominence in his controversial <u>Structure of Scientific Revolutions</u>. In that book Kuhn had startled the scientific community by his distinction between "revolutionary" science and "normal" science and his employment of the notion of *paradigm*. Kuhn's use of the later term for "particular coherent traditions of scientific research"[6] has been vastly influential, and though it is problematic, it is still useful. It points to the fact, which Toulmin would agree with in principle, that scientific development occurs within groups of human beings and according to their needs and goals, not according to some pattern of abstract logicality. What shows up as a problem to be solved, both would agree, is not a matter of eternal truth, but a function of what seems to be interesting and important to the practitioners at the time. Kuhn describes the change of paradigms, those "revolutionary" moments when one paradigm, for example, Newtonian physics, is replaced by another paradigm, for example, Einsteinian relativity theory.

But Toulmin is able to show that Kuhn's strong distinction between "revolutionary" and "normal" science is overdrawn and overdramatic, and that Kuhn himself, in the face of criticism, has had to redefine "revolution" from something occurring in rare and spectacular times of change to something occurring with frequency--a "micro-revolution." But a revolution which happens every month is not really a revolution. Still, the *rate* of change is not really such a crucial issue, after all. What is important is *how* change occurs, and here Toulmin is even more critical. Kuhn can say, in a passage suggestive for theologians (and for that reason dangerous), that

> A decision between alternate ways of practicing science is called for, and in the circumstances that decision must be based less on past achievements than on future promise. The man who embraces a new paradigm at an early stage must often do so in defiance of the evidence provided by problem solving. He must, that is, have faith that the new paradigm will succeed with the many large problems that confront it, knowing only that the older paradigm has failed with a few. *A decision of that kind can only be made on faith.*[7]

This sounds like giving up the search for reasons and relapsing into sheer subjectivism. Kuhn does nothing to help this case, in Toulmin's eyes, when he says, "We may, to be more precise, have to relinquish the notion, explicit or implicit, that changes of paradigm carry scientists and those who learn from them closer and closer to the truth."[8] For Toulmin, the goal of science is

> ...to improve our ideas about the natural world step by step, by identifying problem areas in which something can now be done to lessen the gap between the capacities of our current concepts and our reasonable intellectual ideas.[9]

Kuhn, for Toulmin, not only abandons the search for "truth," but then makes the process of conceptual change in science a matter of Keirkegaardian leaps of faith rather than a combination of rational and causal factors. Is Toulmin's critique well-taken?

Toulmin is on solid ground when he describes Kuhn as provocative and rhetorical and prone to overstatement. And yet, perhaps the two men share more than Toulmin is willing to admit. In his "General Introduction" Toulmin aligns himself with Cartesian radical doubt: "A philosopher is rationally obliged to doubt whatever he can consistently call in question and our inquiries here will merely carry this programme one stage further."[10] But faith and doubt, we have been suggesting, are not so easy to separate. In discussing the preconditions for the rise of that intellectual enterprise we call science, Toulmin pays tribute to the Greeks, who not only invented things like geometry and natural science, but more importantly,

> ...the intellectual traditions without which those disciplines could never have developed as they did. To tolerate, for the first time, such independent thinkers as the Milesians and the members of Plato's academy took great intellectual self-confidence; and it needed greater courage still to see those schools influencing young men from the opinion elite, yet resist the temptation to suppress them.[11]

Or again:

> We find authentic scientific traditions and institutions emerging, or remerging, only where, for once in a while, this frail confidence is achieved. Only there do we see the hard intellectual ideals and institutions of a collective scientific profession appearing, or reappearing; and only within such contexts do we observe the establishment, or re-establishment, of

the crucial public attitudes of conceptual modesty and
tolerance of intellectual innovation.[12]

Granted that Kuhn seemed to speak of an individual
scientist and Toulmin of something collective, yet in both
cases, a kind of faith is operative, either as a background
attitude or as the ground for an individual act of decision.
Toulmin's vocabulary differs from Kuhn's but in the
following passage, it seems that "effort of imagination" has a
function not all that different from Kuhn's "act of faith":

> Thompson's and Rutherford's programme was ...
> based on a new intellectual ideal, and other physicists
> could accept their programme only by
> a corresponding effort of the imagination. Indeed,
> J.J. Thompson's more conservative colleagues, who
> could not make this imaginative leap, began
> by treating his suggestion that the electron was a
> material object of subatomic dimensions as some kind
> of practical joke.[13]

An objection here might be that we may seem to be selecting
quotes without regard to the larger argument. Toulmin's own
program is aptly summarized by his subtitle: "The Use and
Evolution of Concepts." How do concepts change, granting
that they do? Clearly, they can change for two possible sorts
of motivations: "rational" or "causal," i.e., intrinsically related
to the intellectual enterprise or extrinsically so related.[14]
Toulmin has little difficulty in showing that rationality is not
the same as logicality (as against Frege, as we have noted).
And he also boldly argues for the practical inseparability of
causal and rational factors in the development of science. In
theory they may be separated, but in practice not. Toulmin's
book, in fact, is a brilliant account of the interaction of these
two factors, reason and causality, in the use and evolution of
concepts, using as basic metaphor (actually more than a
metaphor) Charles Darwin's notion of natural selection.[15] But
perhaps because Toulmin is so good in his rejection
of absolutism he is at special pains to defend himself against
the charge of irrationality, and this is why he must criticize
Kuhn. The great march of science, embedded as it is in

history, (so that one can speak of "British physics" and "French physics"),[16] is *not* irrational.

Indeed, so inseparable are rational and causal factors, so caught up in an evolutionary process which itself is quite blind, quite without goals apart from the goals of those within the evolutionary process, that the question naturally arises: what, then, is reason? If rationality is not to be identified with logicality and not to be confused with sterile system building, what then, is it? What distinguishes rationality from non-rational causality?

Of course, if we step back for a moment and think about the question, it may sound absurd. To define reason would be to talk about it (presumably) in non-rational terms, and thus engage in reductionism. "The 'rationality' of scientific discovery," as Toulmin points out, "of the intellectual procedures by which scientists agree on well-founded conceptual changes, necessarily eludes analysis and judgment in 'logical' terms alone."[17] If this seems unnecessarily elusive, we can add:

> ... the intellectual content of any rational activity forms neither a single logical system, nor a temporal sequence of such systems. Rather, it is an *intellectual enterprise* whose 'rationality' lies in the procedures governing its historical development and evolution ... In all our subsequent inquiries, therefore, our starting-point will be the living, historically developing intellectual enterprises within which concepts find their collective use; and our results must be referred back for validation to our experience in those historical enterprises.[18]

To say that "rationality lies in procedures" is a bold claim if meant to be taken literally. It may seem at first that Toulmin is completely removing the human factor here: rationality is nothing more than a series of techniques or procedures. This, however, would be to misunderstand him. Rather, reason "lies in procedures' because reason is more like the *way* people do things than it is a Platonic essence or object:

What does mark a man's beliefs as prejudices or superstitions, on the other hand, is not their content, but his *manner of holding* them. In this respect, prejudice and superstition are the converse of 'reasonableness,' both have to do less with what our opinions are than with *how* we seek to enforce them.[19] (Italics ours).

Rationality, it seems, is more like a style than a substance, more a way of being than a thing. Rationality, then, is a way of being, as it were, by which human beings continually display a kind of humility and openness to the real:

We believe, that, as natural scientists, men show their rationality by their readiness to give up the dream of a single universal, uniquely authoritative system of thought; and in being prepared to revise any of their concepts and theories, as their experience of the world is progressively enlarged and deepened.[20]

Essential to that style of interaction we call rationality, then, is "the fact that all claims to act 'in the name of' a discipline are subject to appeal: if not within the framework of any one particular institution, then before the profession at large."[21] The opposite of rationality, then, is not stupidity, but dogmatism, the refusal to stay open to experience, and to change one's conceptions in the light of that experience. But note that rationality is not the possession of an individual who encounters the "objective world" in a disinterested way, and then hands on to others the fruits of contemplation. Rather, all participate in an ongoing rational discipline whose goal is to better explain the world, even in those cases where it seems that great men are proceeding in isolation. And yet, what a Newton or Einstein is doing is to make a judgment precisely about the futures of the communal enterprise of which they are a part, and their judgment will only be important, finally, if it is regarded by the rest of the community of the discipline as truly fulfilling the goals of that enterprise: "Any profound redirection in the strategy of a discipline thus has to be justified by appeal, not to previously established patterns of argument, but to the overall experience of men in the entire history of the rational enterprise concerned."[22]

Let us see if we can sum up the argument so far. "Rationality is a characteristic of human behavior generally."[23] It operates in both intellectual and practical enterprises, both disciplinary and less formal communities. It can be highly organized, as in the present state of physics, or somewhat anarchic, as in psychology or the behavioral sciences, or for that matter, ethics and philosophy. But always it has to do with the way people work together toward common goals, continually improving (or trying to improve) their common procedures and the common standards by which those procedures are judged. As it characterizes human behavior, it too is characterized by a willingness to modify past procedures and standards, and even past goals, in the light of new experience. It is thus comparative rather than utopian: *This* practice *here*, will better serve our purposes than this *other* practice *there*. It is historical, pragmatic, and communal. Like an Aristotelian virtue, it is jeopardized by excess or defect, e.g., by "resistance to procedural changes whose merits ... have been fully demonstrated, or in the premature acceptance of unproved innovations."[24] Finally, it is a matter of practical judgment more than anything else, the wisdom, as it were of the community.

We have devoted some time to Toulmin's analysis of human knowing (or rather, the first volume of his analysis) because the issues with which he wrestles are the ones we think are central, summed up in the title of Richard Bernstein's excellent book: <u>Beyond Objectivism and Relativism</u>.[25] Toulmin begins his analysis by slaying the dragons of "absolutism" in the person of Frege. His corresponding relativist is Collingwood. Throughout the volume, however, one finds oneself asking whether Toulmin himself will be able to avoid relativism. Once one grasps that knowledge is something which is used, as it were, in a continuing human enterprise to reach continuing human goals, then Toulmin's oft-stated concern for an "impartial standpoint" seems contradictory. But if there is not impartial, objective, eternal standpoint, then there is not truth, or rather, truth is just what gets us to where we want to go quicker than something else does.

In his last chapter, "The Cunning of Reason," Toulmin sets out to deal with the objection that has been building in the reader throughout the book, one voiced against Toulmin by Joseph Agassi at a meeting of the American Association for the Advancement of Science. Toulmin sums up Agassi's objection:

> We seem, in the long run, to be confronted by an unpalatable choice. We may leave all decisions about what exactly counts as 'scientific' ... to be taken afresh in every milieu, or we may impose universal, *a priori* definitions of 'science' from outside, on all milieus alike; there seems to be no third way. Depending on which alternative we select, we shall end up ... in one or other of the positions we originally rejected. By allowing each ... culture ... to decide ... what properly counts as 'scientific understanding' ... we plunge ourselves back into relativism; once that is done, the very question, whether some new set of concepts promotes the fundamental goals of 'scientific understanding properly so-called,' will be understood in different senses in different milieus, and answered in correspondingly different ways. By imposing universal, abstract definitions of the 'scientific' and the 'legal,' from outside, we land ourselves in an equally arbitrary absolutism; once that is done, we are laying down *a priori* standards of rationality for anything we shall acknowledge as say 'science' or 'law,' in advance of any consideration of the actual diversity to be found in those enterprises. And such *a priori* standards will immediately run up against the same familiar difficulties. From what source do they derive their supposedly universal authority? And how do we demonstrate their relevance and application to the specific problems of men in the whole range of actual disciplines and milieus?[26]

Perhaps Toulmin hoped that his painstaking attempt to detail the Darwinian evolution of concepts would obviate dealing with this problem. And of course, it would, if he were willing to accept that the fruits of our intellectual enterprises are as arbitrary and lacking in point, finally, as the blind process of natural selection is. But Toulmin refuses to take this last step. And against its necessity he uses two arguments. The first is a variant, a weak variant, of the traditional argument of universal reason. There may not be an impartial standpoint, but we do, as humans, whatever our cultures, face similar problems:

> The possibility of understanding actions, customs, and beliefs of men in other milieus rests on our sharing, not common 'sensations' or 'mental images,' but rather common human *needs and problems*. The cultural patterns and 'forms of life' of other peoples are then open to our understanding, in just those respects and to just the extent they represent ways of attacking shared human problems and meeting shared human needs.[27]

This is a helpful defense of cross-cultural understanding, but it still does not address the crucial point. And that may be stated most bluntly in this way: how does a culture set goals for itself? Goal setting is either "rational" (i.e., not "causal") or we should abandon the term and talk honestly about "causes," not reasons. Perhaps "reason" is simply whatever helps us to satisfy our needs. But Toulmin is not finished. "We must not," as he says, "let ourselves be stared down."[28]

It seems finally, that rationality is, as Toulmin has suggested throughout the book, the ability to learn from life, to stay open to experience, to continually revise one's concepts and procedures in the light of new experience.

What separates us from the animals, then, is just this critical ability:

Men are clearly differentiated from ... other animals in two crucial respects. Men have developed and harnessed to the problems of human life a 'language' which, in its richness and subtlety, has no known animal counterpart. And they are capable, not just of operating with stereotyped perceptual and cognitive routines, but also of criticizing and changing their procedures in the light of experience, so as to achieve a more powerful intellectual or practical grasp on their situation. These two distinctive features of the human species are what make it appropriate to discuss human perception and cognition ... in terms of 'rational enterprises' and conceptual improvements.[29]

We escape from relativism, if we do at all, by the fact that we can continue to learn, refusing to be limited by the cultural fences all around us, real as they are.

This may still seem inadequate as a response to the questions we've raised, specifically, how do human beings choose their goals if not by a process which could ultimately be explained more or less adequately as cleverness, i.e., the ability to manipulate the environment to satisfy one's appetites? A theory of knowledge which moves in a pragmatic direction, as Toulmin's does, bumps up against the larger question of purpose: practical to what end? Why should human beings bother at all? Toulmin's response is more or less negative:

As those 'rational transactions' to which we have committed ourselves continue to work themselves out in the course of subsequent history, the same verdict of historical experience which earlier thinkers called the Cunning of Reason (or Nature, or Providence, or Necessity) will, in the long run, penalize all those who--whether knowingly, or through negligence -- continue playing according to out-dated strategies.[30]

It seems that a theory of knowledge attempting to steer between Scylla and Charybdis--between objectivism and relativism--is going to have to talk about questions which have been traditionally termed "ethical" or even religious. It isn't as if Toulmin is unaware of the ethical dimension. In fact, he seems to take it for granted that we have been making ethical progress over the millennia:

> We can -- surely -- recognize a slow but genuine improvement in the understanding of ethical, as well as of intellectual issues. Most of us would hesitate to accept a one-way journey in a time-machine to fourteenth century Europe or third-century Rome; not merely for technological reasons--because of the smells, the poverty, and the disease against which we should have no protection--but also, in large measure, because we should be unwilling to forego the extra degree of moral discrimination, flexibility, and sensibility that men have developed, slowly and painfully, over the last 500 or 1,500 years.[31]

Toulmin is harsh against those (like Teilhard) who see evolution as "going somewhere," as having any grand goal. And yet, at bottom, he is as optimistic as those he criticizes, but with less justification. To assert that there has been progress over the last 1,500 years in moral and ethical matters requires some practical and theoretical defense. One would have to show, on the empirical level, what it could mean that--questions of comfort aside--living in the world of the 20th century (does one need to list the horrors?) would be preferable to sitting at the feet of Francis of Assisi or being a governess in the household of Thomas More. How could one go about deciding that Nero was worse than Hitler, or that Reagan was wiser than Marcus Aurelius? But the situation becomes really impossible when we ask ourselves the theoretical question of how we could account for moral progress without the kind of structured rational enterprise which Toulmin has been suggesting is essential for development in sophistication.

Toulmin's discussion of ethics is brief and inadequate, but it is enough to suggest to us that our basic orientation in this project is sound and helpful. For we are arguing that one must acknowledge a grounding confidence--faith, for want of a better term,--in the community in which one lives in order for there to be knowledge at all; and that, against the backdrop of this faith, a judgment of prudence must be made whose moral dimension must be acknowledged. It seems to us that Toulmin's whole argument can be used to support these two assertions, even though he himself might not acknowledge them. One of the themes which Toulmin takes up is that of *relevance*. A set of abstract logical relationships do not have anything to do with truth until they are applied to the world, and this application is not a question of abstract logical relationships. To stress this point is to stress the inadequacy of objectivism or absolutism. A philosopher of science whose entire career had dealt with the question of relevance, with consequences which will be instructive for us, is Michael Polanyi, some of whose insights we will now look into.

II. Michael Polanyi: Intelligence as Participational

Perhaps the most telling criticism Polanyi makes of objectivism is in his discussion of Laplace, the 19th century French mathematician. Laplace had put forward an ideal of science which still has a hold on many practicing scientists: the model of the perfect mathematical description of all phenomena of space and time. What we strive for in science, said Laplace, is to know where all the entities of nature are, what forces are acting on them, and their speed of movement. To know this, to have this kind of grid set out before one, would be to know everything. Polanyi's response is sharp:

That such virtually meaningless information was identified by Laplace with a knowledge of all things past and all things to come, and that the stark absurdity of this claim has not been obvious to succeeding generations since his day, can be accounted for only by a hidden assumption by which this information was tacitly supplemented. It was taken for granted that the Laplacean mind would not stop short of the list of p's and q's at the time, but proceed by virtue of its unlimited powers of computation to evaluate from this list the events and, indeed all the events that we might be interested to know.[32]

The only possible interest in the "knowledge" that Laplace offers would arise from the *translation* (interpretation, application) of such data into something human beings can use for their projects, directed by their goals and interests. We sense here the familiar attack on absolutism of Toulmin, but here stated with Polanyi's passionate tone:

The tremendous intellectual feat conjured up by Laplace's imagination had diverted attention (in a manner commonly practiced by conjurers from the decisive sleight of hand by which he substitutes a knowledge of all experience for a knowledge of all atomic data. Once you refuse this deceptive substitution, you immediately see that Laplacean mind understands precisely nothing and that whatever it knows means precisely nothing. Yet the spell of the Laplacean delusion remains unbroken to this day.[33]

For Polanyi, knowing is very much a matter of passionate participation, and is based ultimately, on the *bodiliness* of human beings. Such an insight into the essential corporality of human knowing would have been helpful to Toulmin in his discussion of the use of concepts. But let us step back for a moment and consider Polanyi's account of human knowing as skillful, learned, participatory, and focal.

As a practicing chemist, Polanyi reflected on the fact that some of the most important things he learned as a chemist were things that couldn't be *written* down, but had to be *handed* down. (Toulmin speaks of rationality residing in *procedures*.) There has to be a tradition of science in order for the theories of science to mean anything. A vast amount of money spent by an oil-rich skeikdom could buy a library of scientific books and a laboratory of scientific apparatus, but that is not enough. People have to learn *how* to use these things, and have to learn *why* to use them. These things can only be picked up through an apprenticeship. "I have myself watched in Hungary a new, imported machine for blowing electric lamp bulbs, the exact counterpart of which was operating successfully in Germany, failing for a whole year to produce a single flawless bulb."[34]

What is often overlooked, then, is the fact that the articulable store of knowledge of a science is dependent on an inarticulable store of skills which form a tradition of connoisseurship, a tradition which is in many ways submitted to without explicit awareness either of the particular skill being learned or of the entire process itself:

> To learn by example is to submit to authority. You follow your master because you trust his manner of doing things even when you cannot analyze and account in detail for its effectiveness. By watching the master and emulating his efforts in the presence of his example, the apprentice unconsciously picks up the rules of the art, including those which are not explicitly known to the master himself. These hidden rules can be assimilated only by a person who surrenders himself to that extent, uncritically (sic) to the imitation of another. A society which wants to preserve a fund of personal knowledge must submit to tradition.[35]

At this point Polanyi (Toulmin had done something similar) points to the *law* as an example of what he means. Toulmin had pointed out the odd fact of "French physics" and "British physics"; here Polanyi brings up the comparison between these two nations again. In Britain, the *art* of public debate, the *art* of lawmaking and lawfollowing, were present in the bones, as it were. England had developed a tradition of civility and freedom. But when some of the slogans and principles of the English tradition were transported across the channel, they had no context. The French, as is their wont, took the British articulable principles as the whole show, missing the inarticulable skills out of which they flowed. The result was disastrous.[36]

Polanyi's most famous contribution, perhaps, is his distinction between focal and subsidiary awareness, and what he is attempting to do here is not simply to show that there is a difference between things which have been able to be articulated so far and a reservoir of not-yet-articulable skills which someday may yet be specified. His attempt is to show rather, that some things cannot in principle be articulated without destroying the entire skill to which they contribute. They can be described after the fact or before the fact, but they cannot be alluded to in the event of their use, only relied on. This, obviously, must be explained.

Polanyi asks us to consider what happens when we use a tool, for example, a hammer. One might believe that a person using a hammer is only experiencing pressure on his hand and fingers, but this is incorrect. A person so feeling the hammer does not know how to use it. "When we bring down the hammer we do not feel that its handle has struck our palm, but that its head has struck the nail."[37] In other words, we have a "subsidiary awareness" of the feelings in our palm, but a "focal awareness" of the "business end" (so to speak) of the hammer. We *attend* to the task by *dwelling* in the subsidiary elements. Another example Polanyi gives is of the blind man's stick. It is as if his consciousness is out at the end of the stick, giving him information about the world. If he were to concentrate on his palm while feeling his way about, he would be helpless. For,

> ...subsidiary awareness and focal awareness are mutually exclusive. If a pianist shifts his attention from the piece he is playing to the observation of what

he is doing with his fingers while playing it, he gets confused and may have to stop. This happens generally if we switch our focal attention to particulars of which we had previously been aware only in their subsidiary roles.[38]

Another example of what happens when attention is stuck on the subsidiary level is stagefright, which is cured if we can "succeed in casting our mind forward and let it operate with a clear view to the comprehensive activity in which we are primarily interested."[39]

It is important to realize that the interplay between focal and subsidiary awareness is not simply a helpful psychological description of certain aspects of human behavior. For Polanyi it is basic to all human knowing, the failure to recognize which is precisely the problem of our modern epistemologies. For if all knowing is knowing "from" subsidiaries "to" a focus -- if all human knowing is, as he says "from-to," then the notion of an impartial, eternal point of reference becomes problematic (at the very least). For the capital distinction between focal and subsidiary awareness is itself based on a more primordial distinction: that between our "selves" and our bodies. "Our subsidiary awareness of tools and probes can be regarded now as the act of making them form a part of our own body."[40] It is possible, just as it is possible in the case of the hammer, to look at our hands, for example, as objects, to gaze at this bodily appendage, note that it has five fingers, etc. But, just as in the case of the hammer, we cannot objectify our hands at the same time that we are using them, say to drive a car. In a way, our bodies disappear as our focal awareness, relying on the body, projects outward into the world. When we use a tool, we are merely extending our body's reach, adding to our body's capacity to support our exploration of the world beyond it.

This recognition of the role of the body in knowledge gives Polanyi's account a rootedness and keeps it from any danger of angelism. Whatever one knows, one always knows it *from* someplace. But this does not mean that only material objects can be used as tools. "The most pregnant carriers of meaning are of course the words of a language, and it is interesting to recall that when we use the words in speech or writing we are aware of them only in a subsidiary manner."[41] It appears that the human ability to dwell in the parts of the body in a subsidiary fashion can be extended not only to physical tools, but to concepts as well. In each of these cases, one relies on a subsidiary element (my hand, a hammer, the word "dog") which becomes transparent, as it were, to project one's awareness to the intended point.

In many ways Polanyi's analysis makes use of some of the findings of Gestalt psychology, where it is noted that the whole (of perception) is not simply the collection of its parts, but is in some way greater than they are. Thus, a song is not simply a collection of notes which can be investigated individually and then put together in a mechanical way. The song, rather, is based on but transcends the individual notes. Similarly, the physiognamy is recognized by the way in which the particulars cohere together rather than by their individual qualities. Everyone seems to be familiar with the Gestalt drawing of two faces/a candlestick, which shifts from one image to the other as we gaze at it. Polanyi argues that we find ourselves dwelling in the particulars in a different way, focusing either on the candlestick or on the two faces. Again, to detail the particulars in each of these cases is to lose sight of the whole. Reality is less like a soup, the tasting of a small part of which will reveal what it is, so much as it is like a face, which must be recognized at once, as a whole, rather than from its parts.

In such clear examples as these, we can specify what particulars are being dwelled in, though, obviously, not while we're actually doing it. But as matters become more complex, as Polanyi points out, "the curious thing is that we have no clear knowledge of what our presuppositions are and when we try to formulate them they appear quite unconvincing."[42] When hammers and tools and individual perceptions are replaced by interpretive schemes like the theory of evolution, or the procedures of the community of physical scientists, dwelling in can only be described very inadequately. We learn by doing, and we learn to learn by imitating those around us, whether we are scientists, or simply speakers of a language and citizens of a culture. As Toulmin might say, we become enculturated into the procedures of a group, and in these procedures lies the group's rationality, or, as Polanyi says:

> When we accept a certain set of pre-suppositions and use them as our interpretative framework, we may be said to dwell in them as we do in our own body. Their uncritical acceptance for the time being consists in a process of assimilation by which we identify ourselves with them. They are not asserted and cannot be asserted, for assertion can be made only *within* a framework with which we have identified ourselves for the time being; as they are themselves our ultimate framework, they are essentially inarticulable.[43]

By dwelling in a set of inarticulable assumptions we make knowledge possible; but we also make it suspect, for what guarantee do I have that what I have discovered in this fashion is true? There is none for Polanyi. For anything to count as knowledge, it must so count for some person who is looking at it from within a fiduciary realm, a network of cultural assumptions which he could not question if he tried:

> This, then, is our liberation from objectivism: to realize that we can voice our ultimate convictions only from within our convictions -- from within the whole system of acceptances that are logically prior to any particular assertion of our own, prior to the holding of any particular piece of knowledge. If an ultimate logical level is to be attained and made explicitly, this must be a declaration of my personal beliefs. I believe that the function of philosophic reflection consists in bringing to light, and affirming as my own, the beliefs implied in such of my thought and practices as I believe to be valid.[44]

But can we not doubt even our most basic beliefs? Yes and no. We can, of course, claim to doubt whatever we like, but all formulations of doubt, like all formulations of our convictions, rely on an implicit set of assumptions. There is no place to stand from which to doubt everything, for the act of standing somewhere is always an implicit act of faith. And human beings must stand somewhere.

Truth, then, is not some sort of impersonal statement. "Truth is something that can be thought of only by believing it."[45] Truth is what I can't help but believe, what is obvious, given my personal and cultural history. But has Polanyi rescued us from objectivism only to put us at the mercy of relativism and subjectivism? Surely there has to be an alternative to a knowledge which sees it as a function of someone's conception of subjective whim?

Actually, the last point is unfair, for Polanyi is not talking about whim, but about belief. But the question of relativism is still troubling, and must be dealt with. Polanyi claims that his position "is not solipsistic, since it is based on the belief in an external reality and implies the existence of other persons who can likewise approach the same reality."[46] In a way, this neatly reminds those who stress the objectivity of knowledge that their framework is just as fiduciary as Polanyi's and, in fact is more likely to lead to solipsism than his. But this is not yet adequate as a response to the charge of relativism.

If we ask ourselves what is it that bothers us about relativism, it may be a feeling of being trapped. Situated as I am here in this place and time, I can never break through to "reality," and thus, to truth. Polanyi's effort in this regard is interesting, for, more than Toulmin, he recognizes the fundamental *moral* character of knowledge. Discussing all the many ways in which our conditioning can negatively influence our awareness of truth--the prejudices of our race, the self-justification of our class, the narrowness of our culture, etc., he asks, "How can we claim to arrive at a responsible judgment with universal intent if the conceptual framework in which we operate is borrowed from a local culture and our motives are mixed up with the forces holding on to social privilege?"[47] This is indeed the question, and this is Polanyi's answer:

From the point of view of the critical philosophy, this fact would reduce all our convictions to the mere products of a particular location and interest. But I do not accept this conclusion. Believing as I do in the justification of deliberate intellectual commitments, I accept these accidents of personal existence as the concrete opportunities for exercising our personal responsibility. *This acceptance is the sense of my calling.*[48] (Emphasis his).

We see that epistemology leads to anthropology and anthropology to ethics. We argue about knowledge because, human beings that we are, we find it important to know. We move toward the real. We could regard this very movement toward the real as an absurdity, of course, but this seems to be inadequate to its compelling character. It is, Polanyi suggests, a calling:

I believe, therefore, that as I am called upon to live and die in this body, struggling to satisfy its desires, recording my impressions by aid of such sense organs as it is equipped with, and acting through the puny machinery of my brain, my nerves and my muscles, so I am called upon also to acquire the instruments of intelligence from my early surroundings and to use these particular instruments to fulfill the universal obligations to which I am subject. A sense of responsibility within situations requiring deliberate decisions demands as its logical complement a sense of calling with respect to the processess of intellectual growth which are its necessary logical antecedents.[49]

For Polanyi, then, the reality which is human knowing is at its heart a giving of oneself over to a journey with its own rules and delights, a journey of discovery whose end is never fully in sight, a journey which is undertaken with many others, some of whom are on very different roads, all of whom are tending toward the same goal. The journey requires a commitment which simply cannot be justified in advance. But it is not simply that, if we want to know anything, we have to commit ourselves, though that is true. It is also that we are called to commit ourselves simply to be human, to make the kinds of decisions that humans make, and in making this commitment we can, in a way, transcend our particular situation.

We have not emphasized that for Polanyi, as for Toulmin, this journey is characterized by a constant openness to revision, a humility which is the exact opposite of the fanaticism which might seem to be the logical outcome of a system of knowing based on faith rather than doubt. "But a dogmatic orthodoxy can be kept in check both internally and externally, while a creed inverted into a science is both blind and deceptive."[50] Knowledge based on faith, suggests Polanyi, at least acknowledges its inadequacy; knowledge claiming to be nothing but knowledge (i.e., modern science) is dangerous because it thinks it is no creed, but simple truth. Thus the supposed chief characteristic of science, openness to revision, is shown by Polanyi to be more congenial to faith than to science! But surely there is a vast difference between a dogmatic structure like a Christian church and the scientific community, which operates by free inquiry.

A conception of knowledge which places an emphasis on enculturation, on the uncritical (at first) assimilation of standards from a community of tradition, must have an account of what that community is, from which one derives one's framework. Polanyi's account of the scientific world is at times quite personal, which should be no surprise. In discussing the early rejection of his own theory of the absorption of gases, a theory which later proved to be correct, Polanyi, surprisingly enough, argues that such disciplinary decisions as the rejection of his theory were absolutely necessary for the institution of science, if the scientific community "is not to admit for publication so much nonsense that scientific journals are rendered worthless thereby. Discipline *must* remain severe and *is* in fact severe."[51]

Polanyi's comment here, while from an essay written late in life, is not the mellow reflection of age, but the repetition of an opinion he held as a much younger man. But how can the necessary discipline of the scientific community be kept from becoming tyranny? As we answer this question we will see the influence of the British political experience is often decisive for Polanyi's thought. It may not be an idle or merely humorous comment that Britain is a kind of laboratory of what happens when you reject objectivism in the political sphere, relying, not on written constitutions but on a tradition of civility. At any rate, this is an attractive hypothesis for Polanyi and (to a smaller extent) for Toulmin.

"The authority of science," says Polanyi, "resides in scientific opinion. Science exists as a body of wide ranging authoritative knowledge only so long as the consensus of scientists continues."[52] For Polanyi, any community must solve the problem of combining continuation of the tradition along with encouragement of innovation and discovery. What science has managed, happily, to avoid, is the establishment of some supreme constitutional authority which would pass on the worth of theories. Rather, the community is linked by a broad consensus, which alters imperceptibly by the efforts of individuals within the community. "each scientist is confronted with the criticism of his neighbours, who in their turn are criticized by their own neighbors. Thus the chain of mutual appreciation spreads throughout the body of science."[53] Thus the authority is the authority of a republic rather than of a dictatorship or monarchy. Clearly, for Polanyi, this kind of loose structure of parliamentary democracy provides a model for community in general:

> The realms of science, of law, and of Protestant religion which I have taken as examples of modern cultural communities are each subject to control by their own body of opinion. Scientific opinion, legal theory, Protestant theology are all formed by the consensus of independent individuals, rooted in a common tradition...Thus the life of science, the law and the Protestant church all three stand in contrast to the constitution, say, of the Catholic Church

which denies to the believer's conscience the right to interpret the Christian dogma and reserves the final decision in such matters to his confessor. There is here the profound difference between two types of authority; one laying down general presuppositions, the other imposing *conclusions*. We may call the first a General, the latter a Specific Authority.[54]

The use of Protestantism and Catholicism to show contrasting tendencies in communal authority is from Polanyi's 1946 work, <u>Science, Faith, and Society</u>, and does not show up again in his major work, <u>Personal Knowledge</u> (1958) or later minor efforts. But it remains a helpful clue to Polanyi's notion of good and bad community. A community of General Authority "assumes that individual members are capable of making genuine contact with the reality underlying the existing tradition."[55] This by no means prejudices the fact that the way in which the individual sets up the problems of encountering reality are inevitably reflections of the communal "transmit" (to use Toulmin's word). It simply means that reality is something other than a possession of the community, but exists independently of it. And so, while "every interpretation of nature, whether scientific, non-scientific or anti-scientific, is based on some intuitive conception of the general nature of things,"[56] an intuition which we are given rather than create, nevertheless, there is the Real, and "Real is that which is expected to reveal itself indeterminately in the future."[57]

By contrast to such a community of General Authority,

Specific Authority on the other hand makes all important reinterpretations and innovations by pronouncements from the centre. This centre alone is thought to have authentic contacts with the fundamental sources from which the existing traditions spring and can be renewed. Specific Authority demands therefore not only devotion to the tenets of a tradition but subordination of everyone's ultimate judgment to discretionary decision by an official centre."[58]

It need not bother us that this is a caricature of Catholicism. Like any good caricature, it can point up the issues clearly. And the issue is, in the search for truth, where does faith reside--in the community or in some source of authority above the community? Stated this baldly it may seem that we have an arbitrary choice to make. Unfortunately, Polanyi goes on to take the merits of General Authority for granted, without mentioning Specific Authority again. But their contrast: is instructive beyond clarifying terms. It seems that the two forms of authority are not distinguished in some arbitrary way but are related to each other. The one is a restriction of the other. Certain people or epochs or statements of the community are lifted up and given the truth status which resides authentically in the reality which is the goal rather than the possession of the community. Specific Authority appears as the kind of objectivism we have been at pains to excoriate throughout this effort. It ends the search because it claims achievement of the goal. And, as we have been claiming throughout, such a claim denies the essential bodiliness of human beings, their situation in space and time, their need to apply what counts as truth to each new moment for it to count as truth at all. The claim of a human being or a human institution to possess ultimate, indubitable truth appears in our perspective increasingly as a contradiction in terms.

The contrast between General Authority and Specific Authority, helpful as it is in revealing Polanyi's basic convictions, can be supplemented by another contrast: the contrast between fact and value. In many ways we can helpfully see Polanyi's entire philosophical project as an attempt to deal with the relationship between these two sets of notions and to come up with an alternative to unsatisfactory versions of their relationships. Polanyi's project, then, is among other things, an attempt to provide an alternative to Marxism, where fact is in practice and in theory subjugated to the common good as proclaimed by the state; to a kind of scientific positivism which sees fact as having nothing to do with values, communal or otherwise; or to a Romantic individualism which is tempted to construct a world of personal value apart from the communal world of shared reality and shared values.

> Marxism-Leninism denies the intrinsic creative powers of thought. Any claim to independence by scientists, scholars or artists must then appear as a plea for self-indulgence. A dedication to the pursuit of science, wherever it may lead, becomes disloyalty to the power responsible for the public welfare. Since this power regards itself as the embodiment of historic destiny and as dispenser of history's promises to mankind, it can acknowledge no superior claims of truth, justice or morality. Alternatively, materialistic (or romantic) philoso|phies, denying any universal claims to the standards of truth, justice or morality, may deprive citizens of any grounds for appealing to these standards and thus endow the government with absolute power. The two processes are in fact fused in their joint justification of force as superior to mind.[59]

Polanyi is aware of the irony that, if we flee from the consequences of one error, we find ourselves in the arms of another. If we flee the tyranny of those who demand moral submission to community standards of truth and value (which could be the Communists or the Nazis or certain types of religious communities), we may wind up rejecting the role of communal authority in the discovery of truth entirely, a rejection which will haunt us later when the world becomes a vast moral wasteland of anarchy and relativism. Even the very appeal to universal standards of which Polanyi speaks in this passage can become, in time, just another form of tyranny, depending on the rigidity with which they are understood. And, as Polanyi says, the romantic flight finally succeeds only in making it easier for those who wish to impose their wills on the community.

The ease with which one extreme breeds its opposite may give us pause. There is indeed a danger in trying to be too clear and systematic about one's presuppositions. For the individual or the community, the recognition of the errors of a one-sided

40

position must not be so much the development of an alternative position, which then becomes a fortified town to be defended at all costs, but a recognition of the essential impossibility of specifying all of one's presuppositions and the tentative character of all affirmations, a kind of humility. Stephen Toulmin had made a similar point in criticizing the objectivist Frege and the relativist Collingwood. Both these men, Toulmin insisted, had painted themselves into a corner by making the same mistake:

> The problem of conceptual change is intractable for both Frege and Collingwood just because they both subscribe to the philosophical cult of systematicity, i.e., to the belief that concepts must form 'logical systems', and to the consequent equation of the 'rational' with the 'logical.'[60]

Polanyi's solution to the various unfortunate sunderings of modernity: the sundering of fact from value, of individual from community, of faith from knowledge (and the resulting unfortunate covert relationships between these factors), is, as we have been suggesting, very much along the lines of the British parliamentary system. In this Polanyi is consistent from the beginning of his writing career to the end. Like the community of science, the British system is successful for Polanyi, because it is balanced. It manages to combine respect for the past with the possibility of innovation. It provides for individual freedom and responsibility within the context of allegiance to certain communal symbols which are not tyrannical because they are largely vague, their interpretation being part of the joint program. What it demands of the individual--and the demand is still just that, a demand--is not unthinking allegiance and submission to a set of clearly defined truths and values, but a willingness to take part in the process of searching for the fulfillment of the truths and values symbolized by the traditional icons of King and Fair Play and so on. Again, these symbols and icons do not form a system, but they do form a tradition. Whether the community is the international community of science or the national community of England, at bottom what is required is a kind of faith:

The creative life of such a community rests on a belief in the ever continuing possibility of revealing still hidden truths. In Science, Faith and Society, I interpreted this as a belief in a spiritual reality, which, being real, will bear surprising fruit indefinitely. To-day I would prefer to call it a belief in the reality of emergent meaning and truth.[61]

This conclusion carries Toulmin's argument farther than he would want to do, but we are nevertheless free to see the two thinkers as mutually reinforcing some important truths, i.e., the inadequacy of objectivism, the role of community and traditions in knowledge, the necessity of judgment in the application of theoretic truths, and finally, stronger in Polanyi than in Toulmin, the role of the body and of commitment in the discovery of knowledge.

III. Hubert Dreyfus: Intelligence as Artificial?

It may be helpful at this point to look at the attack on foundationalism from a slightly different perspective. Hubert Dreyfus has been engaged for years in a critique of Artificial Intelligence, or rather, in a critique of the ideas of those men who are convinced that it will be possible, ultimately, to design and construct a machine which will carry on all the important functions of the human brain, a machine which would be, in other words, intelligent. Dreyfus's ongoing debate with these men, as outlined in <u>What Computers Can't Do</u>[62] can clarify for us the difference between human beings and machines, and consequently, between human knowing and what machines do. Dreyfus begins with a brief historical background to the problems of machine intelligence. What philosophical presuppositions lie behind it?

Since the Greeks invented logic and geometry, the idea that all reasoning might be reduced to some kind of calculation--so that all arguments could be settled once and for all--has fascinated most of the Western tradition's rigorous thinkers. Socrates was the first to give voice to this vision.[63]

The Platonic-Socratic enterprise was an attempt to achieve clarity about the presuppositions of life, especially moral behavior. What is justice? What is piety? These are the questions that taxed the early dialogues, and which Socrates, often enough, claimed ignorance about. Along the way to answering these questions another question arises: What would count as an answer? For Plato, says Dreyfus, "what cannot be stated explicity in precise instructions--all areas of human thought which require skill, intuition, or a sense of tradition--are relegated to some kind of arbitrary fumbling."[64]

But Plato's attempt to find clarity does stop somewhere. It may be that we achieve clarity about the definitions of concepts, but we do not have an infinite regress. At some point we must simply know the meaning of the fundamental concepts used in those definitions. Thus, the intuition of basic concepts *and* the judgment by which one knows when these basic concepts apply to the world elude definition. "Plato admits his instructions cannot be completely formalized."[65]

But Plato had begun a process, and "for the Platonic project to reach fulfillment one breakthrough is required: all appeal to intuition and judgment must be eliminated."[66] But how could this be done? It wasn't until Galileo that the tools for the project could begin to be assembled. Galileo had discovered that one could describe motion through the use of mathematical formalisms. Rather than using Aristotelian *metaphors* about objects seeking the center of the earth, the modern physical scientist uses an unerring mathematical *formula* which describes exactly what happens in every possible circumstance of speed, weight and shape. The blinding success of the formalization of physical reality led naturally to the hope that "a Galileo of human behavior might succeed in reducing all semantic considerations (appeal to meanings) to the techniques of syntactic (formal) manipulation."[67] Leibnitz had a clearer vision of where he was heading:

> The most important observations and turns of skill in all sorts of trades and professions are as yet unwritten. This fact is proved by experience when passing from theory to practice we desire to accomplish something. Of course, we can also write up this practice, since it is at bottom just another theory more complex and particular.[68]

It is one thing to call for the existence of something, yet another to actually bring it into being. The latter task required the work of mathematicians like Charles Babbage, George Boole and A. M. Turing, and--most importantly--the development of electrical switching. If all knowledge can conceivably be represented by two things--a set of mathematical notations and a set of rules by which these notations may be employed--then the stage is set for a machine to know: "*Any* process which can be formalized so that it can be represented as a series of instructions for the manipulation of discrete elements, can, at least in principle, be reproduced by such a machine."[69]

It should require no underlining to recognize these descriptions as a particularly clear and distinct version of objectivism; what is worth understanding (for those who might feel that attacking objectivism is beating a dead horse) is the way in which these descriptions of knowledge continue to dominate the thinking of the scientists who dominate the world of artificial intelligence. And, as Dreyfus likes to point out, this is where foundations and governments are spending huge sums of money. Not only is objectivism the dominant way of thought among such people; there is no alternative. Dreyfus's dialogue with the AI people, then, will be a particularly concrete example of the dangers of and alternatives to, objectivism.

Dreyfus suggests that there are four basic presuppositions that underlie the pretensions of the Artificial Intelligence (AI) school, and these four presuppositions can be attacked in turn. They are:

1. A biological assumption that on some level of operation--usually supposed to be that of neurons--the brain processes information in discrete operations by way of some biological equivalent of on/off switches.

2. A psychological assumption that the mind can be viewed as a device operating on bits of information according to formal rules. Thus, in psychology, the computer serves a a model of the mind as conceived of by empiricists such as Hume (with the bits as atomic impressions) and idealists such as Kant (with the program providing the rules). Both empiricists and idealists have prepared the ground for this model of thinking as data processing--a third-person process in which the involvement of the processor plays no essential role.

3. An epistemological assumption that all knowledge can be formalized, that is, that whatever can be understood can be expressed in terms of logical relations, more exactly in terms of Boolean functions, the logical calculus which governs the way the bits are related according to rules.

4. Finally, since all information fed into digital computers must be in bits, the computer model of the mind presupposes that all relevant information about the world, everything essential to the production of intelligent behavior, must in principle be analyzable as a set of situation-free determinate elements. This is the ontological assumption that what there is, is a set of facts each logically independent of the others.[70]

Dreyfus devotes a chapter to each assumption, and we can here simply summarize his conclusions. The first assumption, he points out, is an empirical one; it is subject to verification or falsification in the light of research. As it turns out, the best research to date, even by those people initially predisposed to the comparison of brain and computer, points rather to the immense complexity of the former. What may seem at first to be a classic binary structure of nerves either "firing" or not, turns out to be much different. The biological assumption then, "is an empirical hypothesis which has seen its day."[71]

But though the first assumption falls, there is a fall-back position: the brain may not be wired like a computer, but the mind may still *work* like one. Dreyfus is able to show rather easily that human skills like natural language use, pattern recognition (recall Polanyi's use of the Gestaltists), "zeroing-in", and differentiation between essential and inessential factors in a situation cannot be reproduced by a computer today and probably never will be. Thus, "the empirical results, riddled with unexplained exceptions...are only promising if viewed in terms of an *a priori* assumption that the mind must work like a heuristically programmed digital computer."[72]

Of course, one could argue that even if the brain is not wired like a computer, and even if the mind does not work like one (or cannot yet be shown to work like any computer we know of), it might still be possible, Dreyfus concedes, for a machine to do what the human mind does, but differently:

> Although human performance might not be *explainable* by supposing that people are actually following heuristic rules in a sequence of unconscious operations, intelligent behavior may still be *formalizable* in terms of such rules and thus reproduced by the machine. This is the epistemological assumption.[73]

Of course, one could argue at this point, as Dreyfus does, that nobody has been able to program a computer to, say, speak a natural language, but one would still have to deal with the obvious objection that it's just a matter of time before that actually occurs. Enough things have been declared impossible in the history of science to give us pause. What one must do is to "show that the theoretical claim is untenable on its own terms."[74] The strongest argument against the epistemological assumption is one raised by (among others) Ludwig

Wittgenstein. By attempting to reduce language to a set of rulelike behaviors, he comes up against the problem of needing rules to determine when the rules are applicable. "Wittgenstein is arguing, as Aristotle argues against Plato, that there must always be a place for interpretation."[75] Human beings always seem to find themselves in contexts, and in order to understand behavior, one must understand each context. "To have a complete theory of what speakers are able to do, one must not only have grammatical and semantic rules but further rules which would enable a person or a machine to recognize the context in which the rules must be applied."[76] This is admittedly daunting for the computer theorist, but not fatally crippling. For it may be immensely difficult to program a computer to recognize all possible contexts of everyday life and language--it would mean programming the computer with all the knowledge a human being has--nevertheless, why couldn't it be done *in principle* (if not in practice)? A context, after all, is just a word for a more complicated set of rules by which lower-level rules are ordered.

We are thus pushed back to the recognition that a "full refutation of the epistemological assumption would require an argument that the world *cannot* be analyzed in terms of context-free data"[77] This, of course, is what Dreyfus has been calling the ontological assumption. If one could demolish this, one will have won a final victory.

Dreyfus never does provide a logically irrefutable argument against the ontological assumption, though he does demonstrate that his opponents are unable to put forward a convincing argument in *favor* of it. What he does is to provide an alternative description of human behavior and knowledge, one which is, presumably, more plausible than the AI model.

The focus of the argument continues, of course, to the crucial issue of context. Is human being-in-the-world really a matter of an immense number of facts--and rules to use them-- in every possible situation (which are themselves simply more facts?) But, for human beings, context or situation is by no means merely a matter of "objective" data; rather, the world comes to us as the *place where our concerns are worked out,*

47

and is interpreted according to what our concerns are at the moment. "Everything we experienced in some way, immediate or remote, reflects our human concerns. Without some *particular* interest, without some *particular* inquiry to help us select and interpret, we are back confronting the infinity of meaningless facts we were trying to avoid."[78]

For example, the possible "facts" about the room in which I type are literally infinite. And yet, the *relevant* facts at this moment are functions of my concerns as I type this page. What facts are relevant, of course, will change as soon as this page is done, or I become hungry, or cold, etc. It seems that human beings do not operate out of an on-going "infinite context" and then modify it down to manageable levels in light of an "objective" state of affairs, but rather "we carry over from the immediate past a set of anticipations based on what was relevant and important a moment ago. This carryover gives us certain predispositions as to what is worth noticing."[79] The reason computer theorists can make no sense of such an elementary situation as the one I'm describing is that, says Dreyfus, they have managed consistently to ignore three immensely important areas which underlie human being-in-the- world. These are:

> The role of the body in organizing and unifying our experience of objects; the role of the situation in providing a background against which behavior can be orderly without being rulelike, and finally the role of human purposes and needs in organizing the situation so that objects are recognized as relevant and accessible.[80]

Let us examine these roles briefly, beginning with that of the body in human knowing. There is an irony, Dreyfus notes, in the fact that what computers seem to do very well is precisely what one might have expected to give them the most trouble--those "higher" human skills like abstract logical analysis. But the opposite has happened. "It is the sort of intelligence which we share with animals, such as pattern recognition (along with the use of language...) that has resisted machine simulation."[81] This remarkable fact about perception, i.e., that whatever we perceive is perceived against a background which is experienced as less important, as framing some object in the foreground, is the key for Dreyfus. Because of what Dreyfus, following Husserl, calls the ground, or "outer horizon", human beings simply *ignore* a vast amount of irrelevant data and focus in on what counts, a trait they share with dogs and cats, but not computers. Consider a cocktail party where, one can eavesdrop on various conversations in the room by so focusing one's attention, and ignore the rest of the party's chatter. A tape recording of the party would simply pick up everything.

But this notion of the "outer horizon" is actually less interesting than what Dreyfus (following Husserl) calls the "inner horizon", a concept difficult at first. When we understand a sentence, for example, we do exclude sounds not relevant to the sentence, but this does not explain how each individual word is heard, because each word is, after all, heard precisely as *part of an on-going sentence.* Simply put, "when we perceive an object we are aware that it has more aspects than we are at the moment considering. Moreover, once we have experienced these further aspects, they will be experienced as co-present, as covered up by what is directly presented."[82] We do not build up the picture of the house from the details, oddly enough. Rather, we experience *the house,* and then interpret the details as "details of a house." The Gestalt is made up of parts, in a sense, but it is the Gestalt which determines what the parts are parts of. That this is true of the relationship between words and the sentence they form has been recognized since the 18th century, pointed to by Friedrich Schleiermacher as the famous "hermeneutical circle":

> Complete knowledge always involves an apparent circle, that each part can be understood only out of the whole to which it belongs, and vice verse. All knowledge which is scientific must be constructed in this way.[83]

As in language, so in the perception of an object like a house, the Gestalt is very much a Gestalt, not of houses in general, but of *this* house, not of sentences in general, but of the meaning of *this* sentence. There is a degree of indeterminancy and co-determinancy which is, when one thinks about it, rather amazing and unformulizable.

But we have not yet exhausted the role of the body in perception and, consequently, in knowledge. For we do not perceive the world with our eyes or our hearing or our touch, but often enough, with all of them together. We can coordinate our bodily responses to the world, "not only recognize objects in each single sense modality, but by virtue of the felt equivalence of our exploratory skills we can see and touch the same object."[84] Our senses are not sensors which provide us with data which we can coordinate with data from other sensors. Rather, through our different senses we experience, not colors, sounds, smells, but this *barking dog*, and when we run, it is not because we have run through a series of possible behaviors on a logic tree, analyzing them with lightning speed. Rather, we have learned, as embodied creatures, to act in the world.

> The body can constantly modify its expectations in terms of a more flexible criterion: as embodied, we need not check for specific characteristics, but simply or whether, on the basis of our expectations, we are coping with the object. Coping need not be defined by a specific set of traits but rather by an on-going mastery which Merleau-Ponty calls maximum grasp. What counts as *maximum grasp* varies with the goal of the agent and the resources of the situation. Thus it cannot be expressed in situation free, purpose-free terms.[85]

Thus there are three aspects of bodily functioning in the world which underlie perception, and therefore knowledge, and which cannot be formalized into a set of rules. They are the two forms of "horizonal" perception, inner and outer, by which objects are perceived within a field which defines them, while the field is a function of the objects being perceived; and the way in which the perception of object-in-a-field can be transferred from one sense organ or body part to another without losing the experience of the single unified object-in-a-field. "Thanks to this fundamental ability an embodied agent can dwell in the world in such a way as to avoid the infinite task of formalizing everything."[86]

The importance of the body, then, for our general discussion of knowledge should be obvious. "Indeed, sensory-motor skills underlie all 'higher' rational functions; even logic and mathematics have an horizonal character."[87] But surely to say that embodied creatures perceive everything on the pattern of more important/less important (or object and foreground) must now lead to a discussion of what it means to be important. Importance, or relevance, or interest, becomes an important (as it were) topic for our discussion. But "whatever it is that enables human beings to zero in on the relevant facts without definitively excluding others which might become relevant is so hard to describe that it has only recently become a clearly focused problem for philosophers."[88]

To talk about importance is to ask "Important in what way? Important to whom?" In other words, it is to discuss the last two of the three areas of human knowing we have promised to look at: the situation and purpose. Of course, inasmuch as body, situation, and purposes inevitably interpenetrate we have had to make reference to the latter two in discussing the former. Actually, if Dreyfus is right, any of these only makes sense in relationship with the other two. There is no situation without a body, but no body without a situation either. Dreyfus makes use of Wittgenstein to clarify this inter-relationship of body, situation, purpose:

> Wittgenstein constantly suggests that the analysis of a situation into facts and rules (which is where the traditional philosopher and the computer expert think they must begin) is itself only meaningful in some contexts and for some reasons. Thus again the elements already reflect the goals and purposes for which they were carved out. When we try to find the ultimate context-free, purpose-free elements, as we must if we are going to find the ultimate bit to feed a machine--bits that will be relevant to all possible

tasks because chosen for one--we are in effect trying to free the facts in our experience of just that pragmatic organization which makes it possible to use them flexibly in coping with everyday problems.[89]

It is important to understand the radicality of this perspective. It is not as if Dreyfus (and we) are saying that building up the world out of data is impossibly *hard*, or that we only select the facts we need at any given moment for our purposes from our environment. Rather, data and facts *do not exist at all* apart from the context of a purpose. This room, with its books, decorations, diplomas and furniture, for example, is what it is, my room, only in the context of my dwelling-in-it. As Dreyfus says, "When we are at home in the world, the meaningful objects embedded in their context of references among which we live are not a model of the world stored in our mind or brain; *they are the world itself.*"[90]

Some might object that this is solipsism, that there exists a world-- the physical universe--outside of the world of human beings. One easy response to this objection is to point out that it is easily identified as a question which only makes sense in the very rarified human world known as philosophy. It gains its meaning from its context and its purpose, a purpose which, it is easy to show, most human beings have little time for. This is not a refutation, surely, though it is a demonstration. A refutation might point out that it is only in relationship to human purposes that "physical universe" makes any sense, i.e., as that which human beings cannot control, are in awe of, frightened by, etc. The human world is not necessarily something humans own or control; it is simply the world they live in, a world which expands when the planet Pluto is discovered or an astronomer sights a new star. It is a world of new and surprising discoveries, but it remains *our* world.

Indeed, so used are we to thinking of the world as ultimately simply a set of Laplacean atoms that it takes an effort to realize just how alienating that conception is, how in many ways it too is a product of a set of cultural purposes, purposes which are no longer relevant to our goals as humans. Or better: the question is not between a universe of "impersonal" physical facts and a human world; both are quite human, both are functions of human needs and purposes, both arise out of particular human contexts. The question is: what are our goals?

And so the question is not whether I want to think of my Latin dictionary as a set of atoms, or black marks on paper (on the one hand) or as having meaning in the world of my concerns; both descriptions reflect human concerns. The real question is: does it make more sense to think of my dictionary as something I use to look up Latin words or as a set of ink spots on paper? Most of the time, surely, the former will be the helpful way of looking at my dictionary; i.e., that is what it "really" is.

Our discussion has finally gotten to the crucial question of *concern*, what human beings, in some sense, *are*. Dreyfus notes that we talk a lot in our time about *values*, and about the way facts can be but must not be sundered from values. And there is a general sense that a world of mathematical formalism tends to devalue the world. In debates about economics, nuclear war, genetic engineering and the like, the dilemma becomes--now that we know the facts, what can we *do*? Generally, once one knows the "facts" in these discussions, the only thing to do is to continue the status quo. This should be no surprise, for if we are right, and facts only show up as functions of a goal, then the very "objective" facts presented to us are already oriented toward a goal. To put it strongly,

> ...to speak of values already gives away the game. For values are a product of the same philosophical tradition which has laid down the conceptual basis of artificial intelligence. Although talk of values is rather new in philosophy, it represents a final state of objectification in which the pragmatic considerations which pervade experience and determine what counts as an object are conceived of as just further characteristics of independent objects, such as their hardness and color. A value is one more property that can be added to or subtracted from an object.[91]

In this passage Dreyfus is giving a critique of the attempt of Satosi Watanabe to pursue an object which seems quite in line with that of Dreyfus, namely, to show that machines differ from humans. Machines can be programmed to have *objectives*, says Watanabe, but only humans have *values*. But Watanabe then goes on to assume that values can be assigned quantitative functions which can then be programmed into a machine. The machine can then act as if it had the values of the human being who programmed it. But this misses an important point. And the point is not simply that a machine cannot create values on its own. It is rather than "what Watanabe misleadingly calls values belongs to the structure of the *field* of experience, not the objects in it." Recall that before anything can show up as an *object*, it must be perceived as such against a *background* which is, at the moment, not as interesting (important, "valuable" etc.). The object begins to play a role, as it were, in the drama of human care.

Dreyfus is worth quoting at length here:

Heidegger is also the first to have called attention to the way philosophy has from its inception been dedicated to trying to turn the concerns in terms of which we live into objects which we could contemplate and control. Socrates was dedicated to trying to make his and other people's commitments explicit so that they could be compared, evaluated, and justified. But it is a fundamental and strange characteristic of our lives that insofar as we turn our most personal concerns into objects which we can study and choose, they no longer have a grip on us. They no longer organize a field of significant possibilities in terms of which we act but become just one more possibility we can choose or reject. Philosophers thus finally arrived at the nihilism of Nietzsche and Sartre in which personal concerns can be equally arbitrarily abandoned or trans-valuated.[92]

Thus, if we follow this Heideggerian analysis, man is not so much the being who *has* concerns so much as he is concern or care, within a situation. Man, or *Dasein* ("Being-there") is "ontically distinguished by the fact that, in its very being, that Being is an *issue* for it."[93] Since Being is manifestly not an object among objects, the goals of *Dasein*'s searching are not specifiable in advance. We shall have to develop this analysis further in later chapters, but for the moment we can say that human being (or *Dasein*) *is concern* (speaking broadly) which both knows and does not know its goal. "Gratification is experienced as the discovery of what we needed all along, but it is a retroactive understanding and covers up the fact that we were unable to make our need determinate without first receiving that gratification."[94] The circularity (or wholism) which we have noticed before as characteristic of perception and knowledge is here given a more general expression, in terms of the nature of human being as care.

What have we gained by attending carefully to Dreyfus' analysis of artificial intelligence? We agree with him that:

> We can view recent work in artificial intelligence as a crucial experiment disconfirming the traditional assumption that human reason can be analyzed into rule-governed operations on situation-free discrete elements-- the most important disconfirmation of this metaphysical demand that has ever been produced. This technique of turning our philosophical assumptions into technology until they reveal their limits suggests fascinating new areas for basic research.[95]

What we have been doing so far in this chapter is showing the inadequacy of objectivism, moving from Toulmin's critique, which recognized the necessity of seeing human understanding as operating within a set of procedures employed by a historical entity, to Polanyi, who was able to demonstrate more clearly than Toulmin the fiduciary and passionate character of the commitment underlying the ongoing human enterprises of science, and now to Dreyfus, whose study of artificial intelligence provided us with a surprising confirmation of some of our ideas, and whose employment of phenomenological and Heideggerian categories moved the discussion into deeper waters which will be explored later on in our study.

It may seem that our task in this chapter is done: we have critiqued objectivism and given a glimpse of some alternatives, before embarking on a discussion of the Gadamerian perspective which we will follow. But we sense an omission. The three men we have discussed so far are, in some way, operating as philosophers of *science*. This was deliberate, for if we could make the case against objectivism from within its very citadel, as it were, we could argue *a fortiori*, that the case could be made in human sciences. But we have not pointed to anyone actually operating in what the Germans call the *Geisteswissenschaften*, and we will do that now. We choose the ethician Alasdair MacIntyre for two reasons: first, he explicitly and brilliantly deals with the problem of what could be called ethical objectivism in his latest book; and secondly, he raises themes which complement and illuminate our study so far and our later discussions.

IV. Alasdair MacIntyre: Intelligence as Moral

In his discussion of the place of moral thought in the Enlightenment MacIntyre goes over some familiar ground but also makes some original observations. The rise of calculative reason in the 18th century is a movement which restricts reason even as it purports to make it king. "It can assess truths of fact and mathematical relations but nothing more. In the realm of practice therefore it can speak only of means. About ends it must be silent."[96] But ethics is precisely about the ends of human behavior, if it is about anything at all, and so we are faced with the problem of what to do about ends. If, says MacIntyre, ethics is supposed to help us understand just how it is that we go from where we are to where we should be, the abandonment of the project of finding out where we should be effectively destroys moral discourse: "Without a teleological

56

framework the whole project of morality becomes unintelligible."[97]

If we have lost a teleological framework, apparently there must have been a time when we had one. Perhaps by looking at the past we can gain some understanding of what those words mean.

Consider, MacIntyre ask us, the heroic societies of the Icelandic sagas or the age of Homer. What does it mean to be a "good man" in such a culture? Quite clearly, a good man is a man who functions well in his culture, i.e., in the case of a heroic society, a good man is one who is courageous, loyal, honest, etc. A good watch, suggests MacIntyre, is a watch which does what a watch is supposed to do. "It follows that the concept of a watch cannot be defined independently of the concept of a good watch."[98] A good man, inevitably, is simply a man who does what a man is supposed to do. "Morality and social structure are in fact one and the same in heroic society."[99] In societies whose vision of life and of human being are fairly simple and straightforward, people do not spend time asking whether something was"right" or "wrong" in some abstract sense. These questions arise, of course, but almost always achieve resolution, at least in the eyes of those not blinded by selfish passion. The issue of what I should do is not generally cause for anguish per se, though *doing* it might be.

"A good man," then, is not some abstract conception. "A man in heroic society *is* what he *does*."[100] But what is required for a man to act well? clearly, he must possess the virtue required, virtue being precisely that excellence which makes the hero a hero in all his many facets:

> To judge a man therefore is to judge his actions. By performing actions of a particular kind in a particular situation, a man gives warrant for judgment upon his virtues and vices; for the virtues just are those qualities which sustain a free man in his role and which manifest themselves in those actions which his role requires.[101]

Thus, it would be absurd to judge a man in a heroic society by criteria taken from somewhere other than his own society. As MacIntyre says, "in heroic society there is no 'outside' except that of the stranger. A man who tried to withdraw himself from his given position in heroic society would be engaged in the enterprise of trying to make himself disappear."[102] What relevance does this analysis of the virtues of a heroic society have for the discussion of morality today?

> The answer is that perhaps what we have to learn from heroic societies is twofold: first that all morality is always to some degree tied to the socially local and particular and that the aspirations of the morality of modernity to a universality freed from all particularity is an illusion; and secondly that there is no way to possess the virtues except as part of a tradition in which we inherit them and our understanding of them from a series of predecessors in which series heroic societies hold first place.[103]

That modernity could and did conceive of morality as "universal" as MacIntyre suggests is not surprising, given what we have so far learned about the drive to achieve context-free "truth" in the physical sciences. Faced with a world of context-free facts, the thought of modernity had to see the moral problem as the plight of the individual in a world of arbitrary choice. Men must always act, but the decline of authority and the inability to connect value to fact, leaves us with a naked will standing alone. Traditionally,

> ...to be a man is to fill a set of roles each of which has its own point and purpose; member of a family, citizen, soldier, philosopher, servant of god. When man is thought of as an individual prior to and apart from all roles, 'man' ceases to be a functional concept.[104]

MacIntyre sees the contemporary and modern moral philosophy as an attempt to clothe a naked emperor. Just as Dreyfus showed that the consequences of objectivism show it to be epistemologically bankrupt, so MacIntyre presses home the point that, without a social context for virtue to appear as virtue (as for Dreyfus, there must be a perceptual horizon for an object to be perceived a object), virtue loses all meaning. Indeed, morality loses all meaning. "Each moral agent now speaks unconstrained by the externalities of divine law, natural teleology or hierarchical authority; but why should anyone now listen to him?"[105]

This is the key question of modern ethics; having given up authoritative communal projects, we have apparently achieved the benefit of individual autonomy, but at the cost of any coherent approach to our neighbors. Perhaps MacIntyre's boldest and most provocative critique is his destruction of the one moral modern category which seems to have thrived on the rise of individualism: that of human rights. International organizations like the United nations and the Catholic Church have tended to use the rhetoric of rights, sometimes with effect, as a moral language which can be shared by all, from radical feminists to totalitarian dictators. To attack the "tradition" of human rights seems not only bold and provocative, but unkind. The question really is: do the principles of human rights make any *sense*, i.e., do they have meaning?

MacIntyre is able to show that the word "right" is not present in any ancient or medieval language. This hardly proves that there are no such things, but it does demonstrate that human beings can get along quite well without the language of rights. In fact, says MacIntyre, not only have human beings gotten along quite well without the concept, they have gotten along quite well without the reality: "There are no such rights, and belief in them is one with belief in witches and in unicorns."[106] MacIntyre can not be accused of timidity. Why the confidence?

> The best reason for asserting so bluntly that there are no such rights is indeed of precisely the same type as the best reason which we possess for asserting that there are no witches and the best reason which we possess for asserting that there are no unicorns; every

59

attempt to give good reasons for believing that there *are* such rights has failed.[107]

It makes some sense to argue that, as a Roman citizen or a lord of the realm, one has certain privileges and responsibilities, since such privileges serve a social function and are given precisely because they do serve a function. But when the concept is stretched to include everybody, it is difficult to make sense of it, at least apart from religious language about "God-given" rights, as in the U. S. Declaration of Independence. In other words, it seems that validity-of-rights language is not really demonstrable, a fact conceded by those defending it.

Are we left then with Nietzsche's thesis that all morality is ultimately will-to-power?

> The power of Nietzsche's position depends upon the truth of one central thesis: That all rational vindications of morality manifestly fail and that therefore belief in the tenets of morality needs to be explained in terms of a set of rationalisations which conceal the fundamentally non-rational phenomena of the will.[108]

This is where modernity leaves morality: with a crippling nihilism, masked at times with sentimentality. MacIntyre's positive analysis of moral behavior, as we have seen, pointed out that all moral discourse requires a tradition of goals and practices, a community. If we examine MacIntyre's positive contribution briefly, we will see several helpful insights. Recall that MacIntyre wants to revive the concept of virtue as central to the understanding of morality, and that virtue is a functional term. The virtuous man is the one who, given these circumstances, can perform as he should. This leaves MacIntyre with the task of describing more clearly the context within which the virtue can make sense. To do this he must define three key terms: *practice, narrative order,* and *moral tradition.* These are progressively wider concepts: "Each later stage presupposed the earlier, but not vice-versa."[109] Let us look at each of them.

In many ways, what MacIntyre means by a practice is what Toulmin means by an enterprise, and is not dissimilar to what Polanyi would call, variously, a tradition or a rational framework, etc. At any rate, MacIntyre defines practice as:

> ...any coherent and complex form of socially established cooperative human activity through which goods internal to that form of activity are realized in the course of trying to achieve those standards of excellence which are appropriate to, and partially definitive of, that form of activity, with the result that human powers to achieve excellence, and human conceptions of the ends and goods involved, are systematically extended.[110]

MacIntyre's distinction between external and internal goods is interesting and illuminating. The virtuous man is not the one who does not get pleasure from what he does, but precisely the one who gets pleasure out of doing the right thing. But what pleasures are indeed the right ones in each case? MacIntyre uses the example of chess. One can motivate a child to learn to play the game by rewards of cash or candy, but not until the child begins to enjoy it, as we say, "for its own sake," can we be confident that we have truly initiated him into the practice. Goods internal to chess might include the pleasure of calculating moves or learning how to use strategic principles, or just the thrill of victory, but together they make up what the practice is all about. (Incidentally, such an understanding is alien to the computer.) A person who "enjoys" chess, then can attain the goods of the practice even if she should lose, and could appreciate excellence in others even if they should lose. Experiencing the internal good is essential to judging the performance of others. A person who does not "like" painting or English romantic poetry or driving race cars is by that fact able to judge such performances only inadequately.

Note that the performances of which we speak require initiation into a practice. There may be some goods attendant upon chess which are immediate (like the enjoyment of the beauty of the pieces) but they are minimal and only debatably

61

"internal." Getting the right kind of pleasure is something that one must learn, and learn through a process of relatively blind obedience. Thus,

> ...a practice involves standards of excellence and obedience to rules as well as the achievement of goods. To enter into a practice is to accept the authority of those standards and the inadequacy of my own performance as judged by them. It is to subject my own attitudes, choices, preferences and tastes to the standards which currently and partially define the practice.[111]

Internal goods are therefore a bit odd, at least to a mind accustomed to translating the term "good" into "individual pleasureable state." For external goods like money or fame may be sought simply as useful for one's own pleasure, but internal goods are different. "Their achievement is good for the whole community who participate in the practice."[112] In many ways the pleasure of internal goods is the pleasure of giving oneself over to something greater than oneself, a good (perhaps the word pleasure is already hopelessly individualistic) obtained by "subordinating ourselves to the best standard so far achieved, and that entails subordinating ourselves within the practice in our relationship to other practicioners."[113] It entails suffering a good deal of pain at times; it entails being a responsible participant in the development of the ongoing practice which includes more than me; it entails self-control and a willingness to overlook minor annoyances. "In other words, we have to accept as necessary components of any practice with internal goods and standards of excellence the virtues of justice, courage and honesty."[114]

Thus one does not *seek* pleasure in this conception; one seeks a particular good, with pleasure attending upon the attainment of the good, but not to be confused with it. "Virtue" here becomes that quality by which we can successfully seek the good, but seek it in an unselfish way. "It is of the character of a virtue that in order that it be effective in producing the internal goods which are the rewards of the virtues it should be exercised without regard to the consequences."[115]

In many ways the preceding analysis of pleasure and virtue will be familiar to readers of Aquinas and Aristotle. And though the discussion of virtues as functionally defined as skills within a practice would surprise Aristotle, the next question MacIntyre asks is very Aristotelian. For, to place virtues within practices is to raise the question of the relation of the various practices to each other. To make sense of each practice, MacIntyre must ask himself, "What is the good for man?" Not simply the good at this moment (as within this practice) but the good for his whole life. Answering this question will require answering questions about the meaning of a human life and its unity. But if we have assimilated the discussion about *practice*, it will come as no great surprise that practices are part of a larger order of human acts. This is the case. For MacIntyre, to be human is to be part of a narrative which links birth to life to death as narrative beginning to middle to end."[116]

The introduction of the notion of narrative is extremely important. For "narrative history of a certain kind turns out to be the basic and essential genre for the characterization of human actions."[117] Human actions show up as such, as human actions, only against the background of a story which explains them, which situates them. The basic insight is completely in line with Toulmin, Polanyi and Dreyfus. What MacIntyre is saying is that the horizon or background of human actions is *narrative*. When MacIntyre says that "there is no such thing as 'behaviour', to be identified prior to and independently of intentions, beliefs and settings,"[118] he is simply extending ideas we have noted before in this chapter.

But if our lives are stories, stories must be *told*. There must be conversation. And conversation itself is a kind of narrative, or better, without conversation there can be no "deeds', because deeds are such only against the background story, and story requires words. Conversation, one might say, *is* story. It is "the form of human transactions in general."[119] In our conversations we tell our stories in which our deeds become deeds, and our conversations are themselves stories. We are, in short, embodied narratives:

A central thesis then begins to emerge: man is in his actions and practice, as well as in his fictions, essentially a story-telling animal. He is not essentially, but becomes through his history, a teller of stories that aspire to truth. But the key question for men is not about their own authorship; I can only answer the question 'What am I to do?' if I can answer the prior question 'Of what story or stories do I find myself a part?'[120]

Recall that to make the notion of practice intelligible it had to be put into the larger context of the narrative order, or story, of a person's life. Now we see that a person's life is not a story by itself, but is simply part of a larger story which is being told by someone other than him.

Of course, one could ask at this point, "What, then is a story?", but as Aristotle observed long ago, the most basic terms cannot be defined. If we are story, *are* conversation, we can hardly jump out of our skins, as it were, and define ourselves without conversing. But one can describe, if not define, story. One can say, for example, that "at any given point in an enacted narrative we do not know what will happen next."[121] This simply points to the fact that human actions are explainable, but not predictable. There is a rational relationship between actions (the rational relationship of events in a story) but they could have been otherwise. The problem of freedom and determinism lies here. But here is another crucial characteristic of story: it has a goal, a *telos*:

We live out our lives, both individually and in or relationships with each other, in the light of certain conceptions of a possible shared future in which certain possibilities beckon us forward and others repel us, some seem already foreclosed and other perhaps inevitable. There is no present which is not informed by some image of some future and an image of the future which always presents itself in the form of a *telos*--or of a variety of ends or goals--toward which we are either moving or failing to move in the present. Unpredictability and teleology therefore co-exist as part of our lives.[122]

To argue that human life has the character of a narrative, that it is unpredictable and yet oriented toward a goal, is to raise the question: what goal? MacIntyre points out that the struggle with this question arises when heroic culture breaks down (or changes) into something more flexible and confusing. Aristotle and Plato were, in their various ways, trying to deal with the question of what to do when the story is no longer crystal clear. To talk this way is to talk about the third of the concepts we have promised to talk about: moral tradition. Our practices, chess playing or writing books, fit into the context of the story of a life, and the story of a life is never really the story of a life, but part of the story, if you will, of the moral tradition of which it is a part. But what is the goal of a moral tradition?

One could, or course, say that the goal of a moral tradition is the "good life" for human beings, but then one would have to ask just what the good is, and different traditions will have different answers to the question. MacIntyre does not make the point, but, if we leave the definition there, we will be faced with a relativism which is not helpful. For if we agree with MacIntyre that "all reasoning takes place within the context of some traditional mode of thought,"[123] we may find ourselves feeling trapped. But the truth is that the good life is the life spent, among other things, arguing about the good life:

> A living tradition then is an historically extended, socially embodied argument, an argument precisely in part about the goods which constitute the tradition.[124]

What this means is that, for the tradition, as for the individual, the meaning of life is that it is a quest for the meaning of life: "The good life for man is the life spent in seeking for the good life for man, and the virtues necessary for the seeking are those which will enable us to understand what more and what else the good life for man is."[125] We are in the tricky position of people who have come upon a group telling stories around a campfire, stories which pierce to the heart of the group, and now it is our turn.

Unfortunately, for MacIntyre, that tradition which is an argument about the tradition has pretty much died. The last moment when such a tradition existed was perhaps a century or more ago: "Jane Austen is in a crucial way...the last great representative of the classical tradition of the virtues."[126] In her novels, one finds a world where virtue is practiced--particular virtues suited to a particular world:

> Jane Austen writes comedy rather than tragedy for the same reason that Dante did: she is a Christian and she sees the *telos* of human life implicitly in its everyday form. Her irony resides in the way that she makes her characters and her readers see and say more and other than they intended to, so that they and we correct ourselves. The virtues and the harms and evils which the virtues alone will overcome provide the structure both of a life in which the telos can be achieved and of a narrative in which the story of such a life can be unfolded. Once again it turns out that any specific account of the virtues presupposes an equally specific account of the narrative structure and unity of a human life and vice versa.[127]

When Jane Austen wrote, however, the light was already dying. As our culture has disintegrated, we can now see that "we have all too many disparate and rival moral concepts, in this case rival and disparate concepts of justice, and that the moral resources of the culture allow us no way of settling the issue between them rationally."[128] If we take the position that the life of virtue requires a community within which to flourish, and if one takes the subsequent position that community has broken down in our time, then the conclusion is obvious: the life of the virtues is impossible in our time. This is the crisis for MacIntyre, and its solution is obvious: "What matters at this stage is the construction of local forms of community within which civility and the intellectual and moral life can be sustained through the new dark ages which are already upon us."[129]

One might quibble with this pessimism. If rational debate is now impossible, writing a book about the impossibility of rational debate sounds like the classic attempt of absurdists to communicate to the world that communication is impossible. The success of the enterprise destroys its point. And where would come the possibility for renewal? If virtue can only be virtue within a community, then creating community can hardly be a virtuous act; it would be something like fathering oneself; a *creatio sui ex nihilo* which not even God has done. Perhaps it is useful here to go back to our first thinker, Stephen Toulmin, and his criticism of Frege and Collingwood. Trying to be too neat, we destroy ourselves. Seeing rationality in terms of a rigorous system, whether that system be objectivist as in the case of Frege, or relativist as in the case of Collingwood, obscures what should be the obvious fact that in human affairs, all things are, as Aristotle liked to observe, "for the most part" and "on the whole." A total collapse of community in America would be literally unthinkable: we could only throw stones at each other. It is surely not a reckless assertion that we have not yet gotten to that point.

What we have done in this chapter is to show that, quite apart form the Continental existentialist and phenomenological tradition, a plausible attack on, and a plausible alternative to, objectivism is possible. Moving from Toulmin to MacIntyre we have tried to show that scientific knowledge requires a context of an on-going human enterprise (Toulmin); that this enterprise requires commitment and passion and faith (Polanyi); that human knowing inherently bodily, situational, and purposive, and thus not reproduceable by a machine (Dreyfus); and that human beings are by their nature a part of a story or conversation, which tells them as much as it is told by them. There are many things about which our chosen authors would disagree; this strengthens our case. For the agreements which we have been able to point out along the way are remarkable enough. One could object that two of our writers have been somewhat influenced by phenomenology already (Dreyfus, and, perhaps, MacIntyre), but this does not obscure the unique character of their contribution to this discussion. At any rate,

Dreyfus' arguments by no means require a Heideggerian basis, nor do MacIntyre's.

It would have been interesting to pursue our inquiry in this chapter into other areas. James McClendon's study of Anglo-American linguistic philosophy in many ways parallels our concerns, for example,[130] and the struggle against a "value-free" sociology (and social science in general) does as well.[131] And the entire American pragmatist tradition, Pierce and James Dewey, has many affinities with our perspective. But we must stop somewhere. The point we wished to make in this chapter has, we hope, been made.

Notes

1. Stephen Toulmin, <u>Human Understanding</u>, (Princeton: Princeton University Press, 1972), p.43.

2. Toulmin, p. 44.

3. Toulmin, pp. 56-57.

4. Toulmin, p. 59.

5. Toulmin, p. 95.

6. Thomas Kuhn, <u>The Structure of Scientific Revolutions</u>, (Chicago: The University of Chicago Press, 1972), p. 10.

7. Kuhn, p. 158.

8. Kuhn, p. 170.

9. Toulmin, p. 150.

10. Toulmin, p. 29.

11. Toulmin, p. 219.

12. Toulmin, p. 120.

13. Toulmin, p. 153.

14. Toulmin, p. 252.

15. Toulmin, cf. especially Chapter 5, "Interlude: Evolution and the Human Sciences."

16. Toulmin, p. 247, (discussing Pierre Duheim.)

17. Toulmin, p. 84.

18. Toulmin, p. 85.

19. Toulmin, p. 257.

20. Toulmin, p. 191.

21. Toulmin, p. 281.

22. Toulmin, p. 241.

23. Toulmin, p. 370.

24. Toulmin, p. 370.

25. Richard J. Bernstein, <u>Beyond Objectivism and Relativism</u>, (Philadelphia: University of Philadelphia Press, 1983).

26. Toulmin, p. 496.

27. Toulmin, p. 491.

28. Toulmin, p. 497.

29. Toulmin, p. 494.

30. Toulmin, p. 503.

31. Toulmin, p. 408.

32. Michael Polanyi, <u>Personal Knowledge</u> (Chicago: University of Chicago Press, 1962), p. 140.

33. Polanyi, p. 141.

34. Polanyi, p. 52.

35. Polanyi, p. 53.

36. Polanyi, p. 54.

37. Polanyi, p. 55.

38. Polanyi, p. 56.

39. Polanyi, p. 56.

40. Polanyi, p. 59.

41. Polanyi, p. 54.

42. Polanyi, p. 54.

43. Polanyi, p. 60.

44. Polanyi, p. 267.

45. Polanyi, p. 316.

46. Polanyi, p. 316.

47. Polanyi, p. 323.

48. Polanyi, p. 268.

49. Michael Polanyi, "The Potential Theory of Absorption" in Polanyi, <u>Knowing and Being</u>, ed. by Marjorie Grene (Chicago: University of Chicago Press, 1964), p.93.

50. Polanyi, Science, Faith, and Society (Chicago: University of Chicago Press, 1946), p. 16.

51. Polanyi, p. 16.

52. Polanyi, p. 57.

53. Polanyi, p. 59.

54. Polanyi, p. 57.

55. Polanyi, p. 59.

56. Polanyi, p. 10.

57. Polanyi, p. 10.

58. Toulmin, p. 59.

59. Polanyi, Science, Faith, and Society, p. 17.

60. Toulmin, p. 83.

61. Polanyi, p. 17.

62. Herbert Dreyfus, What Computers Can't Do, (New York: Harper and Row, 1979).

63. Dreyfus, p. 67.

64. Dreyfus, p. 68.

65. Dreyfus, p. 68.

66. Dreyfus, p. 68.

67. Dreyfus, pp. 68-69.

68. Leibnitz, Selections, ed. by Philip Wiener, (New York: Scribners, 1931), p. 48. Quoted in Dreyfus, p. 70.

69. Dreyfus, p. 72.

70. Dreyfus, p. 156.

71. Dreyfus, p. 162.

72. Dreyfus, p. 187.

73. Dreyfus, p. 189.

74. Dreyfus, p. 203.

75. Dreyfus, p. 203.

76. Dreyfus, p. 203.

77. Dreyfus, p. p.205.

78. Dreyfus, p. 222.

79. Dreyfus, p. 222.

80. Dreyfus, p. 234.

81. Dreyfus, p. 237.

82. Dreyfus, p. 241.

83. Friedrich Schleiermacher, <u>Hermeneutics</u>, ed. by Heinz Kimmerle (Missoula, MT:Scholars Press, 1977), p. 113. Cf. also p. 195.

84. Dreyfus, p. 249.

85. Dreyfus, p. 250.

86. Dreyfus, p. 255.

87. Dreyfus, p. 255.

88. Dreyfus, p. 260.

89. Dreyfus, p. 263.

90. Dreyfus, p. 274.

91. Dreyfus, p. 274.

92. Dreyfus, p. 275.

93. Martin Heidegger, <u>Being and Time</u> (New York: Harper and Row), p.32.

94. Dreyfus, p. 277.

95. Dreyfus, p. 304.

96. Alasdair MacIntyre, <u>After Virtue</u> (Notre Dame: 1981), p.54.

97. MacIntyre, p. 54.

98. MacIntyre, p. 55.

99. MacIntyre, p. 116.

100. MacIntyre, p. 115.

101. MacIntyre, p. 115.

102. MacIntyre, p. 119.

103. MacIntyre, p. 119.

104. MacIntyre, p. 56.

105. MacIntyre, p. 67.

106. MacIntyre, p. 67.

107. MacIntyre, p. 67.

108. MacIntyre, p. 111.

109. MacIntyre, p. 174.

110. MacIntyre, p. 175.

111. MacIntyre, p. 177.

112. MacIntyre, p. 178.

113. MacIntyre, p. 178.

114. MacIntyre, p. 178.

115. MacIntyre, p. 185.

116. MacIntyre, p. 191.

117. MacIntyre, p. 194.

118. MacIntyre, p. 194.

119. MacIntyre, p. 197.

120. MacIntyre, p. 201.

121. MacIntyre, p. 200.

122. MacIntyre, pp.200-201.

123. MacIntyre, p. 206.

124. MacIntyre, p. 207.

125. MacIntyre, p. 204.

126. MacIntyre, p. 226.

127. MacIntyre, p. 226.

128. MacIntyre, p. 231.

129. MacIntyre, p. 245.

130. James McClendon and James Smith, <u>Understanding Religious Convictions</u> (Nashville: Abingdon Press, 1974).

131. Norma Haan and Robert Bellah, et. al., <u>Social Science as Moral Inquiry</u> (New York: Columbia University Press, 1983).

Chapter Two
Gadamer: The Recovery of Prudence

We have been concerned in our last chapter with an attack on objectivism, an ideal of knowledge which sees detachment as a goal to be striven for. As we have seen, however, "as long as science remains the ideal of knowledge, and detachment the ideal of science, ethics cannot be secured against complete destruction by skeptical doubt."[1] Indeed, if the Laplacean ideal of placing all atoms on a huge time/space grid were ever achieved, "it would tell us absolutely nothing that we are interested in."[2] If teleology, a larger human context, is absent from our experience of the world, it cannot be imported later from somewhere else.

This rejection of a conception of reason which sees it as primarily "theoretical" i.e., detached, context-free, neutral with regard to purpose, is shared as well by Hans-Georg Gadamer and his famed teacher, Martin Heidegger. Like the previously discussed thinkers, Heidegger and Gadamer are concerned to recover an understanding of knowledge which is not alienating, which re- situates the human person *in* the world and not *above* it. The thesis we develop in this chapter is that the enterprise begun by Heidegger and continued by Gadamer is a rehabilitation of the Aristotelian virtue of *phronesis*, of prudence, and of the rhetorical tradition flowing from that virtue. We will show, further, that the retrieval of *phronesis* is the way to overcome the impasses of objectivistic thinking, to re-establish the humanities and morality, and to regain a concept of knowledge faithful to the historical nature of human being.

To some, especially those only marginally interested in Heidegger, it might appear at first glance that to regard Martin Heidegger as in any way an Aristotelian is a poor joke. Isn't Aristotle the chief representative of precisely that kind of metaphysical thinking which the German philosopher is at pains to "destroy?" Aren't Plato and Aristotle exactly the ones who started us on the road of objectifying, "present-at-hand" consciousness? This is partially true, but there are, in a way, two Aristotles. There is the Aristotle of the <u>Metaphysics</u> and the Aristotle of the <u>Ethics</u> and <u>Politics</u>. It is the latter Aristotle who will be helpful to us. As Gadamer says:

> In considering the structure of the hermeneutical process I have explicitly referred to the Aristotelian analysis of *phronesis*. Basically, I have followed here a line that Heidegger began in his early years in Freiburg...It is true that Aristotle's ontological basis became suspect for Heidegger even in his early investigations, a basis on which the whole of modern philosophy, especially the idea of subjectivity and that of consciousness, as well as the impasses of historicism, is founded (what is called in <u>Being and Time</u> the 'ontology of the present-at-hand'). But in one point Aristotelian philosophy was at that time much more than a counter-model for Heidegger, but was a real vindication of his own philosophical purposes: in the Aristotelian critique of Plato's universal *eidos* and, positively, in the demonstration of the analogical structure of the good and the knowledge of the good, as is the task in the situation of action.[3]

Thus, Gadamer sees Aristotelian ethics as an ally of Heidegger and of himself. As Gadamer says elsewhere in <u>Truth and Method</u>, "Aristotle's analysis is in fact a kind of model of the problems of hermeneutics."[4] Since hermeneutics is the enterprise Gadamer considers himself to be about, this must be considered a strong statement. Indeed, Gadamer goes further: "For moral knowledge must be a kind of experience, and in fact we shall see that it is perhaps the fundamental form of experience, compared with which all other experience represents a denaturing."[5] From the hint offered in this quotation we can be prepared for the fact that the problem of the modern scientific outlook, which we saw in our last chapter, namely, how does one find values in a world of fact, is dealt with by reversing the question. It is not, for Gadamer, that we live in a world of objective fact, which then needs to be related somehow to human concerns. Rather, he follows Heidegger in claiming that "present-at-hand", objective knowledge is derived from, and subordinate to, a more primordial understanding, an understanding from *within* the situation, and not above it. This is the insight the philosophers in our last chapter were moving toward, at least.

The *locus classicus* for a discussion of the distinction between the two kinds of knowledge is to be found in Heidegger's major work, Being and Time, in his famous account of the hammer.

> Where something is put to use, our concern subordinates itself to the 'in order to" which is constitutive for the equipment we are employing at the time; the less we just stare at the hammer-Thing, and the more we seize hold of it and use it, the more primordial does our relationship to it become, and the more unveiledly is it encountered as that which it is--as equipment. The hammering itself uncovers the specific manipulability of the hammer. The kind of Being which equipment possesses--in which it manifests itself in its own right--we call readiness-to-hand *(Zuhandenheit)*.[6]

"Readiness to hand", then, is the the kind of being which equipment-- like the hammer--possesses. Heidegger is now able to contrast this kind of knowledge with theoretical knowledge: "If we look at Things just 'theoretically', we can get along without understanding "readiness to hand." But when we deal with them by using them and manipulating them, this activity is not a blind one; it has its own kind of sight."[7] Heidegger considers this last point worth repeating on the next page: "Action has its *own kind* of sight."[8]

Thus the great shift which Heidegger makes in modern philosophy is to put readiness-to-hand in the primordial position and presence-at-hand (objective or scientific or theoretical knowledge) in a derivative one. Subject-object knowledge, the awareness of things possessed by "I", is not the starting point of all the rest of knowledge, as philosophers have mistakenly thought at least since Descartes; rather it is a *deficient mode of something more basic*: the knowledge which we find ourselves using as beings in a world of care and purpose. This is a thesis clearly more radical than those of Toulmin or Polanyi.

But what characterizes this more basic knowledge, and how does the Aristotelian critique shed light on it? Further, what does it have to do with Gadamer's task, namely, hermeneutics? And lastly, how do both of these questions relate to the problem of the modern scientific outlook (and, ultimately, to the problem of faith)? Recall that Gadamer's chief and general concern, the discipline called hermeneutics, is, to put it another way, the concern about understanding (*Verstehen*). Gadamer wants to "discover what is common to all modes of understanding."[9] But understanding, for Gadamer, occurs in a conversation *with* someone *about* something, whether that someone be a text or a person or a tradition. Anyone who has ever been in a conversation knows that it has, as they say, a "life of its own." It does not proceed by pre-arranged and rigid determinations.

Indeed, the kind of conversation which is undertaken for pedagogical or psycho-therapeutic reasons is not conversation in the best sense of the term; there is a kind of inauthenticity about it. Such discourse, however helpful and necessary it might be for a participant or a pupil, is lifeless as conversation. The understanding which "happens" in language is, then, the basic knowledge for Gadamer. It seems, however, that we have gotten far away from Heidegger's hammer. But not really. For Heidegger, understanding, on a primordial level, is what is going on in the middle of hammering, *in the concernful action itself*, and not in the contemplation of the hammer apart from the action. And though we cannot pursue the point in detail here, even in <u>Being and Time</u> (but especially in the later writing), authentic action, understanding, and language or discourse are not separable. For *Dasein's* job, as it were, the point of its activity, is to allow truth to occur, and truth shines forth most perfectly in discourse:

When we talk in an ontically figurative way of the *lumen naturale* in man we have in mind nothing other than the existential-ontological structure of this entity, that it *is* in such a way as to be its 'there'. To say that it is 'illuminated' (*erleuchtet*) means that as Being-in-the-world it is cleared (*gelichtet*) in itself, not through any other entity, but in such a way that it *is* itself the clearing. (*Lichtung*)...*Dasein is* its disclosedness.[10]

It is the task or vocation of *Dasein*, then, to be the place where understanding occurs, and understanding is primordially present in *Dasein's* practices: "Interpretation is carried out primordially not in a theoretical statement but in an action of circumspective concern--laying aside the unsuitable tool."[11] Nevertheless, "discourse is the Articulation of intelligibility"[12] and the "way in which discourse gets expressed is language."[13] Language, then, is not a set of individual present-at-hand word-things, but concernful discourse, primordial conversation previous to any particular word. Ontically, the discourse may take place in the middle of and be expressive of the concern of building a house; on a deeper level, the discourse reveals *Dasein's* very essence as *Being whose care is Being*, the place where truth shines forth from the darkness of hiddenness. Thus concernful action, conversation--and truth-- are not enemies for Heidegger, but friends. For Gadamer, understanding which happens *within* the conversation, and not apart from it, is the basic understanding.

At this point one might ask, "but how do I know what to say to allow truth to happen authentically in a conversation?" With the asking of this question we have reached the fundamental Gadamerian problematic of *application in a situation*. Toulmin had mentioned the issue, Polanyi had developed a theory of connoisseurship, but for Gadamer, application *is* understanding. Gadamer's great predecessor in hermeneutical theory, Friedrich Schleiermacher, had taken almost exactly the opposite tack in his consideration of the question of understanding bequeathed to him by the 18th century:

Only what Ernesti...calls *subilitas intelligendi* genuinely belongs to hermeneutics. As soon as the *subtilitas explicandi* becomes more than the outer side of understanding, it becomes part of the art of presentation, and is itself subject to hermeneutics. Therefore, by making a special application of the universal rules, hermeneutics may offer suggestions for the proper *use* of commentaries, but not for the writing of them.[14]

What is happening here is of major importance, because Schleiermacher is such a critical figure in theology and biblical hermeneutics. Schleiermacher *separates* understanding from its application, i.e., the writing of commentaries on the scriptures or the delivery of a homily. It is obvious to Schleiermacher that *making use* of knowledge is different from *possessing it*, and he is more concerned here with the latter. But, as we have seen for Heidegger, so for Gadamer, *the employment of knowledge is not another thing beside knowledge*. Understanding is not something present in the mind of the reader apart from a conversation. *It is only in the actual application of knowledge* (Schleiermacher's *explicandi*), only in its actual use, as it were, *that understanding occurs.*

For Gadamer, then, hermeneutics, the art of understanding, is not a set of universal rules for mastering a text, no matter how subtle the rules might be envisioned to be. For such a set of rules would still be present-at-hand knowledge which would *have to be applied* to a novel situation. And how would I know how to apply these rules? It seems that the knowledge we are seeking here is not a method, if method is a set of rules, but something that *precedes* rules and makes their use possible. It is here that the analysis of Aristotle in the Ethics becomes helpful. The point of analogy between Aristotle's Nichomachean Ethics and Gadamer's hermeneutics is not in the actual subject matter, for they are different. Aristotle, in his Ethics, is concerned with moral action; Gadamer in Truth and Method, is concerned with understanding, especially in the human sciences. (Of course, these two domains are ultimately related, as we have seen, but the point we want to make is that Gadamer does not see himself as a moralist.) The immediate point of contact between the two phenomenologies, as it were, Aristotle's description of moral behavior, and Gadamer's description of hermeneutical understanding, is in the issue of *application:*

> This is the point at which we can relate Aristotle's analysis of moral knowledge to the hermeneutical problem....Hermeneutical consciousness is not involved with either technical or moral knowledge but these two types of knowledge still include *the same element of application* that we have recognized as the central problem of hermeneutics.[15] (Emphasis is Gadamer's)

Thus, like Gadamer and Heidegger, Aristotle was faced with the problem of a tradition of knowledge which saw truth *primarily* as presence-at-hand (the tradition of the Academy), and with the need to apply that universal knowledge to a particular situation (*this* text, *this* moral action, *this* conversation). Aristotle's discoveries and struggles in this enterprise show up (at least for us) some of the problems with the Platonic conception, for which the right behavior depended simply on *knowing-that,* or present-at-hand knowledge. The good person is the person who has knowledge; the one who has knowledge is a good person. For it is certainly arguable that the mere possession of present- at-hand knowledge does not guarantee moral goodness. And yet, it is certainly true that there is *some* connection between knowledge (we might use the term "wisdom" is English at this point) and good behavior. How to solve the problem? How do we get at the kind of knowledge that is involved in applying rules to a particular situation?

If it is clear that the kind of knowledge we seek is not *episteme,* theoretical knowledge (for both Plato and Aristotle, this is knowledge proper, science), it should also be clear that it is not to be identified with mere skill, *techne,* though it seems to have affinities with the latter. But moral action is not really a *making,* and moral knowledge is not really *knowing-how,* as if fashioning one's actions were exactly the same as fashioning a pot or a house. Clearly, a pot or a house is external and controllable in a way that our own actions can never be.

Rather, the knowledge we seek has to do with a person's possession of himself or herself in action in a non-present-at-hand way, i.e., not knowledge *about* oneself, how tall one might be, how strong, but something which underlies all these in a mysterious way. How to talk about this knowledge? Gadamer mentions that "Aristotle's ability to describe phenomena from every aspect constitutes his real genius."[16] And in this case, Gadamer suggests, Aristotle's phenomenology of moral action can be instructive for us in our own concernful conversation in *three principal ways*. Let us look at them. First says Gadamer, moral knowledge for Aristotle is a *peculiar* form of knowledge. It is peculiar in that *we do not learn it*. There is never a time before we have moral knowledge. The point that we *always already* know the basics was, of course, classically expressed by Plato. "And he was profoundly correct when he taught that all cognition is only what it is as recognition, for a 'first cognition' is as little possible as a first word."[17]

> What sort of folly is it to say that a child speaks a 'first word'. What kind of madness is it to want to discover the original language of humanity by having children grow up in hermetic isolation from human speaking and then, from their first babbling of an articulate sort, recognize an actual human language and accord it the honor of being the "original" language of creation. What is mad about such ideas is that they want to suspend in some artificial way our very enclosedness in the linguistic world in which we live. In truth we are always already at home in language, just as much as we are in the world.[18]

There is no first word, then, because to speak even one word, to really *speak* one word, and not just babble it, means to speak a sentence, i.e., some statement which makes sense, a *logos*. There is no learning how to do this. One simply does it or not. So *moral knowledge, like hermeneutic understanding, is more like the action of a tradition than it is my action*, just as it is truer to say that language speaks us than that we use language. We do speak and do act, of course, but in each case we are part of something larger than ourselves. It is not difficult to find evidence in Aristotle's Ethics to support Gadamer's interpretations of the ancient philosopher. It is one of Aristotle's characteristic comments throughout the text of the Ethics that "moral goodness is the child of habit, from which it has got its name, *ethics* being derived from *ethos*, habit, by a slight alteration in the quantity of the e."[19] And how do we acquire such habits, such customary ways of acting? Aristotle's answer is that "we acquire the virtues by first exercising them. The same is true of the crafts in general. The craftsman has to learn how to make things, but he learns in the process of making them."[20] It one is good, one does good things; in order to do good things, one must already be good.

But what of the evaluative question, i.e., how do we know that what we are doing is indeed "the good?" Aristotle answers that "we may use the pleasure or pain that accompanies the exercise of our disposition as an index of how far they have established themselves. A man is temperate who, abstaining from bodily pleasures finds this abstinence pleasant."[21] And so Aristotle paints for us a picture of the virtous person. In this picture the virtuous person is the one who does the virtuous thing "by second nature", as the scholastics used to put it: he finds the virtuous action pleasurable ("natural"), the vicious action repugnant. The brave soldier, for example, is not so much the soldier who can overcome his natural fear, but the one who actively *enjoys* the risks of combat.

All well and good, but clearly and unfortunately, most people have *not* achieved, if it is something to be achieved at all, the state of virtue. Why is this the case? The answer, for Aristotle, has to do with *education*, or the lack of it, and education has to do with *the training of the emotional responses*. Aristotle states his point with exemplary clarity:

> Pleasure has a way of making us do what is disgraceful; pain deters us from doing what is right and fine. Hence the importance--I quote Plato--of having been brought up to find pleasure and pain in the right things. True education is just such a training."[22]

Thus a good person is the one who is trained from youth to find good things pleasant and bad things unpleasant; virtue is in such a person's very bones, as it were.

But a skeptical mind might still be unsatisfied. We asked how it is that one can be sure that one is doing good, and were told that the virtuous person finds good things pleasant, the vicious unpleasant. Then we asked how one became virtuous, and were told that one had to be educated. But how do I know that what I have been trained to see as good truly *is* good? In book 10 of the <u>Ethics</u> Aristotle gives perhaps his clearest and fullest answer:

> In all such cases we are guided by the belief that the truth is that which seems to the good man to be true. If this be a sound principle, as it surely is, and if good--that is, the good man in respect of his goodness--is the standard by which we measure the true value of everything, it follows that the true pleasures are what seem to him to be pleasures, and the really pleasant things those which he finds pleasant. And if some things displease him which produce an agreeable impression on others, there is nothing to surprise us in that. Humanity is subject to corruption and abnormality in many forms, and what seems pleasant to persons in such a condition is not really pleasant at all. Clearly, then we are bound to affirm that the admittedly disgraceful pleasures are pleasures only to the depraved. But with regard to the reputable pleasures, what or what sort of pleasure should we affirm to be distinctively human?...We must affirm that it is that or those pleasures which perfect the activity or activities of the perfectly happy man when they are human in the full meaning of the word.[23]

Some might accuse Aristotle here of simply evading the issue. But as the noted Aristotelian scholar, Joseph Owens, says of Aristotle's position:

On the theoretical plane it has to defend itself against the charge of circularity in making correct choice and correct habituation depend reciprocally upon each other. But from the practical viewpoint the Greek *polis* already was there as a fact, and could give the education in which the virtues were developed.[24]

But we no longer live in the Greek *polis*, and so must consider the theoretical issue. As Owens goes on to say, "For Aristotle the moral judgment is of its nature dependent upon the habituation of the person making it. It allows no possibility of rubber gloves to keep it aseptic from the agent's moral orientation."[25]

Thus there is for Aristotle neither in theory or practice any archimedean point *outside* of the human community to judge goodness and badness. It is from *within* a common understanding of goodness, an understanding which *precedes my arrival* on the scene as a sentient individual, that I do the good or evil thing. That this approach raises problems goes without saying, and it is precisely Gadamer's concern to deal with them, as we shall see later on, chiefly in our discussion of the debate between Gadamer and Jurgen Habermas. But for the moment we will postpone further discussion of this point and go on to the second insight Gadamer cites as coming from Aristotle's analysis and helpful for his (Gadamer's) discussion of hermeneutical understanding.

The *second* insight, then, into moral knowledge which Aristotle's analysis provides for us and which is relevant to our concerns is the notion that moral knowledge can *never be knowable in advance:*

> In fact, this means that the end towards which our life as a whole tends and the elaboration of it into the moral principles of action, as described by Aristotle in his Ethics, cannot be the object of a knowledge that can be taught.[26]

Rather, it is more like a *seeing*, an unclouded seeing whose opposite is not mistake but blindness. One sees what has to be done *in* the moment, not before it, and perhaps not even after it. (Recall Heidegger's "Action has its own kind of sight.") Truth, moral truth, appears or does not, *in the situation.* At first, this may appear to be a flat contradiction of what we have just seen--the capital importance of a good upbringing. As Aristotle puts it himself:

> It is notorious that young persons are capable of becoming excellent geometricians and mathematicians and accomplished students in subjects of that nature. Yet the public is not easily persuaded that a young man can be prudent.[27]

Apparently we must make a distinction between teaching and upbringing, between the knowledge which can be communicated in concepts (mathematics and so on) and a knowledge which comes from experience. Principles and concepts can be memorized by a youngster, or, for that matter, stored as data in a computer memory bank. but what cannot be turned into a set of rules or principles is *prudence*: "Prudence involves knowledge of the ultimate particular thing, which cannot be attained by science but only by 'Perception'."[28]

This remarkable virtue of prudence, Aristotle continues, "involves a detailed knowledge which only comes from practical experience, and practical experience is what the young man lacks--it comes only after many years."[29] Note that prudence is not the *same* as practical experience or detailed knowledge, but *involves* them. There is a rather mysterious quality about it indeed, and Aristotle says, vaguely enough, that prudence "perceives a certain kind of truth by a process of a different order,"[30] i.e., a process different from that by which we come to knowledge of unchanging principles.

The *third* insight to which Gadamer points in his analysis of the Ethics is Aristotle's assumption that the exercise of moral knowledge involves a certain kind of *concern for the other person.* We do not seek the good simply for ourselves, but we seek it together with the other; this implies the further fact that we can *think* and *feel* with the other. Moral judgment requires a continuing conversation among *friends*, people who, as it were, are on the same side, who are truly seeking the common good and not trying to score debating points. *Moral judgment,* we have to say, *requires community*, not simply as a matter of formation in the past, but also as a matter of encouragement and challenge in the present. Aristotle takes it for granted that good men seek the company of other good men. But a more specific reflection is found in his discussion of *gnome* in book 6. This he defines as:

> . . . the quality in virtue of which we describe some men as persons of good feeling or as having fellow-feeling for others...an aptness to form a correct judgement of what is equitable. This is shown by our habit of saying that equitable men are especially prone to have sympathy or fellow-feeling for others and that it is equitable to have sympathy in certain cases. But sympathy involves a correct judgment of what is equitable, which comes to the same thing as saying a judgment of what is *truly* equitable. Reflection will show that all these qualities have the same reference: we attribute right feeling, understanding, prudence and intelligence to the same persons.[31]

In the light of our contemporary passion for distinguishing, even segregating, the cognitive and affective domains, it is remarkable that for Aristotle, the ability to make a correct moral judgment according to right reason is bound up with one's ability to feel another's pain and joy.

In the last few pages we have been examining three aspects of Aristotle's account of *phronesis*, or prudence, as laid out in the <u>Ethics</u>. But we have not been looking at them for themselves, but because they throw light, according to Gadamer, on hermeneutical understanding. We can now see that the three aspects of prudence we have been discussing are also aspects of the essential hermeneutical problem (as Gadamer poses it), i.e., the problem of application. Just as for Aristotle, the right action is not known ahead of time, *but in the situation* (though this does not deny that general principles and guidelines can be very helpful), so too, understanding in a conversation cannot be determined in advance. If it could, in fact, be determined in advance, then the real understanding would already have occurred: there would be no possibility of real surprise, real advance in knowledge.

And, just as for Aristotle the *right action is not exactly learned,* so too with understanding. In order to perform the right action I need prudence; in order to understand I need a kind of principle of understanding. To learn either of these two things would presuppose that one already had them; *the very learning would already be an exercise of the thing to be learned.* Thus we can see that the hermeneutical circle is inescapable, and not just in hermeneutics. Whenever it becomes clear that knowledge is not best seen as primarily present-at-hand but rather participational (to use the Polanyian word), its essential circularity will be obvious.

Finally, to conclude this Aristotelian phenomenological analysis, just as moral knowledge requires the virtues of *friendship,* so too does hermeneutical understanding require a kind of friendship with the interlocutor or the text. For neither Aristotle nor Gadamer is this friendship a kind of mystical communion or what Christians would call charity. This relationship, as we shall see more fully later on, is characterized by two things: not overlooking the *claim* of the other, and *listening* to what he has to say to us.[32] For to refuse to be changed by the text or the interlocutor or the work of art, to refuse in advance to even listen, would obviously make understanding impossible.

In these three aspects of prudence or *phronesis*, then, we see that the application is the understanding. Only in the actual *doing* of the thing does the right thing to do emerge:

> We were totally sure of this, that application is not an additional and casual (*gelegentlicher*) aspect of the phenomenon of understanding, but co-defines it right from the start and completely ... The interpreter who is concerned with a tradition seeks to apply it to himself. But this does not mean that the traditional text would

be received and understood by him as something public and then only later applied to specific uses. On the contrary, the interpreter wants to do nothing at all but to understand this public thing, the text. He wants, that is, to understand what the tradition is saying, which constitutes the meaning and significance of the text. But to do that, he is not allowed to lose sight of himself and of the concrete hermeneutical situation in which he finds himself. He must apply the text in this situation if he wants to understand at all.[33] (my translation)

By going back to Aristotelian *phronesis*, Gadamer is not only retrieving Aristotle, he is also retrieving one whole strand of the Western tradition which has its roots in Aristotle, namely, the tradition of rhetoric. In a world in which present-at-hand knowledge is the only knowledge regarded worthy of the term, then moral discourse, as MacIntyre points out, is not possible as rational speech, but is only comprehensible as an expression of one's emotional preference.

It is important to underline the point here that understanding, for Gadamer, is *rational*, difficult as this may be to grasp for those who can see knowledge only as present-at-hand. In fact, *the disagreement is precisely over what qualifies as rational.* But where "all evaluative judgments and more specifically all moral judgments are nothing but expressions of preference, expressions of attitude or feeling,"[34] then clearly *rhetoric* can only be the art of manipulating people's emotions in order to cause them to do your own (arbitrary) will. And this is precisely what the word has become for many people.

We might add that the modern notion of rhetoric is not only cynical about *reason*, but it is also, or especially, cynical about *emotions*, characterizing them as little more than animal impulses useful in controlling people. That an emotion is not a dispensable epiphenomenon of human being is hard to accept when one's concept of what is important is present-at-hand knowledge. Gadamer's vision is, among many other things, a defense of human feeling much more profound than that of the Romantics, who were still caught in the conceptual framework of their opponents.

But there is, fortunately, another, older tradition of rhetoric, which sees it as *the art of uncovering the truth in this situation.* A tradition which believes only in a truth discovered *outside* the situation obviously has no use for rhetoric. But a tradition which *does* see it that way will obviously take rhetoric very seriously indeed. Rhetoric in *this* tradition is not so much the art by which the truth is sought, but the art by which truth is sought *together*:

> According to Vico, what gives the human will its direction is not the abstract generality [*Allgemeinheit*] of reason, but the concrete generality [*Allgemeinheit*] that represents the community of a group, a people a nation, or the whole human race. Hence the development of this sense of community is of prime importance for living.[35]

The Jesuit-influenced pedagogue Vico placed the claim to significance and independence of the art of rhetoric on the fact that it deepened the ability to see what is staring one in the face, *the obvious (verisimile).* This kind of knowledge is obviously not based on logical argumentation alone, for logical argumentation, to get anywhere, depends on the general sense of right and wrong, true and false, plausible or implausible, which is what rhetoric is all about. This general sense of which Vico speaks is a communal possession, *a sensus communis.* The common sense recognizes what is clear, what is obvious, what is convincing and plausible in a situation. It "works instinctively [*instinktiv*] and *ex tempore* and for this very reason cannot be replaced by science."[36]

And so Gadamer uses Vico as an exponent and an exemplar of a tradition, already embattled in Vico's own time, which Gadamer wishes to retrieve: "Vico's appeal to the *sensus communis* belongs, as we have seen, in a wider context that goes right back to antiquity and the continued effect of which into the present day is the *subject of our book.*"[37] Vico's concern was educational, i.e., he was interested in the question of how one inculcates the young into the traditions of the community, as opposed to the rationalists and fideists of his day, Vico insisted that what was important was to possess a common sense which could not control or predict the future, but which could navigate in the present, and that it was "acquired through living in the community and...determined by its structures and aims."[38]

Vico's emphasis on education as a *growing into the goals of the community*, goals which must appeal to the imagination of the young, and not simply to their minds, makes him a natural ally of the modern Aristotelian whom we have investigated earlier, Alasdair MacIntyre. It is helpful at this point to note that, for MacIntyre, "the chief means of moral education is the telling of stories."[39] It is not that we decide to be a story as individuals. Nor do we find ourselves at one point in our lives in a story and at other point in our lives, not. Rather, the story, like the language we speak, is the horizon of our understanding. To understand at all is to understand within the context of the story which our community tells as its own. MacIntyre sounds a Gadamerian theme when he says that:

> ...conversation is the form of human transactions in general. Conversational behavior is not a special sort or aspect of human behavior, even though the forms of language-using and of human life are such that the deeds of others speak for them as much as do their words. For that is possible only because they are the deeds of those who have words. I am presenting both conversations in particular, then, and human actions in general, as enacted narratives.[40]

The fact that the Aristotelian ethicist MacIntyre sounds so much like Gadamer simply underscores the point we have been trying to make, the influence of Aristotle on Gadamer.

We should be able to see at this point the central role the rhetorician would play in the Gadamerian community. The rhetorician would have the role of telling the story of the community persuasively (which means truly), so that everyone in the conversation would be able to see clearly what his or her role should be. Nor would this be telling people something new and alien; it would be recalling to them the story which they already *are*. But neither would this be telling people something old and stale; for the meaning of the story is discovered only as the story unfolds. In an essay written some years after Truth and Method, Gadamer expresses this thought in the following way:

> In all our knowledge of ourselves and in all our knowledge of the world, we are always already encompassed by the language that is our own. We grow up, and we become acquainted with men and in the last analysis with ourselves when we learn to speak. Learning to speak does not mean learning to use a pre-existent tool for designating a world already somehow familiar to us; it means acquiring a familiarity and acquaintance with the world itself and how it confronts us."[41]

To summarize: what we have seen so far is that Gadamer's enterprise in Truth and Method is an appeal to an ancient tradition stemming from Aristotle and continuing up until modern times in the tradition of rhetoric and in humanistic studies. This ancient tradition to which Gadamer appeals, the tradition we are calling the *phronesis* tradition, rests on a very different concept of understanding than that which prevails in positivistic philosophies of science. Specifically, it depends on a communitarian, participatory, fiduciary (to use the Polanyian word) notion of what is means to *know*.

Gadamer's provocative retrieval of the word "prejudice" from its enlightenment tarring and feathering is in line with this general program: "The fundamental prejudice of the enlightenment is the prejudice against prejudice itself, which deprives tradition of its power."[42] If the only way I can understand is in conversation in commmunity within a language tradition, then "prejudice" is no longer a bad thing. Indeed, "historical analysis shows that it is not until the enlightenment that the concept of prejudice acquires the negative aspect we are familiar with."[43] It is, rather, a part of the tradition on which I stand. In a sense, I *am* my (our) prejudices. Prejudices are, or can be, the sedimented wisdom of the tribe, the story into which I am born and away from which I am like a word without a sentence: I am, literally, illogical.

But at this point a certain familiar uneasiness may begin to arise. Doesn't this conception of prejudice--indeed, the whole notion of *phronesis* we have been expounding so far--take for granted that the tradition, the community, the language world in which we live, the story of which we are a part, the set of prejudices by which we are formed--is *valid*? We have come up against this assumption before, but is it justified? Are there no evil traditions, oppressive languages, dehumanizing prejudices?

How can we be *sure* that the language into which we have been born is not at least partially corrupt? Is it possible that the very rhetoric of freedom so prized in the Western world, especially in this country, might not be simply a subtler form of mind control than drugs or forced entry into mental hospitals? Doesn't Gadamer's thought lead us into a passive acceptance of authority? Perhaps it is not out of place, considering the emphasis on context and community in their thought, to point to the fact of Heidegger's and Gadamer's native land, which has been so guilty of excessive respect for authority. Is Gadamer simply raising German obedience to the level of philosophy? Quite apart from such a (perhaps unfair) *ad hominem* line of thought, have not Freud, Marx and Nietzsche, Paul Ricoeur's "masters of suspicion", shown us that behind the rational conversations of our interlocutors lies hidden a host of irrational motivations, chiefly the will to power, and that the attempt to understand conversation requires that one disregard what the conversations *say* and pay attention to their economic or libidinal or power *motivations*? The question has been hovering over our heads, and it is time to look up at it courageously.

Notes

1. Michael Polanyi and Harry Prosch, <u>Meaning</u> (Chicago: University of Chicago Press, 1975), p.27.

2. Polanyi, p. 29.

3. Gadamer, <u>Truth and Method</u> (New York: Seabury Press, 1975), p.489. This quote is from a supplement to the second German edition. In general, quotations from <u>Truth and Method</u> (hereafter TM) are from the 1975 English translation, with reference, where possible to the German text. Where the translation is my own, I so note.

4. Gadamer, TM, p. 289. cf. <u>Wahrheit und Methode</u> (Tubingen, 1960) p.307.

5. Gadamer, TM, p. 288. cf. WM, p.305.

6. Martin Heidegger, <u>Being and Time</u>, translated by John MacQuarrie, (New York: Harper & Row, 1962), p.98.

7. Heidegger, BT, p. 98.

8. Heidegger, BT, p. 99.

9. Gadamer, TM, p. xix. Also a quote from the second German edition.

10. Heidegger, BT, p. 171.

11. Heidegger, BT, p. 200.

12. Heidegger, BT, pp. 203-204.

13. Heidegger, BT, p. 204.

14. Schleiermacher, <u>Hermeneutics</u> (Missoula, MT: Scholar's Press, 1977), p.13.

15. Gadamer, TM, p. 281. cf. WM, p.298.

16. Gadamer, TM, p. 283. cf. WM, p.300.

17. Gadamer, "The Scope and Function of Hermeneutical Reflection" in Philosophical Hermeneutics (Berkeley: University of California Press, 1976), p.25.

18. Gadamer, "Man and Language," in PH, p.62.

19. Aristotle, Ethics, translated by J.A.K. Thompson, (New York: Penguin Books, 1955) (Book 2, ch 1), p.55.

20. Aristotle, (Book 2,1), p.56.

21. Aristotle, (Book 2,3), p.59.

22. Aristotle, (Book 2,3), p.59.

23. Aristotle, (Book 10,5), p.300.

24. Joseph Owens, "Aristotle's Contribution on the Nature of Ethical Norms" in Listening, Fall 1983, (18:3), p.231.

25. Owens, p.232.

26. Gadamer, TM, p. 287. cf. WM, p.305.

27. Aristotle, Ethics, (Book6,8), p.182.

28. Aristotle, p. 182.

29. Aristotle, p. 182.

30. Aristotle, p. 182.

31. Aristotle, (Book 6,11), p.186.

32. Gadamer, TM, p. 324.

33. Gadamer, WM, p. 307. cf. TM, p.289.

34. MacIntyre, p. 11.

35. Gadamer, TM, p. 21. cf. WM, p. 18.

36. Gadamer, TM, p. 21. cf. WM, p. 18.

37. Gadamer, TM, p. 23. cf. WM, p. 21.

38. MacIntyre, p. 114.

39. MacIntyre, p. 197.

40. MacIntyre, p. 197.

41. Gadamer, "Man and Language," in PH, p. 63.

42. Gadamer, TM, pp. 239-240. cf. WM, p. 255.

43. Gadamer, TM, p. 240. cf. WM, p. 255.

Chapter Three
Gadamer and Habermas--the Debate Over Doubt

Jurgen Habermas, the thinker whose critique of Gadamer will take up this chapter, might seem at first to be an unlikely adversary for Gadamer. For Habermas, as a sociologist of knowledge, has attacked objectivism with, if anything, more venom than Gadamer, and has explicitly identified himself with large portions of Gadamer's analysis flowing from Schleiermacher. Habermas' best known work in this country is probably <u>Knowledge and Human Interests</u>, a book in which the attempt to sunder those two realities is shown up as inauthentic, a project with which Gadamer would agreed wholeheartedly. Let us look briefly at Habermas' project in this book. In a programmatic lecture appended to the main body of the work, Habermas points to the concept of "theory" that is at the source of our problems: "The only knowledge that can truly orient action is knowledge that frees itself from mere human interests and is based on Ideas--in other words, knowledge that has taken a theoretical attitude."[1] But the word *theory* was not always so understood in Greek thought:

> The word 'theory' has religious origins. The *theoros* was the representative sent by Greek cities to public celebrations. Through *theoria*, that is through looking on, he abandoned himself to the sacred events. In philosophical language, *theoria* was transformed to contemplation of the cosmos. In this form, theory already presupposed the demarcation between Being and time that is the foundation of ontology...It reserves to *logos* a realm of Being purged of inconstancy and uncertainty and leaves to *doxa* the realm of the mutable and the perishable. When the philosopher views the immortal order, he cannot help bringing himself into accord with the proportions of the cosmos and reproducing them internally.[2]

Thus, the traditional understanding of theory was by no means divorced from life. Through theory, one was educated into conformity with the highest life. Nevertheless, the elevation of *theoria* from the world of everyday life, its restriction to an aristocratic class, the existence of slaves to do the work of the world, and the removal of the Greeks from a place in the political system, all helped move an elevation into a chasm. Thousands of years later, "there is a real connection between the positivistic self-understanding of the sciences and traditional ontology."[3] For both modern positivistic views of science and traditional ontology:

> ...are committed to a theoretical attitude that frees those who take it from dogmatic association with the natural interests of life and their irritating influence; and both share the cosmological intention of describing the universe theoretically in its lawlike order, just as it is.[4]

What the modern sciences have lost, of course, is just the *interest* which made classical ontology human: the interest in the good life, to be achieved through contemplation. By sundering (apparently) knowledge from interest, science can claim, ironically, a kind of purity of intention which can then be used to dominate. "Whether you like it or not, this is the way things are." This is the claim of science. The fact that the findings of science are just as "value-laden", just as much the products of human interest, as any other human enterprise, is conveniently hidden, beyond critique. This leaves "humanists" to spend their time trying to import "values" back into a world of "facts", an enterprise which is inherently impossible: "The very term 'value', which neo-Kantianism brought into philosophical currency, and in relation to which science is supposed to preserve neutrality, renounces the connection between the two that theory originally intended."[5]

Habermas criticizes Husserl's attempt to re-found science on the ground of phenomenology because Husserl, while recognizing the interest-coupled nature of science, presumes that at least a disinterested study *of* science (or anything else) is *possible*. In the face of Nazi attempts to manipulate science,

99

this was understandable, says Habermas, even admirable, but it still managed to miss the real point, the essential relationship between knowledge and human interest.

The task of a truly critical philosophy of science, then, (that of Habermas) is precisely to demonstrate the connection between knowledge and interest in each of the three great areas of human understanding: science ("empirical-analytical science"), what we could call the humanities ("historical-hermeneutical science"), and critical theory itself ("emancipatory cognitive interest"), which might be regarded as philosophy proper.[6] It is quite clear that it is the last concern, the emancipatory, which is Habermas' real interest.

Once one has gotten through unmasking the pretensions of objectivism, whether the objectivism of pure science, or the equally pernicious objectivism of humanists who reduce hermeneutical understanding to technique, one is face to face with the fact that, yes, indeed, all knowledge, including our own, is conditioned by interests. This seems to leave us with the feeling that knowledge is nothing more than a way of satisfying our needs. Knowledge is nothing more than a sophisticated tool with which to manipulate the environment in accordance with my desires. Is there a way out of this counter-intuitive reduction of knowledge to manipulation? Indeed there is. Humans indeed "use" knowledge in their struggle with nature. But there is more to being human than this kind of knowledge:

> The human interests that have emerged in man's natural history, to which we have traced back the three knowledge constitutive interests derive both from nature and *from the cultural break* with nature. Along with the tendency to realize natural drives they have incorporated the tendency toward release from the constraint of nature. Even the interest in self preservation, natural as it seems, is represented by a social system that compensates for the lacks in man's organic equipment and secures his historical existence *against* the force of nature threatening from without. But society is not only a system of self preservation.

> An enticing natural force, present in the individual as *libido*, has detached itself from the behavioral system of self-preservation and urges toward utopian fulfillment.[7]

For Habermas, then, knowledge does indeed transcend mere self-preservation, because, as he goes on to say, through knowledge, humans can become *aware* of their interests and the way in which their knowledge is determined by them. True, even the critical function of knowledge is subject to the law of interest. "But the mind can always reflect back upon the interest structure that joins subject and object *a priori*: this is reserved to self-reflection. If the latter cannot cancel out self-interest it can to a certain extent make up for it."[8]

Habermas' enterprise has been called "transcendental" by many, referring to Kant's belief that he had found the fundamental conditions for the possibility of knowledge, the *a priori,* or transcendental structures of human consciousness. Habermas has not always enjoyed this designation, but the fact that he uses the word *a priori* three times in 14 lines is an indication that the adjective is not totally off the mark. For, in this programmatic lecture, Habermas makes it clear that "the standards of self-reflection are *exempted* from the singular state of suspension in which those of all other cognitive processes require critical evaluation. *They possess theoretical certainty*."[9] This is a remarkable statement. Does it mean that, finally, knowledge can be separated from human interest? Not really, for in this case, *the struggle to be free of particular interests is itself an interest:*

> In self-reflection knowledge for the sake of knowledge attains congruence with the interest in autonomy and responsibility. The emancipatory cognitive interest aims at the pursuit of reflection as such. My *fourth thesis* is thus that *in the power of self-reflection, knowledge and interest are one.*[10] (Italics his)

This his sounds like Habermas is having his cake and eating it too. Is it really so easy to sort out the drive for autonomy (legitimate) from other drives, like the will to dominate (illegitimate)? Is Habermas being naive? Actually, it is only at this point that we begin to reach the source of the disagreement between Habermas and Gadamer, and it does have to do with the accusation of naivete, but *by* Habermas *against* Gadamer. Let us see why this is so.

Habermas readily acknowledges, in fact, that his fourth thesis sounds utopian; that's the point. In the present state of affairs, power and knowledge are indeed so clandestinely and completely intertwined that true self-reflection is made extremely difficult. Only in a society where the "emancipatory cognitive interest" is given a chance to breathe can "knowledge and interest" be "one". The *a priori* possibility of autonomy and responsibility is present in the very fact of *language*, that incredible human invention (using the word in its etymological, not current definition), for in speech humans look for agreement which is unforced and lasting. But language, in the present condition of humankind, is corrupt, and therein lies the problem:

> Only in an emancipated society, whose members' autonomy and responsibility had been realized, would communication have developed into the non-authoritarian and universally practiced dialogue from which both our model of reciprocally constituted ego identity and our idea of true consensus are always implicitly derived. To this extent the truth of statements is based on anticipating the realization of the good life. The ontological illusion of pure theory behind which knowledge-constitutive interests become invisible promotes the fiction that Socratic dialogue is possible everywhere and at any time. From the beginning philosophy has presumed that the autonomy and responsibility posited with the structure of language are not only anticipated but real. It is pure theory, wanting to derive everything from itself, that succumbs to unacknowledged external conditions and become ideological. Only when philosophy discovers in the dialectical course of history the traces of violence that deform repeated attempts at dialogue and recurrently close off the path to unconstrained

> communication does it further the process
> whose suspension it otherwise legitimates:
> mankind's evolution toward autonomy
> and responsibility.[11]

It is precisely the task of critical theory, then, to *seek out the embedded inauthentic power relationships in our language.* Until this is done, and done well, conversation will remain what it is now--a utopian dream. The fact that the word "conversation" is, as it were, an eschatological term, is what Habermas accuses Gadamer of overlooking. While agreeing with Gadamer wholeheartedly in his attack on objectivism, Habermas insists that Gadamer is too quick to assume that the problem is solved once objectivism is done away with. Gadamer forgets, says Habermas, that live discourse has problems of its own. What must never be forgotten, according to Habermas, is the *conflictual* and *unequal* character of most discourse. The partners in the average conversation are inevitably possessors of differing amounts of wealth, power, linguistic ability--even such subtle determinants as looks and charm. In such conversations the inequality of the participants will result in conclusions which will not be valid, even if they are apparently acceptable to all the discussants. The coercion is hidden, which of course, makes it all the more pernicious. And thus the story (to use MacIntyre's vocabulary) is really only the story of a few--the few with the power to make their opinions count.

And, as we have seen, it is not simply a matter of obvious power, but of power doubly hidden--in the very language used by the participants. The classic example for today is perhaps that of women's liberation. If a woman is born into a culture in which women--albeit half the population--are not regarded as capable of speech, she will most likely internalize the lie and regard herself as justly excluded. Great historical figures like Joan of Arc and Queen Elizabeth of England would remark about their "feminine weakness" but their "manly" courage. So that, even if reality threatens to burst the bubble and destroy the lie embedded in the language, it is quickly re-interpreted quite naturally in the light of the prevailing misconception. Such examples could be multiplied in terms of every oppressed minority, whether of class, race, age, sexual orientation or anything else. Indeed, as Walter J. Ong has shown, the very rhetorical tradition of which Gadamer speaks so highly, is adversative to the core, and an absolutely male preserve. The presence of women alters its fundamental "agonistic" structure drastically.[12]

We are thus faced, say Habermas, with an unpleasant possibility: What if the very language which we speak, the ground on which we walk, as it were, is *itself* so corrupt that we are not even aware as we speak of how we are hiding--even from ourselves--our complicity in crime? As Habermas points out:

> We would only be justified in equating the supporting consensus, which is, according to Gadamer, at any given time prior to a successful agreement, with the factual having come to an agreement in any particular situation *if* we are certain that each consensus which has already become customary within the medium of a linguistic tradition had come into existence *without pressure* and in an *undistorted* way. But the depth-hermeneutical experience teaches us that, in the dogmatics of the tradition context, not only the objectivity of language in general prevails, but also the oppressivity of a relationship of force which deforms the intersubjectivity of an agreement as such and systematically distorts colloquial communication.[13]

Thus, on Habermas' account, Gadamer is indeed guilty of naivete. To say that the truth must emerge in the actual doing of the activity of the conversation and not before or after, as Gadamer does, ignores the fact that the conversation itself could be corrupt, and that the "truth" which emerges might not be truth at all, but covered-up domination.

Of course, it is only fair to admit that Gadamer does observe that "in every dialogue a spirit rules, a bad one or a good one, a spirit of obdurateness and hesitancy or a spirit of communication and of easy exchange between I and Thou."[14]

but surely this is not to the point. The question still remains: how do I recognize a *true* spirit of communication from a sham one? Nor, as we have noted, can we accuse Habermas of lacking appreciation for Gadamer's basic insights, and thus arguing from ignorance. As we have seen, he has praised Gadamer for his "first-rate critique of the objectivistic self-understanding of the cultural sciences", a critique (Habermas continues) which "hits not only historicism but also the false consciousness of the phenomenological and linguistic executors of its legacy."[15] And Gadamer is right, Habermas goes on to say in his review of Truth and Method, that the impartial and disinterested observer of the myth of scientism is an inadequate model for the act of understanding, not only for the human science, but for knowing in general. But Gadamer's critique in incomplete.

Up to this point it has been hard to say what the crux of the disagreement between Habermas and Gadamer might turn out to be. Granted that Habermas regards Gadamer as not giving sufficient attention to the masked oppression within the conversation, but this is surely a matter of emphasis, not substance, for Gadamer would not deny that language can contain a vicious prejudice within it, as it can contain a virtuous one. But Gadamer has indeed missed a substantial point, says Habermas, and it is this: in stressing the truth that all knowledge is knowledge-in-a-situation, Gadamer overlooks the necessity of judging the coming-to-be of knowledge by impersonal methodological criteria which can be developed by an analysis of successful communication. "The confrontation of 'truth' and 'method' should not have misled Gadamer to oppose hermeneutic experience abstractly to methodic knowledge as a whole."[16]

The mention of words like "impersonal", "method" and "abstract" sound a challenge. For Habermas, a "transcendental hermeneutics" (by that name or not) *is* possible, a setting up of the conditions for the possibility of successful interpretations. If conversations or interpreta|tions do not meet our conditions, we will be able to see how they could have been improved and just where they went wrong. Thus, method can serve the purpose of truth, and should not simply be opposed to it, as Gadamer does. So Habermas.

But if it is possible for us to derive from successful communication the transcendental conditions for its possibility, conditions which could achieve a "theoretical certainty" and form a part of an "impersonal methodology", then we are entitled to know that whose conditions are. Habermas does not disappoint. The basic criterion he wishes to employ is that of *symmetry*. This may sound a bit odd at first, but what it means is that neither of the partners in a dialogue can be favored in any way. No dialogue partner must have an "authoritative" role, because this would mean that the conclusion is determined from the start. Rather, every dialogue partner must in practice and not just in theory be interchangeable with any other dialogue partner. Elaborating on this central concept, Habermas speaks of several different kinds of symmetry. Let us look at them more closely.

First, say Habermas, there is a symmetry of *asserting* and *opposing*, by which each partner is equally free to say what s/he wants to say and to reject what his or her partner says; secondly, there is a symmetry of *revealing* and *concealing*, whereby each participant is confident in presenting him or herself and accepting of the self-presentation of the other; finally there is a symmetry of *rights* and *duties*, whereby neither party has privilege but each party expects of the other exactly and only what he or she expects of him or herself. In some ways this list reminds one of Aristotle's discussion of friendship, though the differences will be obvious if they are not so already. The three symmetries are not simply interesting phenomenological descriptions of conversation. They are much more. Habermas maintains that

> ...these symmetries of the choice and practice of acts of speaking *guarantee* the equality of the participants in the maintenance of their roles in dialogue, a maintenance which makes *structurally possible* a distinction between true and false statements, truthful and deceptive remarks, and right or wrong actions."[17] (Italics mine.)

Habermas concludes his argument by claiming that, if these conditions are met, we can be sure that "a consensus would have to result which would be *per se* a true consensus" assuming the ideal conversation (for that is what it would be) goes on long enough.[18]

In the preceding quotations from Habermas' articles on Gadamer, the operative words are, I think, "guarantee" and "structural". Habermas is after, or rather, thinks he has found, a *formal* tool by which the content of any conversation can be critiqued with *certainty*. By definition, structure is different from what it supports or contains; form is different from substance. What this means, then, is that Habermas is arguing that the claim of a statement to truth can be decided *apart from* the actual meaning of the statement, by looking at *how* the statement was arrived at. If all the rules were followed, then the statement is true; if the rule were not followed, then the statement is false (the action is wrong, the remarks deceptive) precisely to the degree that the rules were not followed. Notice that Habermas is not simply saying that statements only have meaning against a background; this would not bring him into conflict with Gadamer. Rather, he is saying that *the background itself can be judged*, and, *a fortiori*, the statements within it. Habermas would no doubt want to nuance this analysis, and he is not always perfectly clear, but I believe that, in principle, this is what he is saying.

At first glance, this solution may seen to set our minds at rest. The uneasiness which resulted from our suspicion of the tradition can be cured at last. The desire, programmed, apparently, into our genes, to free ourselves from the domination of nature *can* be fulfilled. Armed with the tool of impersonal method, we can set to work distinguishing between those aspects of the received tradition which have been handed down through coercion and condemnation and those aspects which have resulted from free and unfettered conversation. Of course, Habermas does not deny the unfortunate fact that there probably never has been such a thing as an ideal speaking situation--this actually bolsters rather than subverts his case--but that does not take away from the fact that the ideal speaking situation is able to act as a norm to judge all those situations (namely and precisely *all* situations) which deviate from that norm.

With Habermas' intention there can surely be little disagreement. But has Habermas really escaped from Gadamer's (and his) attack on objectivism? First of all, and most obviously, there is the question of whether "symmetry" is capable of functioning as the self-evident *a priori* norm of an ideal speaking situation. Is it really self evident that the ideal situation is one in which neither of the partners has any advantage over the other? A student working with a revered teacher on a common project would presumably never be able to have a real conversation with his or her mentor. The earnest wrestling in Plato's <u>Phaedo</u> between Socrates and his students over the question of immortality must fall into the category of inauthentic discourse because all deferred to Socrates. Habermas might reply that the conversation would be ideal only to the extent that everyone contributed equally and freely to the discussion, but it's hard to see why such a conversation could not reveal truth if the more learned and the less learned still took each other seriously, precisely for what they were-- teacher and disciple--and if the questions arose naturally and not from manipulative or purely pedagogical purpose. What is needed here, perhaps, is not so much *symmetry*, as *gnome*, the kind of fellow-feeling Aristotle prized.

But let us assume, for the sake of the argument, that Habermas has indeed been completely successful in establishing self-evident, *a priori*, norms for the ideal speaking situation. But let us allow ourselves a question: *Where did these norms come from*? How did we learn to recognize and accept them as norms? (Surely not on the sheer authority of Habermas!) But if we are already able to recognize them as such, how can they function to judge the very conversation in which we decided that they were indeed, the norms for conversation in general? Was *that* conversation ideal? For any possible norms would either have to be developed out of a human conversation or from a revelation from outside of the human race.

Thus, we seem to have come upon an infinite regress: we need norms by which to judge the norms. And if we obtained *these* norms, we would then need still more norms to judge the judging norms, etc. But they are self-evident! They derive from an impartial analysis of conversation! But *whose* impartial analysis, and isn't it naive to suppose the analysis is impartial, or better, motivated by the sheer emancipatory interest Habermas speaks of? But there is more.

The problem of justifying the norms is really the other side of the classical hermeneutical issue, the issue Habermas joined with Gadamer in pointing to: the issue, that is, of *application*. Habermas, after all, agreed with Gadamer that knowledge is *not* a matter of applying universal rules to individual cases, where the rules are known clearly beforehand, but that the truth occurs only in the application and not before. This is an aspect of the paradox of the hermeneutical circle, and Habermas has learned too much from Heidegger to deny its validity. But it seems that his enterprise is precisely an attempt to escape *from* the hermeneutical circle, and, not incidentally, to escape from the whole problematic of *phronesis* which Gadamer has been developing over the course of a lifetime. In order to *apply* Habermas's rules to a concrete situation (what other situation is there?), we would have to possess a *principle* by which would be able to know how to apply the rules in this particular situation. For rules change in their application, and their meaning only appears in their application. That principle, that dynamic reality which we all need in order to apply the rules in a human and not a machine-like way, is, of course, that prudence of which Aristotle spoke:

> The art of understanding, whatever its ways and means may be, is not dependent on an explicit awareness of the rules that govern and guide it. It builds, as does rhetoric, on a natural power that everyone possesses to some degree. It is a skill in which one gifted person may surpass all others, and theory can at best tell us why. In both rhetoric and hermeneutics, then, theory is subsequent to that of which it is abstracted; that is, to praxis.[19]

The "skill" which Gadamer refers to is, it need hardly be stated, the hermeneutical analogue to the "habit" which Aristotle called prudence. It is almost amusing to note that in this passage Gadamer accuses Habermas, who has been so heavily influenced by the thought of Karl Marx, of ignoring the centrality of *praxis* in relationship to *theory*!

Perhaps we have said enough to justify the conclusion that Habermas can be indicted at least (if not convicted outright) of what Martin Heidegger attacks as the grand error of the western philosophical tradition. He is trying to establish true knowledge as present-at-hand and objective in a way which ignores the primordiality and primacy of ready-to-hand, situational, historical knowledge. He is, in fact, trying to establish a theoretical knowledge by which one could escape in some way from the historicity of <u>Dasein</u>, *There*-being, not *everywhere*-being. Such an enterprise, as Heidegger and Gadamer (and at times Habermas) tirelessly argue, is precisely what is at fault with modernity. Habermas' attempt to cure the problems of the contemporary world is precisely the old Enlightenment nostrum which has gotten us into the trouble in the first place. The attempt to free *Dasein* from the bonds of historicity (body, situation, purpose, prejudice, community, tradition) can only propel it into what is literally a no-man's-land, an inhuman place.

To this last point Gadamer comments that "unconsciously the ultimate guiding image of emancipatory reflection in the social sciences must be an anarchistic utopia."[20] If Habermas ignored his mentor Marx before, perhaps, suggests Gadamer, he is ignoring his other mentor, Freud, now. If we re-examine that libidinal urge for freedom, is it really as benign as it appears at first? Throughout this debate, it appears as if Habermas is the heir of the Enlightenment's attack on the past and its prejudices, while Gadamer looks like the champion of tradition. So put, the question of which to choose is a difficult one, for even if we agree that Habermas' solution to the questions he poses of Gadamer are inadequate, and don't do justice to Gadamer's analysis, nevertheless, something of the uneasiness he raises remains with us still. Are we not, in a Gadamerian world, condemned simply to a repetition of past mistakes? Does the Gadamerian perspective entail a static and blind traditionalism in which nothing new and better can ever arise, or worse, an unthinking allegiance to totalitarian nationalism cloaking itself in the symbols of the nation's past? The answer to these questions is, quite clearly, no. But Gadamer is barred by his own arguments from proposing a set of Gadamerian rules by which conversation--or society--could be bettered, either generally or in specific instances. Such rules would still require application, and put us once again back into the center of the hermeneutical circle.

What Gadamer *can* do, however, is to show how conversations *do* go wrong or right in practice. He can do this, not so that we can then develop a set of rules to make sure that conversations in the future will never go wrong again, but to allow us to glimpse, in an inadequate but still helpful way, what we already always know, not as a set of present-at-hand rules but as speakers of a language which speaks through us. Indeed, only if we *recognize* Gadamer's phenomenological description of conversation as what *truly* goes on when things are going well, can we understand what he is talking about at all.

There is a real, and delicate problem here, though, the problem common to Gadamer and to the whole tradition of ethical reflection, in fact. If *phronesis* cannot really be learned, what do we gain by talking about it? Do we not risk simply adding to the store of present-at-hand knowledge to no end? Can one--should one--talk systematically about the inadequacy of systematic talk?

The accusation is bothersome, but perhaps one helpful response to the objection is that, after all, *we do not choose our conversation*--it chooses us- -or, as Gadamer likes to say, we "fall into it". Gadamer speaks with us about this topic because the topic, the question, has arisen in his own conversation and presumably ours as well.

As to why it has arisen--all we can do is point to the obvious fact that all conversation is purposive, as we have said before, but that does not mean that the purpose need always be specified or even that it *could* always be specified, beyond Heidegger's assertion that <u>Dasein</u> is the being whose concern is Being. And though this is extremely difficult, almost impossible, it is nevertheless a valid subject for discourse because anything that can be spoken is a valid topic for discourse, and this, obviously, can be spoken. So, it appears that Gadamer could only be faulted for choosing this topic if the choice of it--to bring up a Habermasian theme--were forced and therefore inauthentic. If Gadamer's enterprise were not a real conversation with the tradition, but rather an attempt to manipulate or coerce or dazzle, then also he could justifiably be criticized. But this is not the case.

But perhaps we can say more. Gadamer, or any ethician, cannot be telling us what we in some sense already know, but he *can* clarify what we know, make us more confident in it, and less susceptible to panaceas and present-at- hand methodologies like that of Habermas. This is no small thing. To explain this point, Gadamer turns, not surprisingly, to Aristotle's discussion in the <u>Politics</u>:

> He compares the intention of such a practically oriented pragmatics with the target being sighted by the archer when he aims at the goal of his hunt. He will more easily hit the mark if he has his target in view. Of course, this does not mean that the art of archery consists merely in aiming at a target like this. One has to master the art of archery in order to hit the target at all. But to make aiming easier and to make the steadiness of the direction of one's shooting more exact and better, the target serves a real function.[21]

Ethics, and hermeneutical discussion in general, then, cannot turn bad people into good, but *it can make good people more conscious of their goals,* and thus help them to attain them. As Gadamer says, "practical philosophy presupposes that we are already shaped by the normative images or ideas in the light of which we have been brought up and that lie at the basis of the order of our entire social life,"[22] but it does not presuppose that those images are always clear to us or even that they cannot be changed. But as always, "the point here is a notion of science that does not allow for the ideal of the non-participating observer but endeavors instead to bring to our reflective awareness the communality that binds everyone together."[23]   Thus, a conversation which focuses on conversation need not come up with a set of present-at-hand rules in order to be helpful in making future conversation better. It need only so describe what is really going on that we can recognize the picture and use it to do what we do more clearly. But the picture is not infallible, is not in any way authoritative except insofar as in the situation it seems to the discussants to be authoritative, helpful, illuminating. Or, as Gadamer himself puts it, "practical philosophy is not the virtue of practical reasonableness."[24] It is not the virtue, but it assists its exercise.

But to speak of a phenomenological description of conversation, of an account of what makes conversations go wrong or go right in practice, is to raise the hope that that such an account actually exists somewhere. Does Gadamer have an account of conversation which avoids positing present-at-hand rules but which still, after the manner of the Aristotelian bull's eye, helps us see what we are about in the practice of human speech? Indeed he does, and it is to this account we must now turn explicitly, for it will advance the fundamental point of this chapter: the problem of faith and doubt. We have shown that *the attempt to find certainty in theory apart from the conversation is a dead end.* Perhaps Gadamer's phenomenology of speech will put the question in a more helpful light and suggest a way out of the difficulty. We begin by recalling that for Gadamer (as for MacIntyre), what human beings *are* is conversation. Thus, to speak well is not an optional issue for humans. It is the only issue.

But to speak is to be in dialogue, a dialectic, a back-and-forth between persons, and to get to its core Gadamer calls upon the analysis provided by Georg Hegel. Just as Hegel analyzed the dialectic between the "I" and the "Thou", so can we, says Gadamer, analyze the hermeneutical experience of being-in-a-tradition, because the tradition in which we stand confronts us not as an object, but as a person. Not that the tradition actually *is* a person, an individual consciousness, only that the analysis of the relationship between "I" and "THOU" can throw useful light on certain aspects of the hermeneutical relationship.

Gadamer begins his Hegelian analysis by noting what the *inadequate* approaches to the "I" and "Thou" relationship have been. For example, one could say that I experience the Other by trying to understand human nature as an objective thing, an essence. Once I have done this I can then predict the behavior of the Other. It simply becomes a matter of gathering enough supplementary information. Quite clearly, this is inadequate. The Other-- whether that Other be the "those" or the tradition in which I stand--cannot be reduced to present-at-hand, to objective knowledge. To do this is precisely to miss the fact that the relationship between us is not one of observer and observed, but is a *moral* one. It is precisely this attitude (of disinterested observation) which Gadamer is at pains to excoriate throughout Truth and Method. We need not rehearse that argument again here.

The *second* inadequate approach to the understanding of the Other seems at first to be more "humanistic." Rejecting objective knowledge of the Other as "putting the Other in a pigeon-hole", I (quite rightly) search for another, less mechanical way of relating to him or her. And this way is the way of seeing him or her as someone just like myself. Is this not the ultimate compliment? This is the attitude we associate with the name of Friedrich Schleiermacher. Schleiermacher--at least the later Schleiermacher--claimed that there are two ways by which we can venture to understand a person--or a text. The first way is the "comparative method" which we can call a kind of objective knowledge: "The comparative method proceeds by subsuming the author under a general type. It then tries to find his distinctive taints by comparing him with the others of the same general type."[25] Obviously, this type of knowledge is important and, at times, indispensable. But there is another type of knowledge, which Schleiermacher refers to as "divininatory." This is the *intuition into the uniqueness of the Other*, achievable, paradoxically enough, because, in some mysterious way, the uniqueness of the Other is reflected in the uniqueness of the "I". Schleiermacher goes on to say that,

...the divinatory (knowledge) is based on the assumption that each person is not only a unique individual in his own right, but that he has a receptivity to the uniqueness of every other person. This assumption in turn seems to presuppose that each person contains a minimum of everyone else.[26]

Schleiermacher calls comparative knowledge "masculine" and divinatory knowledge "feminine." Like the two sexes, both are necessary. For Schleiermacher, understanding a friend's conversation and understanding an historical text both require a constant interplay between the comparative and divinatory methods: the comparative, by which the text is set next to other texts, subsumed under a type, and the divinatory, by which an individuality is intuited by another individuality. An intimate friend, says Schleiermacher, is known from within, just as a favorite author (Schleiermacher, of course, was famous for his attachment to his friends, and even made theological use of fellow-feeling in Christmas Eve).[27]

Though this approach seems to be most respectful of the Other's individuality, in reality, ways Gadamer, when we claim to understand the Other by reading between the lines, as it were, in his or her conversation or writing, we are claiming to know something that the speaker has not explicity revealed (by definition), or even that the speaker may not even know about him/herself. What is wrong with this?

One contemporary name to describe what is wrong with this approach is "paternalism". To use Gadamer's words: "One claims to express the Other's claim and even to understand the Other better than the Other understands himself. In this way, the Other loses the immediacy with which it makes its claim."[28] Thus, rather than listening to what I say, my interlocutor, claiming a sympathetic insight which is denied even to me, insists that she knows what I *really* mean, or better, what is really *behind* my speech. Anyone who has been subjected to this conversational ploy, not uncommon in a culture which likes to play with psychological terms like "projection" and "repression", knows how maddening it is, for there is no reply. One can either place oneself on the couch or refuse to do so, but in neither case is the <u>Sache</u>, the subject of the conversation, advanced.

Gadamer argues that where such a notion of understanding between persons is operative, the relationship must inevitably be inauthentic. But, as we have suggested earlier, one must be willing to admit that there are times when such inauthenticity may be entirely appropriate and necessary. To give examples: in a pedagogical relationship, classically it is not amiss for the instructor to know the student better than the student knows him or herself, at least in some defined area of instruction. Thus the teacher's questions will arise, not spontaneously, as they would in an authentic conversation, but by design, the design of leading the student into the subject matter. Of course there can exist a certain spontaneity even here, and I would argue that, the better the teacher, the more will the pedagogical conversation approach the authenticity of ordinary conversation. One could argue that the ultimate goal of all pedagogy is precisely authentic conversation.

Another example of inauthentic but valid speech is that of the therapist. Even more than the teacher, the therapist must take a God-like attitude over the patient, revealing to the patient just who the patient is. But again, as with the teacher, it could be argued that therapy must at least move toward authentic conversation as a goal, the therapist slowly turning from therapist to mentor to friend.

What seems to be common to both these forms of inauthentic conversation is that one partner in the dialogue takes the role of parent, the other, that of child. Such a relationship is valid, of course, only insofar as the partners really are parent and child, in some extended sense of those terms, at least. The key point Gadamer wishes to make, however, is that however valid they might be, such therapeutic, pedagogical or paternal relationships *must not be regarded as paradigms for conversation in general*. That would mean that we would regard our friends (or texts or tradition) as patients, students, or children--in the classroom, on the couch, or in the nursery. "By understanding the Other, by claiming to know him, one takes from him all justification of his own claims."[29]

This *second* form of relationship, then, seeing the Other as another Self, shows itself now as a disguised form of the will-to-power which is at the core of the reduction of all knowledge to present-at-hand objectivity! The attempt to escape the problems raised by treating the other as object by moving in the (apparently) only alternate direction--treating the Other as subject--is still caught in the subject-object scheme, which was the real problem in the first place. Ironically, subjectivity winds up becoming another form of the objectivity which is seen (correctly) to be dehumanizing. By claiming to see behind the Other's actual words, the interpreter takes for granted that his or her *own* insight is real, i.e., need not be interpreted away later on as an expression of an inner truth to which he or she is blind. The *interpreter's* claim need not be shown to be in the final analysis, a claim for something else, something which only still another interpreter could know. In other words, by seizing the pedagogical or therapeutic or paternal high ground, Schleier|macher's "I" pretends to step out of the ongoing relationship of claim and counter-claim which makes up human life. A child may beg or ask, and it certainly has needs, but it cannot make a claim for itself. Its needs are interpreted *for* it. Aristotle, in the <u>Politics</u>, had pointed out that women, children, and slaves were all in the same category of being subject to the rule of the head of the household, i.e., they were not *free*. In Schleiermacher's conception, friends, texts, and traditions turn out to be more like women, children, and slaves in a Greek *polis* than like equals who can challenge us. Schleiermacher's "I", then, escapes from the conversation of equals and friends, away from the only place where someone can actually make a claim on me.

An unconvinced Schleiermachian might offer the rebuttal that the 19th century scholar never claimed that divinatory insight was infallible, and, indeed stressed that it was part of a continuous process. In fact, such a person might go on, one might even see the divinatory knowledge we have of particular individuals as akin to that very *phronesis* which Gadamer retrieves from Aristotle, which is also a knowledge of the ultimate particular thing. Possibly so, we reply, but it misses the point. The *real* point of contention between Gadamer and Schleiermacher is in the *what*, not the *how*. That is, for Schleiermacher, the important thing is finally to *know* the Other, the indefinable person. For Gadamer, the important thing is to *share with* the Other in the indefinable enterprise of being human. The trouble with the Schleiermacher position, as David Tracy says, is that:

> The meaning of the text becomes an object for our insatiable curiosity as to the strange possibilities of the human spirit. The text itself has simply nothing to say to us any longer, for its questions and answers, its subject matter, are now merely historical curiosities. The text is simply a clue to the mind of the author or to a particular social and historical situation. And neither of these realities, we assume, has any more to say to us than the text which articulates them.[30]

Or, in Norman O. Brown's vivid metaphors, when the first concern is with the *mind* of the (usually dead) author, rather than with the meaning of the text, we seemingly "let the ghost of the dead author slide into, become one with the reader's soul. It is necromancy, or shamanism; magical identification with ancestors; instead of living spirit, to be *possessed* by the dead."[31] Here the Romantic desire to know the Other (person, text) is unmasked as a desire to be possessed by the Other, (conceived as thing)and therefore to become lifeless oneself. We escape, in other words, from the world of claim and counter-claim which is *life*.

But if these two ways of relating to the "Thou", and (by analogy) to the tradition, are inadequate as central paradigms, what do we have left? What characterizes the person who is speaking *well*, who possesses the prudence we have characterized as central, if it is not simply the possession of objective knowledge (first option) or the possession of subjective insight into the Other (unmasked in the second option as another form of objectivism)? "The important thing

... is to experience the Thou truly as a "Thou", i.e., not to overlook his claim and to listen to what he has to say to us." Continuing on in this passage, Gadamer suggests that the key to such an experience of the "Thou" can be described by the word *openness*. He goes on to say that "without this kind of openness to one another there is no genuine human relationship. Belonging together always means being able to listen to each other."[32]

Gadamer earlier used the example of the therapist to illuminate a kind of inauthentic conversation. This example can again be clarifying at this point. For, while it appears as if the therapist is precisely and almost by definition the one who listens to the Other, in reality this cannot be the case, for to listen means more than paying attention to phenomena. To listen means to be jolted out of complacency at times. In fact, the therapist who expressed surprise at what a patient tells her ("My heavens! I never heard *that* before!") would immediately raise suspicions in her client that this was her first case. To be surprised would mean that she does not possess a godlike understanding of her patient, and is therefore not a good therapist. Rather, everything the patient says must be "interesting", which keeps the therapist in the disinterested (ironically enough) observer status.

Unlike the therapist, then, the one who is *open* is capable of being surprised, even shocked by what he or she hears. Also unlike the therapist, the one who is open is capable of hearing something *new* and actually learning something. And just as this pattern is found in the experience of human conversation, so, says Gadamer, is this true in the analogical experience of interpreting a text or a tradition. The *important thing*, says Gadamer, a great 20th century Plato scholar, is surely just that Plato may be *right* about many things which are still of interest to us. *Why else should we read him?*

But openness is admittedly a vague word. We have described its implications casually so far, but now we must ask: *what exactly characterizes this openness of which Gadamer speaks?* What is really involved in listening to the

Other without overlooking his or her claim on us? Gadamer's contention is that:

> ...the hermeneutical consciousness has its fulfillment, not in its methodological sureness of itself, but in the same readiness for experience that distinguishes the experienced man [*den Erfahrenen*] by comparison with the man captivated by dogma [*dogmatisch Befangenen*].[33]

Gadamer introduces some new concepts here, important ones. It seems, then, that there are two kinds of people: those people whom Gadamer calls "captivated by dogma: and those who are "experienced." To be captivated by dogma is to face reality with a predetermined set of expectations which are conscious and (in Heideggerian terminology) present-at-hand. Here Dreyfus' discussion of computer intelligence is helpful. For the dogmatist, the program, as it were, has already been written, and cannot be changed. "Learning" is a matter of adding to the store of facts. Thus, for this kind of person, reality can never disclose anything new, because in principle, truth has already been achieved. Recall Polanyi's dictum that the real is what reveals itself in the future in new and surprising ways. Like our caricatured therapist, the dogmatist can never be surprised.

The dogmatist is without "experience" in Gadamer's terminology, not because he or she might be young and/or has not had a chance to encounter very many of the possibilities of life (which is the way Aristotle would have talked about experience), but because to *have* an experience in the first place requires a particular kind of attitude, an attitude which allows things to happen: that is, what Gadamer calls openness. But is the problem really formal dogmatism itself or simply the material dogmas themselves? What if, in other words, the dogmatist's ideas, by sheer luck, let us say, are actually *true*? The dogmatist remains a sad case even in this (highly unlikely) event, because, even if his tenets are "objectively" accurate, he would still have to face the problem of application of these tenets to the particular situation, with all its confusions and pitfalls and changeability, a task for which he is eminently unsuited.

Of course, one could refuse to deal with the question of application (insofar as that is possible) preferring to regard one's tenets as simply true apart from application. Then, presumably, the dogmatist must learn to live in a world increasingly more and more distant from the world the rest of the human race inhabits, progressively smaller and smaller in its scope. Even the "truth" which she has enshrined in her rigid categories become more and more a strait jacket. Finally, one who lives her life by turning truth into an object begins to take on the lifeless character of an object herself: something with clear boundaries which doesn't move.

If this is a portrait of the dogmatist, what can we say to paint a picture of the man or woman of experience? Clearly, we must turn the picture of the dogmatist upside down, as it were. Chiefly, the experienced person is the individual whose expectations have been *overturned* time and time again by reality. For such a person, things have often been not what they seemed. That which fulfills our expectations, for Gadamer, cannot be called experience. We learn nothing from it; it confirms, in a deadening way, what we already knew (adds more data of the same kind to our memory bank.) "Every experience [*Erfahrung*] worthy of the name runs counter to our expectation."[34] But why is this so? Why does every experience worthy of the name experience need to be a surprise, to be, inevitably, somewhat painful and disagreeable? (Note the Latin root of the English word experience is the verb *experior*, "to try, test. prove, put to the test", an active verb with a passive form). Because the basic experience is the experience that the (present-at-hand) knowledge I have is simply not enough to deal with reality, that life finally cannot be perfectly controlled.

> What a man has to learn through suffering is not this or that particular thing, but the knowledge of the limitations of humanity, of the absoluteness of the barrier that separates him from the divine. It is ultimately a religious insight.[35]

Note that it is not necessarily a *Christian* insight, but a religious one common, then to archaic religions as well as to revelational ones. To be human, then, is to be *limited*, bound by our very bodiliness. We are in space and time and history, and therefore for us to be wise means to be able to function precisely as limited creatures who have come to terms with their limitations. To be wise means to know that we do not know, that all our wisdom is subject to revision tomorrow--or in the next moment. One thinks, classically, of Socrates, who knew only that he did not know. We do not know, then, but must act. This is the painful dilemma of being human, the dilemma we wish at all costs to avoid. But it is, fortunately, something we "always already" know how to do, since we "always already" are human. To be wise, to be "expert" (*experitus*, "having tried"), means to be able, *first* (as we all must be), to make decisions without having all the necessary information, and *second* (as only some of us are), to be able to judge well between foolish decisions and wise ones. (And, of course, the wise decision can very well be wrong. The child who picks the outcome of an athletic contest better than the veteran fan is always available.) And thus, in a round about way, we are brought back once more to that virtue which has been our theme in this chapter: prudence. Prudence and experience, as Aristotle knew, are intimates. It is impossible to have one without the other. Those who, as the saying goes, have "forgotten nothing and learned nothing" have never really *experienced* anything, though they might have lived a long time.

It may look like we have long since forgotten the debate between Habermas and Gadamer. But actually the detour through the discussion of finitude has now enabled us to see even more clearly why the Habermas critique ultimately fails against Gadamer. For if, in the Gadamerian perspective, the important thing, in a sense the only thing, is to remain open to experience--to keep open the conversation which we *are* and do not simply *have* --then the one thing we must be careful *not* to do is to short-circuit the conversation by developing norms for truth to be applied by someone who is not talking. Of course, we do not have to argue that Gadamer is sufficiently sensitive personally to the problem of systematic distortion of communication in modern culture. That conversation is, in our words, an eschatological ideal, a truth which Habermas brings forcefully to our attention. Depth psychological (Freud) and economic (Marx) motivations are concealed, even to the ones who are propelled by them; there is a place for a hermeneutics of suspicion, even in conversation itself. But it is precisely because we are sensitive to the issues of domination and freedom that we must argue that Habermas' solution is a form of that dogmatism which is at the heart of the very domination he decries so well, and the liberation from which is his central theme. To do transcendental metahermeneutics in the Habermasian way is to fall prey to the ultimate sin in the Gadamerian catalogue--it is to try to get a strangle hold on reality. To do this is to render oneself more and more incapable of experience, *real* experience, that experience which involves surprise and suffering.

We could use a Christian symbol here and say that this attempted stranglehold, this "captivation by dogma" is the original sin of humankind, for if we *are* conversation, then to try to get out of the conversation (even with the purpose of making the conversation better in the long run) is to become *less* than human in the very act of trying to become *more* than human. Aristotle's familiar claim--that the one who is not in community must be either a beast or a god--applies here. Neither a god nor a beast has language. For a god, everything is known at once; there is no need to learn, and thus no place for dialectic. Aquinas (and later, Rahner) liked to use the angelic intellect, in fact, as a counter-example for human knowing. And of course, for the beast, there is only the world of immediacy--a habitat rather than a world. But in between the beast and the god (or angel) is the human being, who must speak. And by speaking, the human person is placed in a very definite spot and moment and into a community of those who also speak, for speaking cannot be done alone, unless by carrying the community along with us in some way, right into the wilderness.

But this speaking, this conversation which we are and do not simply take part in, is not idle chatter or gossip

(Heidegger's <u>Gerede</u>), which would be still another form of escape from the demands of the truth: talking, but not really risking a conversation, never making a real claim or allowing a claim to be made on us. It is, rather, a real *discipline* in which the question which arises is given room, and the answer which emerges is paid attention to as the source of the next question. For what we are as a conversation is a dialectic of question and answer. It is a game we learn by the playing of it and not by studying the rule book, a game which imposes its own discipline and provides us with its own rewards: "So it is well grounded for us to use the same concept of play for the hermeneutical phenomenon as for the experience of the beautiful. When we understand a text, what is meaningful in it charms us."[einnimmt][36] With the event of truth, so too with the event of beauty, we cannot decide in advance of its arrival what it is going to look like. "In understanding we are drawn into an event of truth and arrive, as it were, too late, if we want to know what we ought to believe."[37] Gadamer's mention of belief here brings us back to the central theme of our project. Despite our finitude, despite our inability to lay hold on truth and pin it to the wrestling mat, we can still somehow be confident that truth and beauty *will* occur for us, as long as we remain patient and do not attempt to compel them to occur by force.

It is not method *per se* which Gadamer is opposed to, but that violence which method can too easily degenerate into when it is taken as ultimate. But it is not the last word and it cannot achieve everything. "What the tool of method does not achieve must--and effectively can--be achieved by a disicpline of questioning and research, a discipline that guarantees truth."[verburgt][38]

And so, the search for the answer to the riddle of human knowledge--a search which has so far led us through a critique of positivist methodologies and into a discussion about the problem of the doubt at the heart of understanding, that search has now led us into a seemingly modest and yet suggestive conclusion: *the one who can understand is the one who can play*, the one who can be given over to the rhythm of conversation, the one who can be open to the unexpected, *the one who can suffer.* These are the insights with which Gadamer, after his own conversation with Aristotle and Heidegger and Habermas and others, leaves us. We might want to add our own conclusion: the one who can understand is the one who can have *faith.* But is this faith which we have been pursuing in our critique of knowledge and doubt the same thing as, or at least analogous to, that "faith" which the Christian community talks about in its own conversation? Can this philosophical analysis of "faith" and the Christian supernatural virtue of "faith" cast light on each other? One obvious way to answer this question is to turn to those writings which Christians--all Christians--recognize as authoritative and open ourselves to whatever they many tell us. This is our next task.

Notes

1. Jurgen Habermas, translated by Jeremy J. Shapiro, Knowledge and Human Interests, (Boston: Beacon Press, 1971), p.301. Hereafter KHI.

2. Habermas, KHI, pp. 301-302.

3. Habermas, KHI, p. 302.

4. Habermas, KHI, p. 303.

5. Habermas, KHI, p. 304.

6. Habermas, KHI, p. 308.

7. Habermas, KHI, p. 312.

8. Habermas, KHI, p. 314.

9. Habermas, KHI, p. 314.

10. Habermas, KHI, p. 314.

11. Habermas, KHI, pp. 314-315.

12. Walter J. Ong, S.J., Fighting for Life: Context, Sexuality and Consciousness (Ithaca: Cornell University Press, 1981), esp. 118-144.

13. Jurgen Habermas, "Summation and Response," in Continuum 8, (Summer, 1970), p. 125.

14. Habermas, "A Review of Gadamer's Truth and Method" in Understanding and Society: An Inquiry, edited by F. Dallmayer and T. McCarthy (Notre Dame: Notre Dame University Press, 1977), p.344.

15. Habermas, "A Review ...," p. 356.

16. Habermas, "Summation and Response," p. 132.

17. Habermas, "Summation and Response," p. 132.

18. Habermas, "Summation and Response," p. 132. For concrete suggestions on how this could be done, see "What is a Universal Pragmatics?" in Habermas, <u>Communication and the Evolutionary Society</u>, translated by Thomas McCarthy (Boston: Beacon Press, 1979).

19. Gadamer, "On the Scope and Function of Hermeneutical Reflection," in Gadamer, <u>Philosophical Hermeneutics</u>, pp. 20-21.

20. Gadamer, "On the Scope and Function of Hermeneutical Reflection," in Gadamer, <u>Philosophical Hermeneutics</u>, pp. 20-21.

21. Gadamer, "Hermeneutics as a Theoretical and Practical Task" in <u>Reason in the Age of Science</u>, translated by Frederick G. Lawrence. (Cambridge, MA: MIT Press, 1976), p. 134.

22. Gadamer, "Hermeneutics as a Theoretical and Practical Task," p. 135.

23. Gadamer, "Hermeneutics as a Theoretical and Practical Task," p. 135.

24. Gadamer, "Hermeneutics as a Theoretical and Practical Task," p. 117.

25. Schleiermacher, p. 150.

26. Schleiermacher, p. 150.

27. cf. Schleiermacher, <u>Christmas Eve</u>, translated by Terrence N. Tice (Richmond: John Knox Press, 1967).

28. Gadamer, <u>Truth and Method</u> (New York: Seabury Press, 1975), p. 322. Hereafter TM. Cf. Gadamer, Wahrheit und Methode (Tubingen, 1960), p.341.

29. Gadamer, TM, p. 323. cf. WM, p. 342.

30. David Tracy, The Analogical Imagination (New York: Crossroads, 1981), p.105.

31. Norman O. Brown, Love's Body (New York: Random House, 1966), p.199.

32. Gadamer, TM, p. 324. cf. WM, p. 343.

33. Gadamer, TM, p. 325. cf. WM, p. 344.

34. Gadamer, TM, p. 319. cf. WM, p. 338.

35. Gadamer, TM, p. 320. cf. WM, p. 339.

36. Gadamer, TM, p. 446. cf. WM, p. 465.

37. Gadamer, TM, p. 446. cf. WM, p. 465.

38. Gadamer, TM, p. 447. cf. WM, p. 465.

Chapter Four
Some Reflections on Scripture

Our concern is with an explication of Christian faith, and its relationship to knowledge and community. So far our analysis has focused on a critique of knowledge. We have gained the insight of the communitarian (and therefore fiduciary) character of all knowledge. The one who can understand, we agreed with Gadamer, is the one who can be given over to the rhythm of conversation, a surrender we described as faith. But if these reflections are not to be empty and formal, they must be confronted with the concrete experience of Christian faith, as authoritatively conceived. It is possible that what Christians call "faith" is something different, something esoteric and unrelated to our philosophical rumination. It is possible that what Christians call "faith", on the other hand, may illuminate our philosophical account. In this chapter, therefore, we will make a preliminary attempt to encounter Christian faith, via reflections on the scriptures. In later chapters we will attempt to make explicit use of traditional and contemporary theological analysis.

Of course, it would be absurd and dishonest of us to pretend that we are going to reach the pristine core of Christian self-understanding, untouched by contemporary theology. Our reflections on the scriptures will, inevitably, be the reflections of a 20th century American Catholic with a particular kind of theological, social, professional, etc. background, writing for a particular purpose. If what we have said so far makes any sense at all, we need not be bothered by that fact, since it is the basis of all knowing to be already-in-a- situation. Rather, our hope is that truth will emerge in our honest encounter with these basic Christian texts.

But *which* texts? The element of arbitrariness in choosing some texts over others makes us uneasy. Is there no "canon within the canon" to give us a clear starting point? If our reflections so far are accurate, there is not (indeed, the whole question of canonicity becomes problematic). All we can do is give reasons for our choices. We start with scripture. We propose to survey, all too briefly, the synoptics (especially Mark), the Johannine corpus, and Paul. These three major divisions of the New Testament revelation are the traditional ones. If there is something distinctive about Christian faith, it will surely show up in an analysis of the gospels and Paul. But even dividing our task up into three parts is only a gross beginning of the task of selection. To treat adequately of our topic would require several studies like this one on the scriptural revelation alone. The wager we are making in this chapter is that we can discover something illuminating and helpful despite the limitations of this project.

We choose the gospel of Mark as the center of our discussion of the synoptics for all the obvious reasons. It is probably the gospel which is the oldest, that on which the others based their accounts, perhaps in many ways closest to the dominical traditions. Of course, the notion that Mark is an "uninterpreted" gospel or an "untheological" gospel, if it ever was seriously held, has now been exploded. We are under no illusions that here, at last, is a way to get to the "real" historical Jesus.[1] Rather, we simply agree with W. D. Davis that "no understanding of Jesus which ignores Mark's starkness can be true."[2] What we find in Mark is 1) a bluntness, a severity which makes a special claim on us; and 2) a concentration on the issue of faith. Some of the statements in Mark on faith are indeed, among the sharpest (and most annoying, as we shall see) in the New Testament. They demand our attention.

If there is one thing that Mark's Jesus insists on, it is faith. The very first words spoken by Jesus in Mark are the famous programatic proclamation of 1:15: "The time is fulfilled, and the kingdom of God is at hand; repent and believe in the gospel."[3] But what does it mean to believe in the good news? What is the object of the command? How is it a response to an event ("The Kingdom of God is at hand")? This famous verse bursts with possible meaning. But it is Mark's telling of the miracle stories that best reveals what he means by faith.

It is a cliché to say that faith is required for a miracle in the gospels. But note that Jesus *admires* the faith of others and is distressed when it is not present. The amusing (to this writer) miracle story of chapter two is a case in point. Jesus' cure of the paralytic, told most bluntly in Mark, shows Jesus' awareness and approval of faith, to be sure. But the fact that Jesus is in his own home, and is not at all bothered by the hole in his roof caused by the zealous friends of the paralytic; and the fact that it is the faith of the friends of the paralytic rather than the man himself which is commended, are both suggestive. Apparently 1) faith is necessary for a cure to be effected; 2) the faith need not be that of the one to be cured, but may be that of friends; and 3) ingenuity can be an admirable part of the working out of faith.

Exactly the same elements are present in the cure of the daughter of the Syrophoenician woman (7: 24-30). Here we see Jesus at first rejecting the pleas of the mother for a cure for her daughter. Her faith, and her clever retort to Jesus win the day ("For this saying you may go your way; the demon has left your daughter." v. 29).

Note the somewhat embarrassing statement in 6: 5, 6: "And he could do no mighty work there, except that he laid his hand upon a few sick people and healed them. And he marveled because of their unbelief." (Note Matthew 12:58, where the inability of Jesus is toned down to simple refusal.) Two things in this passage are important for us. 1) It is not Jesus' faith that is the issue, but that of those who wish a cure; and 2) Jesus' reaction to unbelief is spontaneous and strong surprise. He cannot believe, as it were, that people cannot believe. Faith is apparently something (to Jesus, at least) which is *natural* in the order of things. People, obviously are supposed to have faith; when they do, wonders happen; when they don't nothing happens. Why, then, don't they believe? This seems to be exactly the reaction of Jesus when his disciples are unable to cast out a dumb spirit: "O faithless generation, how am I to be with you? How long am I to bear with you?" (9: 19)

131

Unfortunately, that faith which is so natural and productive of good is not always present, its absence in Jesus' own disciples being a favorite Markan theme. What makes it so hard to have faith, then? In the Markan pericope of the stilling of the waters, we get an answer. During a storm, the disciples in the boat with the sleeping Jesus awaken him in their fright. After calming the waves, "He said to them 'Why are you afraid? Have you no faith?'" (4: 40) Or again, to the ruler of the synagogue: "Do not fear, only believe." (5: 36) The opposite of faith, then, is fear, a fear which seems to exasperate Jesus as much as faith pleases him. When the father of the boy with a dumb spirit beseeches Jesus, "*if* you can do anything, have pity on us and help us," Jesus replies, "If you can! All things are possible to him who believes." (9: 22-23) The father's reply has for centuries been part of the prayer of Christians: "I believe; help my unbelief!" (5: 24) For with faith, as with all matters pertaining to human beings, we speak, as Aristotle reminds us, "for the most part" or "on the whole." Faith is not an absolute, either totally present or totally absent; it is, rather a question of degree, just as fear, faith's enemy, is never total.

So powerful is faith that Jesus makes apparently outrageous statements about it: "Truly, I say to you, whoever says to this mountain, 'Be taken up into the sea,' and does not doubt in his heart, but believes that what he says will come to pass, it will be done for him." (11: 23) Matthew repeats the thought (Mt 17: 20 and 21: 21) not once but twice; Luke tones the mountain down to a tree (Lk 17: 6); and Paul's use of the saying in his famous hymn to love in 1 Corinthians 13: 2 shows that it had become a familiar part of the Christian tradition that faith can move mountains (though Paul was at pains to point out that, though faith can of course move mountains, it is useless without love).

So familiar is Jesus' statement about the mountain, so well attested in the tradition, that its essentially scandalous quality is covered over, and one must make a mental effort to return to childhood to grasp once again the essential wonder of it, and perhaps, the disappointment with it when it does not

132

work.   If we allow ourselves to experience the painful bluntness of the statement, what can it say to us?

One popular interpretation of the "all things are possible" or "faith can move mountains" motif is especially congenial to the American temper. And it is certainly true that there is such a thing as "the power of positive thinking." It is true that if one believes that one can do something, one has a much better chance of actually accomplishing it.   Once the four-minute barrier is breached, it becomes *possible* for others to go that fast. And if we grant that Jesus was engaging in Semitic hyperbole, all our problems of interpretation seem to vanish. Jesus is saying, simply, that belief can bring surprising results.

We could stop there. But, as Eduard Schweizer points out in his article on "The Portrayal of the Life of Faith in the Gospel of Mark,"

> when we try to describe what the title of this essay
> expresses, we might pick up this or that favorite word
> of Jesus handed down in Mark, or we might prefer to
> keep to the stories about Jesus...Whatever we would
> do, it would be a more or less casual choice of our
> own. Should we not, first of all, look at the totality
> of his Gospel in order to detect what he has to convey
> to us?[4]

That there is something bothersome about the *logion* is obvious from Luke's downgrading of the "mountain" to a "sycamore tree" and by Paul's comment that "if I have all faith so as to remove mountains and have not love, I am nothing." (1 Cor 13: 2) As it stands, the statement is almost an example of Paul Ricoeur's first naivete. It speaks about an untroubled, unwounded way of being in the world, in contact with the springs of joy and power in life, a way of being in the world in which the world stands forth as creation, and creation as gift. It is the way of being of the child in the arms of its mother. And, if it is not too presumptuous to say this, it is a way of being which cannot quite understand the woundedness of those without faith (though it has compassion for them).

As James D. G. Dunn points out,

> It was characteristic of Jesus that he looked for faith in those to whom he ministered. Faith was the necessary complement to the exercise of God's power through him, hence his inability to perform any mighty work in Nazareth because of their lack of faith. (*apistia*--Mark 6.6/Matt. 13.58) Faith in the recipient as it were completed the circuit so that the power could flow. In other words, there was nothing automatic, nothing magical in the power of Jesus, either in its exercise or in his consciousness of it. It was not something he could use or display at will, nor did he want to (Mark 8.11f. pars.; cf. Matt. 4.5-7 par.). It is this *dependence* on winning a response, on winning people to faith, which distinguishes Jesus' *dunameis* from the possible parallels in Jewish or Hellenistic circles, where faith plays no part. It is this *consciousness of supernatural power which is yet not solely at his own disposal* which marks Jesus out as a charismatic rather than a magician.[5]

Whether the logion of Mk 11:23 is primary or secondary to that of Matthew (Dunn argues that it is not primary), the untroubled nature of its faith is obvious. It is, as Dunn suggests in another place, a pre-Easter faith. It is not faith in *Jesus* which is the issue, but faith in *God*: the faith of Jesus in God, the faith which he expected to find in others.

If we return now to Schweizer's point that the logion must be understood against the background of the totality of Mark's gospel (or, we might say, against the entire story of Jesus' life), it becomes obvious that if the *logion* is isolated from the passion of Jesus it will be misunderstood. Not for nothing does Mark situate Jesus' statement after the third of Mark's predictions of the Passion (8: 31; 9: 31; 10: 33, 34) and on the very road to the city of Jerusalem where he would be killed. It is the cross and resurrection which, for Mark (and the entire Christian tradition) compose the essence of the Christian story.

We do not have to go so far as Jurgen Moltmann, when he says that, besides being rejected by human beings, Jesus "was also, and most completely of all, abandoned by his Father, whose immediate presence he proclaimed and experienced in this life."[6] But he is certainly right when he claims that "Christians who do not have the feeling that they must flee the crucified Christ have probably not yet understood him in a sufficiently radical way."[7] The cross is the test of all overly optimistic assessments of the Christian life.

Several chapters after Jesus' confident assertions about prayer we find him in prayer himself, a prayer which is not answered: "And he said, 'Abba, Father, all things are possible to thee; remove this cup from me; yet not what I will, but what thou wilt." (Mk 14:36) Mark's version here is different from that of Matthew and Luke in important respects. Mark's use of the Aramaic term of filial affection, *abba*, is missing from Matthew and Luke. And so is Mark's ironic echo of Mk 9: 23: "And Jesus said to him, '*If* you can! All things are possible to him who believes.'"

In their telling of this story of the healing of the possessed boy, Matthew and Luke omit this verse. But Mark is not only confident enough to use it, he is also willing to put Jesus in the same position as the distraught father who asked for a miracle "if it were possible." Like that man, Jesus asks for a favor. But note that the tone of possibility is sounded in two different ways. Mark says that Jesus prayed "that if it were possible, the hour might pass from him" (v. 35) (just like the father in 9: 22), but then he has Jesus saying (like the Jesus of 9: 23) that all things are *indeed* possible for God. The tension between the two stories is obvious, and strong, and exclusively Markan. Mark invites us to ask the embarrassing question: if all things are possible to the one who has faith, then why were not all things possible when Jesus himself prayed to his father? Could it be that he did not have faith?

Jesus' conclusion to his prayer, "Yet not what I will, but what thou wilt" (Mk 14: 36b) is repeated by Matthew and Luke. It adds an important corrective to the earlier statement. Without it, the praise of faith which moves mountains and for which all things are possible might seem (and has become in the hands of some) an exercise in ego-aggrandizement. Faith itself has a horizon, and that horizon is "the will of God". What does this mean? How can faith be all-powerful and yet limited? Faith is indeed all-powerful, but its power is not the *possession* of any one person, even Jesus, nor is its use the exclusive *right* of any person, even Jesus, nor for the exclusive *sake* of any person, even Jesus. "The will of God" here might say two things: 1) that confidence does not automatically work for the immediate satisfaction of a particular individual and 2) that that's all right, because there is a larger horizon of meaning which is not always clear to us, but which is still to be trusted. The childlike faith which throws itself upon the lap of Reality must confront the fact that there are times when it will crack its skull.   But is it really all right? If faith finally leads to a cracked skull, and, ultimately to death, isn't faith at best a helpful illusion which can at times cause miracles to happen, but which is finally exposed as a house of cards? "The true critique of the preaching of Jesus is the outcome of his life and his end upon the cross."[8] It is a critique which Mark, in his starkness, leads us toward.   Unlike the Jesus of Luke, who forgives from the cross, or the Jesus of John, whose crucifixion is already a revelation of his glory, the Jesus of Mark (and Matthew, who here follows Mark closely) cries out, "My God, my God why hast thou forsaken me?" (Mk 15. 34; Mt 27: 46)

That the verse is the beginning of Psalm 22, which ends in the vindication of the speaker, is often commented upon as a refutation of the superficial interpretation that Jesus is here really feeling abandoned. But two factors make an easy elimination of the scandal here difficult. For one thing, quoting a line from a prayer from memory in a moment of crisis is not the same thing as reciting the entire prayer. We are all skillful at using biblical quotations out of context, and so, in fact were the commentators of Jesus' time. The atomizing of biblical   texts   was   not   invented   by contemporary fundamentalists; it was, in fact, raised to a high art at Qumran. Secondly, even if Jesus did have the whole psalm in mind, that hardly takes away from the pain and abandonment of the first lines. They are as real as the confidence at the end of the prayer. However one looks at the issue, we are far away here from the serenity of "All things are possible to the one who has faith."

Moltmann overstates his case, but his words are suggestive here:

> In the words 'My god, why hast thou forsaken me?' Jesus is putting at stake not only his personal existence, but his theological existence, his whole proclamation of God. Thus ultimately, in his rejection, the death of his God and the fatherhood of his Father, which Jesus had brought close to men, are at stake, From this point of view, on the cross not only is Jesus himself in agony, but also the one for whom he lived and spoke, his Father. In the words of Psalm 22, Jesus in making a claim upon his own being in the particular relationship of his life and preaching to the Father. If we take this as our starting point, then in the death of Jesus more is at stake than Yahweh's covenant fellowship with the righteousness of his people Israel. In the death of Jesus the deity of his God and Father is at stake.[9]

And so Jesus dies, in pain and with a loud cry. The contrast between the death of Jesus and that of other great leaders of the human spirit has often been made. Unlike Socrates, Jesus does not go "gentle unto that good night." Unlike even the martyrs, those witnesses to Jesus whose courage in the face of death inspired countless legends, Jesus died afraid and crying out for release,

> According to Mark 15: 37 he died with a loud, incoherent cry. Because, as the Christian tradition developed, this terrible cry of the dying Jesus was gradually weakened in the passion narratives and replaced by words of comfort and triumph, we can probably rely upon it as a kernel of historical truth."[10]

And so Jesus died, seemingly abandoned by God. As Moltmann says, "The life of Jesus ends with an open question concerning God."[11] We might prefer: an open question, perhaps, about the possibility of faith.

The Markan resurrection account offers a kind of answer to that open question though hardly a completely satisfying one. Jesus is "risen", and the meaning of those words has troubled and intrigued Christians for two thousand years. Mark's own account emphasizes the Galilean setting of Jesus' promised appearance; other resurrection accounts emphasize appearance in Jerusalem. But of all accounts Mark's is the most chaste. In the very place of death, the tomb, the announcement is made that life has triumphed--we might say that faith itself has triumphed. Note that in the stark Markan account (ending, as practically all scholars agree, at 16: 8, whether because this is where Mark himself ended it, or whether the actual ending has been lost; we incline to the former[12]) there is no experience of Jesus as risen, merely the *promise* that "he is going before you to Galilee" (v.7).

Even in the fuller appearance accounts in the other gospels, the element of faith is not eliminated. Jesus does not appear to one who does not have faith. Dermot Lane has summarized nicely the scholarship of C. H. Dodd and X. Leon-Dufour on the common pattern of the resurrection appearances in the new Testament. There are basically five elements of these appearances:

> (a) The circumstances of the appearances are the same in that the followers of Jesus are despondent and disappointed. 'But we had hoped he was the one to redeem Israel' (Lk 24: 21; cf. also in Jn 20: 19).

> (b) The initiative for the appearances comes from Jesus. 'Jesus came and stood among them' (Jn 20: 19; cf. also Lk 24: 15; Mt 28: 9, 18).

> (c)There is some form of greeting from Jesus. 'Peace be with you' (Jn 20: 19; cf. also Mt 28: 9, 17).

> (d) A moment of recognition follows. 'It is the Lord' (Jn 21: 7; cf. also Jn 20: 20; Mt 28: 9, 17).

(e) A word of command from Jesus concludes the experience. 'Go therefore and make disciples' (Mt 28: 19; cf. also Mt 28: 10,; Jn 20:21; Jn 21: 15ff; Lk 24: 266ff).[13]

Resurrection is a thoroughly Jewish concept, a fact which cannot be over- emphasized. The Jesus who is raised by God is no ghost. Nor does he simply lay aside his body and ascend to the realm of the Ideas. Rather, he exists still in some bodily way (though not bodily in the way he was before he died: he is not merely resuscitated), and he is in charge. But again, the fact of Jesus' resurrection is not some Laplacean atomic reality. It shows up as a fact, *only against the background of Jewish categories, Jewish faith and Jewish hope.* And, specifically, it shows up as a fact--though a surprising one-- against the background of Jesus' teaching on the possibility of God's nearness. Or as Kierkegaard put it classically, "for God *is* that all things are possible, and that all things are possible *is* God; and only the man whose being has been so shaken that he became spirit by understanding that all things are possible, only he has had dealings with God."[14] Jesus' trust in God, in possibility, passes through the fire of ultimate testing, through abandonment to brute necessity, and it comes through the other side to victory. This is the experience which the disciples called resurrection, and it was not available to someone who had not learned Jesus' trust, at least as a possible way of being in the world, at least at this moment, at least in a small way.

Resurrection is not a *factum brutum,* then; *it is an event within the horizon of expectation of particular people.* Who are these people? They are the gathered ones, the *ecclesia,* the church. In the moment of experiencing Jesus as risen, they become church; in the moment of becoming church they experience Jesus as risen. As John Knox puts it:

It would be a great mistake to suppose that the event first occurred, and then the community came into existence. On the contrary, the occurrence of the event and the rise of the community proceeded together...The career of Jesus of Nazareth, simply as a human career, was...a relatively unimportant incident in Jewish history. The event of Jesus Christ the Lord was historically the important thing; and this event happened only in the life of the church.[15]

Something had happened, for sure. But what had happened, happened within the life of the church, and continued as a possibility within the life of that church. This new life is described in many different ways in the New Testament. If community is conversation, as we have suggested, then Robert W. Funk is right when he uses the expression "language gain" to describe the change. Or, as he says, "Language is gift, out of which man is born; and the Word of God is gift, out of which faith is born."[16]

What resurrection means, then, is a *new kind of life in a new kind of community*. The classic story in the synoptics on the meaning of the resurrection is Luke's account of what happened to the disciples of Jesus when they were walking dispiritedly toward Emmaus. Here in fraternal conversation over the scriptures and especially in the breaking of the bread, Jesus is revealed as still alive. Fear and sadness turn to joy and a desire to share the good news with the other disciples. What we want to lift up here is the liturgical setting of the story. In the Eucharist, the rite which Christians are ordered to carry on "in memory of me," Christians experience the empowering presence of the Lord, just as they do in the community experience of interpretation and re-interpretation of the community's writings.

Our discussion of Mark has inevitably broadened into a discussion of resurrection-faith, a faith which must always pass through the narrow gate of doubt and death. The meaning of that resurrection-faith slowly comes into focus for us as we investigate the recurrection accounts. It is a new way of being-in-the-world, now available to those who unite themselves to the community formed by the resurrection of Jesus. "Christ, without ceasing to be the man and master whose death was remembered, is now known as the Spirit; the event, without losing its character as historical event, is perpetuated in the community."[17]

Recognition of the role of the community in the development of the gospel of John has become a commonplace of recent scholarship on the fourth gospel. Louis Martyn's work has shown the existence of "bi-levels" in the gospel, with the stories of Jesus being used as analogues for the encounters of Johannine Christians with the synagogue, from which they had been expelled.[18] The struggle with a hostile Judaism gives context to another commonplace of scholarship on the Johannine corpus--the heavy emphasis on belief/unbelief, and all the attendant dualities: light/darkness; death/life; truth/lies; blindness/sight. The division of the world into two camps makes the needs for *choice* obvious. Under attack, the community of John did not have the luxury of irenicism. Those who were under pressure to leave the community had to be strengthened by being reminded that only within the community was there salvation.

The magnificent ninth chapter of John is perhaps the clearest example of the way all these themes mesh together. The blind man receives his sight, but the more important healing is the healing of his ability to see *truth*, and not simply physical objects. His enlightenment of spirit (unlike his enlightenment of the flesh) takes place in stages. John presents the blind man as a shrewd empiricist. He never does anything but report the truth as he see it: "I am the man." (9) "The man called Jesus made clay and anointed my eyes and said to me, 'Go to Siloam and wash'; so I went and washed and received my sight." (11) When asked the whereabouts of Jesus he simply says, "I do not know." (12)

With familiar Johannine irony, John shows us the investigation into the "truth" conducted by the friends and neighbors and then by the Pharisees, an investigation which leads them deeper and deeper into the darkness rather than the light. At the same time, the former blind man simply refuses to "see" anything but the truth. The scandalous fact that Jesus cured on the Sabbath leads the Pharisees to conclude that he is a sinner. Reality conflicts with dogma. How could a sinner cure a man blind from birth? The parents must be called in, to testify that the man was not truly blind. John describes them as frightened of "the Jews" because "the Jews had already agreed that if anyone should confess him to be the Christ, he was to be put out of the synagogue." (22) This anachronistic note reveals the real character of the struggle here depicted between Jesus and the Pharisees: it is the struggle between the Johannine community and early Judaism, which had expelled the Christians from synagogue fellowship. When the parents, through fear, put the onus again on their son ("He is of age, ask him"), he again shows his devotion to truth:

> So for the second time they called the man born blind, and said to him, 'Give God the praise; we know that this man is a sinner.' He answered, 'Whether he is a sinner, I do not know; one thing I know, that though I was blind, now I see.' They said to him, 'What did he do to you? How did he open your eyes?' He answered them, 'I have told you already, and you would not listen. Why do you want to hear it again? Do you too want to become disciples? (24 - 27)

What the Pharisees "know" is a lie. The blind man, regarded as a sinner from birth, nevertheless is ahead of the Pharisees. He may know very little, only "one thing", in fact, but it is enough. He uses the same foundation as the Pharisees, that a sinner could not work a miracle, and, by not ignoring the evidence, comes to the only possible conclusion: Jesus is not a sinner: "If this man were not from God, he could do nothing." (33) This is too much for the Pharisees, who then commit the act to which their blindness has been leading them: they throw the truthful man (no longer blind in any way) out of their community. This effectively constitutes their community as the community of darkness. (For a softening of the seeming anti-Jewish character of John's use of the term "Jews", see M. Lowe's article on the subject.)[19]

Expelled from the community of darkness, the blind man is on the way to the light. When Jesus asks him if he believes in the Son of Man, the blind man professes his ignorance as to who that might be. Jesus' reply is direct: "You have seen him, and it is he who speaks to you." (37) This is a typical Johannine recognition scene. There is something intensely moving about the phrase, "You have seen him", because, of course the gift of sight was the gift of Jesus. Here you are looking at the one who gave you the power to look at him. But Jesus uses the perfect tense: "You have seen him." This is not literally, physically true, since the man only began to see physicaly after he returned form the pool of Siloam. But it is profoundly true that the recognition of Jesus is not the recognition of a stranger, but of someone we have always already known. The Greek connects the perfect tense of the verb *to see* with the present participle of the verb *to speak* by the connective *kai* (like the Latin *et...et,* it is more literally translated as "both...and"). Thus, we have, literally, "You have both seen him and he is now speaking to you." The "always already" event is made present, as it were, in the present conversation. In this community, we can say, using language at once Johannine and Heideggerian, that light appears in the conversation, the light of truth, while in the anti-community, there is only darkness and the lie. In this community, the hidden truth becomes manifest, "the light shines in the darkness, and the darkness did not overcome it." (1:5)

The reaction of the former blind man is faith and worship (38). This is the end of the search for truth. But the journey of the blind man to sight is paralleled by the anti-journey of the pharisees, whose journey is into deeper darkness. Their own investigation is exposed as lacking in honesty; at its end, there is *less* light than at its beginning. Jesus sums up with harsh words: "For judgement I came into this world, that those who do not see may see and that those who see may become blind,." (39) This is exactly what has happened in the story of chapter nine.

As Edward Schillebeeckx puts it,

Seeing, bound up with being drawn by the Father, sees the mystery of the person of Jesus in the events of his earthly life. Thus John speaks of 'seeing god' and 'seeing his glory'. The experience of divine salvation, in the communion of life and love between Jesus and the Father, takes place in human perception. *The 'Joahnnine seeing' is a matter of understanding the historical life of Jesus in his presence as Lord in the Church.*[20] (Italics mine)

The Jesus who is pictured in the gospel of John performing his signs and entering into his glory, is the same Jesus who is available, through the Spirit, in the life of the Johannine community. The immense self-confidence of a writer who could put words in the mouth of Jesus might seem like *hubris* to literal-minded moderns afflicted with an excessive respect for "facts". But if the Lord is present here in this community, the only Lord there is, then the question of whether the "historical Jesus" *really* said this or that becomes a second-order question. The important question is: what is Jesus *really* saying right now? In other words: what is the truth which is happening for the community at this moment? How is God's faithfulness working itself out for us?

Lester J. Kuyper points out that the Johannine notion of truth has deep roots in the Hebrew *emeth* (truth as fidelity):

I would like to submit...what appears to be a consensus of scholars that in this gospel there is a fusing of the Hebrew idea of *emeth* with the Greek concept of *aletheia*. It is not difficult to detect the concept of faithfulness or dependability in some of these passages. Let us observe a few. 'He who does the truth comes to the light' (John 3:21). This indicates the practice of fidelity and steadfastness. In this Gospel the Spirit is called the spirit of truth. He is to be the manifestation of Jesus, who has ascended into heaven. If we may equate the fullness of grace and truth in Jesus with the redemptive faithfulness of God in sending his Son to save the world, then the Spirit of truth is to lead the disciples into that redemptive faithfulness of God. This is to say that the disciples will time upon time, and in increasing measure, receive and experience the gracious faithfulness of God's redemption. In this setting

Jesus declared, 'All that the Father has is mine; therefore I said that he will take what is mine and declare it to you' (16:15). If all that the Father has may be compressed into the Prologue statement--full of grace and truth--then it is clear that the Spirit of truth would take this fullness of God, his faithful redeeming action (so abundantly demonstrated in the Old Testament) and lead the disciples into it.[21]

Within the "works" of the community of the Spirit of Jesus, God's faithfulness is clearly manifested to those who can see it:

Philip said to him, 'Lord show us the Father, and we shall be satisfied.' Jesus said to him 'Have I been with you so long, and yet you do not know me Philip? He who has seen me has seen the Father; how can you say, 'Show us the Father'? Do you not believe that I am in the Father and the Father in me? The words that I say to you I do not speak on my own authority; but the father who dwells in me does his works. Believe me that I am in the Father and the Father in me; or else believe me for the sake of the works themselves. Truly, truly I say to you, he who believes in me will also do the works that I do; and greater works than these will he do, because I go to the Father. Whatever you ask in my name, I will do it, that the Father may be glorified in the Son;' if you ask anything in my name, I will do it. If you love me, you will keep my commandments. And I will pray the Father, and he will give you another Counselor, to be with you forever, even the spirit of truth, whom the world cannot receive, because it neither knows him nor sees him; you know him, for he dwells within you, and will be in you (John 14: 8-14)

The scandalous Markan claim that "all things are possible" is now repeated in a more explicitly Christian context. The community shares in the power of Jesus, who shares in the power of the Father; the community *is* the presence of God

145

in the world, a presence manifested and proven by the works which the community does. Claims as grand as these would sound hollow unless they came from a community which was convinced that within it, the life and truth and love of God could be found. There is no doubt that the "works" referred to included the kinds of healings which Jesus himself did ("If I had not done amongst them the works which no one else did, they would not have sin" 15:24), and perhaps the very process of the missionary work of the early church. But there is an even more profound work:

> I do not pray for these only, but also for those who believe in me through their word, that they may all be one; even as thou, Father art in me and I in thee, that they also may be in us, so that the world may believe that thou hast sent me. The glory which thou hast given me I have given them, that they may be one even as we are one, I in them and thou in me, that they may become perfectly one, so that the world may know that thou has sent me and hast loved them even as thou hast loved me. (John 17: 20-23)

The love which unites the community is here called the very glory of God. That "glory" which manifested itself to the Jews in a variety of ways now shines forth in the human love of this community. The great work which faith makes possible is love, and love, in turn, as the expression of faith, makes possible the faith of those who look upon it, or better, who experience it for themselves.

The intimate relationship between faith and love is a Johannine commonplace, of course. It is the beloved disciple, not Peter, who looks into the empty tomb and believes. (20:8) It is the weeping Magdelan who recognizes the risen Christ when he calls her by name. (20:16) (Doubting Thomas, of course, is invited to put his fingers in the crucified hands of Jesus, but he is not praised).

But it is in the letters of John that the relationship between faith and love is most clearly spelled out: to believe in Jesus is to love the brothers; to love the brothers *is* to believe in Jesus.

146

In 1 John we find perhaps the most quoted lines in the entire New Testament: "We know that we have passed out of death into life, because we love the brethren" (1 John 3:14); "And this is his commandment, that we should believe in the name of his Son Jesus Christ and love one another, just as he has commanded us" (3:23); "Beloved, let us love one another; for love is of God and he who loves is born of God and knows God. He who does not love does not know God; for God is love. In this the love of God was made manifest among us, that God sent his only Son into the world, so that we might live through him" (4: 7-9) "No man has ever seen God; if we love one another, God abides in us and his love is perfected in us." (4:12) And, finally:

> By this we know that we abide in him and he in us, because he has given us of his own Spirit. And we have seen and testify that the Father has sent his Son as the Savior of the world. Whoever confesses that Jesus is the Son of God, God abides in him, and he in God. So we know and believe the love God has for us. God is love and he who abides in love abides in God, and God abides in him. (4;13-14)

There is perhaps no stronger testimony in the New Testament to the fact that believing in Jesus and fraternal charity are distinguishable but inseparable aspects of some deeper unity, that life which is both the life of the community and glory of God. By uniting ourselves with the community in which the spirit of Jesus dwells, we experience salvation, and, by that very fact, provide a witness to the world of what salvation really is.

This Johannine vision lends itself to easy use by those who, like us, tend toward an ecclessio-centric theology. In such a theology, the church, as extension of Christ through the power of the Spirit, is the sacrament of God in the world. Paul, on the other hand, has often appeared to have a different vision, at least in the eyes of the Protestant tradition. Paul's concern with justification by faith and not by works is a struggle within the individual Christian conscience, with the community playing at best a supportive role. Luther's brilliant retrieval of Paul was, of course, colored by his own search for a sense of salvation. But it should not have required Krister Stendahl's famous essay ("Paul and the introspective conscience of the West") to underline the fact that Paul was no brooding existentialist, and that his passionate championing of justi- fication by faith rather than by works was very much a creative response to the struggle between Jewish and Gentile Christians.[22] "Creative" here is not a synonym for "cynical". Paul's genius, if we can call it that after Kierkegaard, was to penetrate to the core of the meaning of Christian faith. Once having done that, the law falls into place, a secondary place, and exaggerated devotion to the law, or rigidity in its use, shows up as what we have been calling objectivism: trusting in rules rather than in the conversation. Indeed, if the Jewish proscription against images was the first great religious protest against objectivism, Paul's relativization of the law was a profound radicalization of that protest: not only material things could become idols, but so could spiritual ones, and all the more pernicious because less obvious.

Liberated from the Law, one might be adrift, but the liberation *from* law is also a liberation to the new life in Christ. Life *in* Christ is life in the community of Christ, which is the body of Christ: "Do you know know that your bodies are members of Christ?" (1 Cor 6:15). As Jerome Murphy-O'Connor says, "In the concrete the being of the Body of the New Man is constituted by an array of *social virtues* (cf. Gal 5:22-23; 1 Cor 13:4-7) which are but facets of love. It is the creative force which binds the diversely gifted members into a complete unity."[23] The New Man is Christ; the community is Christ. But this could lead to confusion: do we really want to say that the historical Jesus of Nazareth is not only present in the community but somehow is the community? Is the expression "body of Christ" meant literally, metaphorically, or both?

Murphy-O'Connor's analysis here is quite interesting:

It would be absurd to imagine that by predicating 'Christ' of the community Paul intended to identify the community with the historical individual

Jesus Christ. In Col 1:18 he makes explicit the distinction between the Head and the Body which is implicit in previous letters. If an explanation in static terms is thereby excluded, we are forced to consider an explanation in terms of *function*. In this perspective the name "Christ" could be predicated of the community if it is possible to conceive Christ and the community as performing *the same indentical function*. Once the problem has been posed in this way it becomes easy to see how Paul's mind worked. The community mediates Christ to the world.[24]

If the community *is* Christ in the world, it shows the world what existence is like when people consciously rely on the fact that "all things are possible to the one who has faith." The world sees revealed a kind of freedom and boldness which characterize people living in their own home. Ingo Hermann's discussion of one of Paul's favorite words, *parrhesia*, boldness, is suggestive. In the ancient world, "free" was the opposite of "slave", not some abstract state of being able to do whatever one wants. The free-born children of the household were *liberi*, a word which simply came to mean children, and later, the young of animals. The point was that the *liberi* could speak their mind because they belonged. In the Septuagint, Hermann points out, "*parrhesia* becomes a free stance in the presence of God (see Job 22:23-27; 27:9f.; Wis. 5:1), and its sign...is the blossoming of joy and the free outpouring of self in prayer."[25] The openness and boldness which is *parrhesia* is clearly brought to its perfection in the New Testament where the Holy Spirit enables us to call upon God as *abba* with the assurance of *liberi*, the free-born children of the household. But there is a deeper sense to *parrhesia* than simply freedom from servile fear. Openness is not simply openness in the abstract, but openness for something, boldness on behalf of something. Hermann puts it well:

In Paul, *parrhesia* is an element of the nature of Christian existence. In Philippians 1:20 we read: 'In accord with my eager longing and hope that in nothing I shall be put to shame, but that with complete assurance (*parrhesia*) now as at all times Christ will be glorified in my body, whether through life or through death.' That Christ be publicly glorified in the earthly life of the believer--this appears here to be the quintessense of the believer's longing. The sense of *parrhesia* is seen in the fact that the 'open' man is transparent for Christ. Thus the New Testament goes beyond the Old: from openness to God comes openness to Christ, the transparency of the Christian for his Lord, who is to be glorified through life and death.[26]

Once fear is conquered, then, it becomes possible to live in such a way that truth can be revealed. Stripped of our bonds, we are free boldly to proclaim the truth--the glory of God. Now it is clear that all the crutches--the idols, the rules, the frantic search for certainty--were not only unnecessary, but destructive. By giving ourselves over to the life of this community, we can at last live without narcoticization, without idolatry, without objectivism, for truth.

Nevertheless, how it would be possible, in practice, to live without the easy answers has been a crisis for Christians whenever they have allowed it to surface as a question. Paul's troubles with the unruly Christian community at Corinth have been used for centuries to show just how difficult it is to live by the Spirit. Positively, however, Paul's pastoral instructions offer revealing glimpses of what it could possibly mean to offer moral advice to people after telling them that "all things are lawful."[27] In his first letter to the Corinthians, Paul has to deal with the fire which he has himself helped to light. By stressing the freedom from the law, he seems to have backed himself into a corner, a corner which today we might call relativism: is there then no standard by which to judge? The delicate question of eating meat sacrificed to idols provides a helpful test case for the discussion of Christian freedom.

That idolatry is *the* sin in the Jewish tradition almost goes without saying; anything, therefore, which would even hint at approval of idol worship must be disapproved of in the strongest terms. In the so-called "Council of Jerusalem"in Acts 15, the compromisers win the case about imposition of Jewish law on the Gentiles, swayed by Peter's speech: "Now therefore why do you make trial of God by putting a yoke upon the neck of the disciples which neither our father nor we have been able to bear? But we believe that we shall be saved through the grace of the Lord Jesus, just as they will." (15: 10-11) Whatever the historical character of this point (or of the actual "Council" itself), the interesting point for our analysis is the letter which the assembly would send out to the Gentiles, refusing to impose upon them the yoke of the law. The letter is, let us recall, the victory of the grace-over-law mentality:

> For it seemed good to the Holy Spirit and to us to lay upon you no greater burden than these necessary things: that you abstain from what has been sacrificed to idols and from blood and from what is strangled and from unchastity. If you keep yourselves from these, you will do well. Farewell. (Acts 15: 28-29)

Luke presents the Gentile congregation at Antioch as "rejoicing" at the reading of the letter (31). Eating meat which has been sacrificed to idols is explicitly placed on the short list of the fundamentals which even the most liberal of the early Christians of Jewish tradition had to insist upon. But Paul's congregation at Corinth was taking a much more radical position.

It must be remembered that the eating of meat sacrificed to idols was a difficult thing to avoid in ancient times. The meat offered for sale in the public marketplace was meat which had been ritually slaughtered, "offered to idols." Diaspora Jews had developed their own network for such matters; should Gentiles do the same? For the Corinthians, the answer was clear: why bother? Idols simply do not exist, and therefore have no power. Why, then, should we take any notice at all of what meaningless rituals have gone on with regard to the food we eat?

To this reasoning, Paul gives a qualified answer:

'All things are lawful', but not all things are helpful.
'All things are lawful', but not all things build up.
Let no one seek his own good, but the good of his
neighbor. Eat whatever is sold in the meat market
without raising any question on the ground of
conscience.   For 'the earth is the Lord's,
and everything in it.' If one of the unbelievers invites
you to dinner and you are disposed to go, eat
whatever is set before you without raising any
question of conscience. (But if some one says to
you, 'This has been offered in sacrifice,' then out of
consideration for the man who informed you, and
for conscience sake--I mean his conscience, not
yours--do not eat it.) For why should my liberty be
determined by another man's scruples? If I partake
with thankfulness, why am I denounced because of
that for which I give thanks? (1 Cor 10: 23-30)

The important thing for Paul is precisely what has been
overlooked by the individualistic Corinthians: the building up
(*oikodomei*) of the community. The English word "edification"
aptly conveys the idea of physical building and moral building
contained in Paul's use of the Greek. The question, "Can I
do this?" really misses the moral point, which is not an
individual issue, but a communal one. As Murphy-O'Connor
puts it, "a choice cannot be good for a Christian unless it is
also good for the others in the community to which he belongs.
The touchstone of moral truth is the edification of the
community (1 Cor 10:23-29)."[28] It is not that the Corinthians
are evil but that they are operating out of an incorrect
framework.

The framework out of which the Corinthians have been
thinking is one not all that unfamiliar to our project: it is an
attempt to escape from finitude. Paul is constantly telling the
Corinthians that they do not "discern the body" (1 Cor 11:29),
and the Eucharistic body and blood of Christ to which he here
refers is quite definitely linked to the Eucharistic body of
Christ which is the community itself, racked by divisions
between rich and poor. It is this community, and not some

abstract notions of freedom which forms the basis of Christian moral thought. "An authentic moral decision is one which intensifies the unity of the community."[29] Gunther Bornkamm's description of the Corinthians is helpful at this point:

> The mark of the 'enthusiasts' was that they disavowed responsible obligation toward the rest and thus sought to transcend the limits of time and history imposed on the Christian life. This is the reason why the great chapter in 1 Corinthians, chapter 15, insists, against those who believe themselves to be already partaking in the life of heaven, that the resurrection of the dead lies still in the future. Bewildering as are the manifestations of extravagant enthusiasm in the Corinthian church, both in number and oddness, and various as are the apostle's counter arguments and directions, the key motif, which runs through the whole letter, is perfectly obvious here. Paul erects even the supposedly trivial and isolated into a matter of principle and judges it in the light of the gospel of salvation viewed in its entirety. As guiding lines he takes the saving word concerning the Crucified One, regarded as 'the foolishness of God' which negates the validity of human wisdom; the true freedom which alone opens a man's eyes to see his neighbor in love (cf. 1 Cor. 13); the voice of reason as opposed to all fanaticism; the emphatic reminder that living in time imposes limitations; and finally, the gospel concerning the future when, and only when, the whole man will be renewed.[30]

It is precisely because the Corinthians do not "discern the body" that they can find consorting with temple prostitutes to be a trivial matter. While Paul's argument is not always clear, the central point is: because we as Christians together form the body of Christ, what we do with our bodies is immensely important. No less than for John, Paul sees the community-- this, very physical, very limited group--as the manifestation of God's glory in the world. (6:19-20) We cannot flee from it into another world, whether that world be imagined as heaven or the realm of Ideas or the world of Law.

That the ascetic and the libertine may have something in common is not a new idea, but it is nicely illustrated when we move from the Corinthians, who, believing they had transcended this little world of flesh and blood, insisted that what they did here did not matter very much, to the Galatians, who were tempted to believe that, in order to be saved, they had to do very specific things in the world of flesh and blood, especially circumcision. The difference between the two communities is stark; the similarity will have to be clarified.[31]

It is interesting that in both cases, what Paul sees is "flesh", *sarx*. The phrase "hermeneutic of suspicion" is quite apt for Paul here. The person who claims to have transcended the world is to be suspected; is this claim simply a backdoor way of satisfying some very down-to-earth libidinal drives? And what about the person who, like the Galatians, shudders at the thought of such immorality and devotes himself or herself to religious practices? This person, too, perhaps more subtly, perhaps not, is satisfying the flesh. Generations of Catholics have used Paul's statement, "Those who belong to Christ Jesus have crucified the flesh with its passions and desires" (Gal 5:24) as a justification for the very kind of ascetical practice which Paul found pernicious and was, in fact condemning in this passage, namely, rigid adherence to a written law.

But what is so terrible about rigid adherence to a written law, especially a religious one? Doesn't it at least provide us with protection from gross sins? Of course, if one regards "sin" as primarily a question of sexual behavior (by no means an uncommon attitude in our own culture), it will be harder and harder to see what indeed is so terrible about such devotion to the letter:

> You are severed from Christ, you who would be
> justified by the law; you have fallen away from grace.
> For through the Spirit, by faith, we wait for the

hope of righteousness. For in Christ Jesus neither circumcision or uncircumcision is of any avail, but faith working through love. (Gal 5:4-6)

The clear danger here is being cut off from Christ. To rely on anything other than Christ is obviously to not need him: "If justification were through the law, then Christ died to no purpose.", (2:21) But so what? Isn't this belief vulnerable to the charge of mythology? We are supposed to rely on a person who lived some years ago (whether 30 or 3000 really doesn't matter), a person we don't know, and only heard of through the preaching of the man who tells us that he is the only way to be saved. Is this not magic and mythology, an extra-ordinarily cheap way of getting out of the human condition?

In response, one might point to the experiential and communal character of the Christian faith:

Let me ask you only this: Did you receive the spirit by works of the law or by hearing with faith? Are you so foolish? Having begun with the Spirit, are you now ending with the flesh? Did you experience so many things in vain? Does he who supplies the Spirit to you and works miracles among you do so by works of the law, or by hearing with faith? (3:1-5)

We do not simply experience Jesus as a mythological figure, but as the one whose Spirit is now in our midst, an experience which is, of course, a communal, rather than simply individual one:

To some it may seem trite and obvious, but today it can hardly be stressed too much that fundamental to Christian community for Paul was the shared experience of Spirit/grace...And it is the (experienced) Spirit who creates community in the first place, so it is the spirit experienced in charismata who sustains community.[32]

Dunn's comment here is echoed by Herbert Muhlen: "If we consider Paul's accounts of worship in the apostolic church, then it becomes clear that the experience of the Spirit has something to do with the *social* experience of God."[33]

But if we say all this, we have not yet said enough. For ecstatic communal experiences, wonderful as they can be, are notoriously ambiguous, and by no means limited to Christians. Paul himself was well aware, for example, that Hellenistic cults provided moments for their adherents similar to those which occurred among the Galatians, including miraculous deeds, ecstatic speech and instantaneous healings. One forgets too easily that Jesus' reputation as a miracle worker was an aid, not a stumbling block, to faith in him, in ancient times.[34] (In this the ancients were probably cleverer than we are.) As Peter Berger says, with typical astringency, "to have a conversion experience is nothing much."[35] An Illustration of the non-special character of such phenomena is not at all difficult, and John Bennett provides us with a contemporary example. Bennett was a spiritual seeker who at one point in his life found himself attracted to Subud, a religious movement of great simplicity focused on the sheer experience of the Life Force. His experience of initiating a group of men into Subud is striking for its parallels with the Pauline experience:

> I went into the hall with the men. There were not far short of fifty. As I faced them, I said to myself: 'They cannot possibly be opened. It is all wrong...' I pronounced the formula usual at the opening, asked them to keep their eyes closed..and commended myself to God. At that very moment the hall was filled with such a sense of Presence; and immense Peace decended on me...After ten or fifteen minutes I opened my eyes...Nearly all the men in the room were already responding to the *Latihan*...I became convinced...|that the Power that works in Subud has nothing to do with me or any other person.[36]

"Christ" is not simply a word for ecstatic religious experiences. If that were the case, he would not be set in opposition to the libertinism of the Corinthians, and for that matter *pace* Paul, would not be incompatible with the budding legalism of the Galatians. Bennett's disillusionment with Subud points to a deep truth here. He found that, powerful as the Subud experience was, it lacked a continuing character. It exhausted itself in the initial ecstatic experience. One might say it lacked a communal and historical basis (Bennett later converted to Catholicism.)[37] This enables us to progress to an understanding of "Christ" in the phrase "severed from Christ", and why one should fear to be so severed.

"Christ", for Paul, as we have noted before, is very much an analogical word. It can refer of course to the historical Jesus, but also to that community, that *soma*, which functions in the world as Jesus did, which reproduces Jesus, as it were, in the world. Salvation is not doing this or that: salvation is possessing the Spirit of this particular historical community (being *in Christ*), a community which has some profound differences (and some profound similarities) with all other human communities. Like many other human communities, it provides a place for ecstatic experiences; like other human communities, it struggles with fidelity and betrayal; but unlike other human communities, this community is the body of Christ, is the place where the Spirit of Christ dwells. What this means is that there is a particular way-of-being peculiar to these people. It can encompass many (sometimes a bewildering variety of) forms; but they all possess this "family resemblance"--they all possess in some way the Spirit of Christ. They continue, as we have said, the body of Christ in the world.

But we might be tempted at this point to go back to our somewhat impertinent question: so what? Granted that being "severed from Christ" would mean being delivered from the community which bears his name and shares his Spirit, a community which by that very fact is unique in the world--are there not other, equally valid communities? For Paul, of course, there are not. There are in the world two possibilities: living in the flesh and living in the Spirit. In the eighth chapter of Romans he describes the contrast:

> Those who are in the flesh cannot please God. But
> you are not in the flesh, you are in the Spirit, if in fact
> the Spirit of God dwells in you. Any one who does
> not have the Spirit of Christ does not belong to him.
> (Rom. 8:8-9)

Paul here characterizes the state of those who are not in Christ
as being incapable (powerless) of pleasing God. To be unable
to please God is no small thing, "for if you live according to
the flesh, you must die." (8:13) The issue here is a matter,
literally, of life and death:

> If the Spirit of him who raised Jesus from the dead
> dwells in you, he who raised Christ Jesus from the
> dead will give life to your mortal bodies also through
> his Spirit which dwells in you. (8:11)

Note that the Spirit which the Christian receives is a life-
giving Spirit, the same life-giving Spirit which gave life to the
dead body of Jesus. Actually, the Spirit is identified so closely
with Jesus in Paul that sometimes it is difficult to know
whether Paul is talking about the Spirit or Jesus: "Anyone who
does not have the Spirit of Christ does not belong to him. But
if Christ is in you ..."(8:9-10) A clearer picture of what Paul
might mean by life and death is obtained as we move on into
chapter eight.

> For all who are led by the Spirit of God are sons of
> God, for you did not receive the spirit of slavery to
> fall back into fear, but you have received the spirit of
> sonship. When we cry Abba! Father! it is the Spirit
> himself bearing witness with our spirit that we are
> children of God. (Rom. 8:14-16)

What happens here is that the Spirit of God, the same Spirit
which raised Jesus, puts us in the same relationship with God,
the *abba* relationship. What this means in practice should be
easier to discern. To be in this community is, among other
things, to be freed from servile fear. Now we understand
the source of that boldness *parrhesia* of which we spoke
earlier. In this community we experience the state of being

truly alive, in the Spirit, powerful, children of God, i.e., at home in this world just as children are at home in their family dwelling. In such a community of faith, the need to escape from the human condition by the various forms of objectivism-- legalism, libertinism--has been conquered. We do not need to grasp after certainty when we already have the Spirit. We can rely on the Spirit at work right now and do not have to worry about whether we can control its functioning tomorrow.

In Paul's version of Christian community, then, the community, just as that of John, is a living witness to the world of what life is truly for. Christians are to "present their bodies as a living sacrifice" (12:1). Each person has his or her function, or charism, within the community. Some are to prophesy, some to serve, some to teach, some to exhort, etc. A helpful indication of Paul's mind can be obtained by examining verse 11 more closely:

> Never flag in zeal, be aglow in the Spirit, serve the Lord:

> *te spoude me okneroi*

> *to pneumati zeontes,*

> *to kurio douleuontes.*

Here Paul, in a rhetorical series of datives (which extend before and after this verse) parallels "burning" in the Spirit with serving the Lord and zeal for the welfare of the brothers. In the first letter to the Corinthians Paul expands on the outline provided in Romans:

> Now there are varieties of gifts, but the same Spirit; and there are varieties of service but the same Lord; and there are varieties of working but it is the same God who inspires them all in every one.
> (1 Cor. 12: 4-6)

This threefold parallelism shows us Paul's vision in a nutshell: God is the source of the energy, the Spirit, the giver of gifts, and Christ is the one who is served in the community. The "variety" here shows us clearly that, for Paul, the Christian community is not simply a group of people, but an organism within which the various parts perform different functions. The metaphor of body is endlessly helpful for Paul to describe both the variety and unity with the living Christian community.

This is, admittedly, a rather sunny view of Christian community. It reminds us of the pre-cross view of faith which we saw in the healing stories in the gospel of Mark. We have to probe a little more deeply into Paul's theology of Spirit, faith and community. We might have made it seem as if casting out the demons of fear were comparatively easy. Obviously this is not the case. Indeed, nothing could be more Pauline than the constant reference to the cross of Christ:

> We have this treasure in earthen vessels to show that
> the transcendent power belongs to God and not to us.
> We are afflicted in every way so that the life of Jesus
> may also be manifested in our bodies. (2 Cor. 4: 7-10)

A community whose style is to "carry about the death" of anyone is certainly a unique group of people. For Paul, there is no doubt that openness to the life of the Spirit of Christ is only possible because of the death and resurrection of Jesus, a death and resurrection which is not simply a mythological or historical event, but an event which reverberates in the community, which forms the community, in fact. If there is no family resemblance between the style of this community and the death and resurrection of Jesus anymore, then clearly, for Paul, the community would have ceased to be the community of Jesus. But what does it *mean* to "carry about the death of Jesus" in the community so that the "life of Jesus" might show itself? What does death and resurrection *mean* in the concrete?

Answering this question would require a profound grasp of the deepest mysteries of all: life and death. But it is possible for those of us who make no claim to special profundity to say something at least. We can say that the kind of life Paul talks about can only be had at the cost of *suffering*. The reason for this suffering, in part, is that learning to give up one's own self- centeredness, learning to direct one's power away from sheer self-gratification and toward the service of the rest of the body of Christ, is intensely painful. The Christian tradition has always labeled this experiential reality "original sin." Gadamer refers to the finitude of the human person, as we have already seen. So fragile and over-reaching a creature! Able to be snuffed out in a sudden wind, while holding the universe in the palm of his mind. Perhaps Ernst Becker has expressed the paradox of being human as well as anyone recently: "He is out of nature and hopelessly in it; he is dual, up in the stars and yet housed in a heart-pumping, breath-grasping body that once belonged to a fish and still carries the gill marks to prove it."[38]

Becker's modern question: "Who wants to face up fully to the creatures we are, clawing and gasping for breath in a universe beyond our ken?"[39] is not simply modern, but human, as human as the fear of death and misfortune, as old as Gilgamesh and Job, and, for that matter, Adam and Eve. The answer, of course, is that no one does. We would much rather try to control what we can, in whatever way we can, rather than surrender ourselves to the frightening unknown. Thus, in Gadamerian terms, suffering is necessary for any experience. In Pauline terms, what is necessary is a participation in the death and resurrection of Jesus: "For you know the grace of our Lord Jesus Christ, that though he was rich, yet for your sake he became poor, so that by his poverty you might become rich." (2 Cor. 8: 8,9).

What we have in the story of Jesus is a man who really did face up to creaturehood. In 2 Corinthians, Paul is in the process of pursuing that most prosaic of occupations, asking for money (namely, the collection for the "poor" of Jerusalem), and so naturally calls upon the example of the most sublime form of giving of which he can think. The point here is not to stress the quasi- mythological elements of the descent-from-heaven theme, but the clear fact that, in some sense, *Jesus did not have to die*, and that he *did* die "for us." There was, in other words, an element of free self-gift in the death of Jesus, a refusal to take any of the easy ways out.

In an article entitled "The Event of Jesus--Power in the Flesh", James Reese discusses this form of giving--the courageous self-emptying of Christ--in the context of the famous hymn in Philippians 2: 5-11:

> Have this mind in you which was also in Christ Jesus, who, though he was in the form of God, did not count equality with God a thing to be grasped, but emptied himself, taking the form of a servant, being born in the likeness of men. And being found in human form he humbled himself and became obedient unto death, even death on a cross.

Note that the important thing here, again, is not the mythological language, but the attitude, the mind of Jesus, which must be reproduced in the community. This, says Paul, is what you are to be *like*. In his exegesis of the passage, Reese especially focuses on the Greek word *harpagamos*, "grasping", which, he says, Paul uses as

> a deliberate understatement to portray the way that Jesus grasped the divine power that he shared. The hymn presents Jesus as recognizing that being on equal terms with God means in its profound dimension to be "not grasping". Thus, the self-emptying of Jesus is the revelation that to be God is to be unselfishness itself. Because he shared God's existence, Jesus knew God perfectly and mirrored him fully. In his life, then, Jesus necessarily pursued a style of service even to the act of total self-giving. He did not do so simply as a model of conduct, but as a revealer of divine reality. Being God means being the Giver, the ever-creative author of all goodness. God can know no holding back, no selfishness, no fear of loss of power...For God, no dichotomy exists between creative power and saving care towards those he has made capable of enjoying his friendship and presence. Far from being

isolated from mankind's needs and longings, God is powerfully involved in human destiny to the point of breaking down the barriers that enslave men. As revealer of that power, Jesus necessarily came "not to be served, but to serve" (Mk 10:45) and to give men life (Jn 10:10). Since this power is eternally creative, it makes those who trust it into a "new creature" (see 2 Cor. 5:17).[40]

But this trust of which Reese speaks, this non-grasping of security, is difficult even for Jesus. As we have seen in our discussion of Mark, the kind of faith which allows miracles to happen, to experience the Spirit-power flowing through one in, for example, the miracle of healing, is possible for many; indeed, the whole point of Paul's many denunciations of the Corinthians was that, in one sense, charismatic phenomena are cheap. But there is a deeper, chastened kind of faith which is needed if we are ever to use our powers well, and this kind of faith is very like death. Initiation into it is provided for by the believer by participation in the very special death and resurrection of Jesus, as mediated by the community.

What the "very special death and resurrection of Jesus" means is a "hope against hope" and a faith which seems to be mistaken. As John Howard Yoder says about the Philippians hymn and Jesus, "his emptying of himself...is precisely his renunciation of lordship, his apparent abandonment of any obligation to be effective in making history move down the right track."[41] Whatever the truth might be about non-attachment as practiced by Gandhi and others in the Eastern spiritual traditions, the renunciation of the Christian is by no means a rising above all hopes. This is why it is so painful and so tragic:

> What Jesus refers to in his call to cross-bearing is rather the seeming defeat of that strategy of obedience which is not strategy, the inevitable suffering of those whose only goal is to be faithful to that love which puts one at the mercy of one's neighbor, which abandons claims to justice for oneself and for one's

own in an overriding concern for the reconciliation of the adversary and the estranged.[42]

What Yoder reminds us of here is that Jesus' cross is not *simply* a sign of human finitude confronted with death--the inescapable human dilemma. It is that, certainly, but it is more, because, as we have pointed out earlier, it is in some sense *chosen*. It is one thing to speak of faith in the face of life's vicissitudes; it is quite another to speak of faith as obedience, faith in the service of love, what we might call fidelity. What the cross and resurrection must be saying is not only that we can *trust*, but that we should be *trustworthy*; not only that we can believe that, as Juliana of Norwich put it, "all will be well", but that we can and must be faithful, must commit ourselves to acting so that "all will be well" for the neighbor, even unto death, and even in the face of total failure. Yoder is quite right when he says that "this vision of ultimate good being determined by faithfulness and not by results is the point where we moderns get off."[43]

To claim that it is possible to both have faith *in* and fidelity *toward* life itself is to open oneself up to being considered a sentimental dreamer, a romantic. Saying, with the Christian community, that "the cross of Christ is the model of Christian social efficacy"[44], that the ultimate power is the power of suffering in faith with no visible support for one's position, has it problems. It "has the peculiar disadvantage--or advantage, depending on one's point of view--of being meaningful only if Christ be the one whom Christians claim him to be, the Master."[45] The Christian community's claim that it is possible to live out a life in faith and fidelity from within a tradition shaped by the event of Jesus' cross and resurrection may be mistaken. It may be that the community's experience of resurrection is illusory and that Paul is simply wrong when he says that "all things work together for good for those who love God" (Romans 8:28). But it is surely the claim that arises out of the New Testament witness.

As we said at the beginning of this study, Christians did not invent faith, but they certainly brought it to clarity and centrality. Christianity brought to awareness and importance the fact of faith and the need for fidelity, but the *reality* of faith in God's power and the obligation to be faithful to it, are easy enough to discern in the Jewish tradition (and no doubt, in the tradition of other religious people):

> The faith of the pious Israelite was nourished by a body of what the cultural anthropologists will call "legend," the central themes of which were that God himself will take care of his people...and that therefore man's preoccupation with his own power as the instrument of his own surviving or prevailing is misdirected.[46]

Throughout the history of the Jewish people, from the story of Abraham through the Exodus, the history of the judges and the monarchy, the chastisement of prophecy, the experience of exile and return, it is Yahweh who saves, not the controlling power of human beings. The New Testament story of the cross, then, is an absolutely Jewish story, but also in some way a break with such stories, for to bring a tradition to the point of absurdity, to draw it to its logical conclusions, is to bend it to the breaking point. *For the cross and resurrection are the ultimate experience of our helplessness and our fidelity, our trust unto death, and the experience that such trust and fidelity are not foolish.*

But is this true? Is it possible to test such statements? We have seen that statements can be verified or falsified on the basis of evidence, but that what counts as evidence, and what shows up as a question is always a factor of communal concerns. This is the burden of our second chapter. Scientific questions make sense within the scientific community. Exactly how long this piece of metal is, to the millimeter, is only meaningful to the person who wants to use it in an automobile, and so on. And, as we have seen, there must be a basic prejudice or trust, if you will, in the general rightness of the community's goals and methods. I not only *can* give myself over to this community, but in some sense I *should*. The conversation, which sometimes appears to be an argument, goes on within a framework which is unquestioned.

And the Christian community is not without its inner-communal frameworks of discernment. As we have seen, Paul rejects literalistic methods of moral judgement, and proposes the basic principle of building up of the body of Christ as the ground of morality. Since such a principle is by no means simple to apply, Paul resorts to lists:

> Now the works of the flesh are plain: fornication, impurity, licentiousness, idolatry, sorcery, enmity, strife, jealousy, anger, selfishness, dissension, party spirit, envy drunkenness, carousing, and the like...But the fruit of the Spirit is love, joy, peace, patience, kindness, goodness, faithfulness, gentleness, self-control; against such there is no Law. (Gal 5: 19-23)

For Paul, these vices are "plain." He is not telling the Galatians something he expects to be novel to them, as if they should say, "We never knew that selfishness was wrong!" What he is doing is recalling to their minds what both he and they regard as true, but which, like all human beings, the Galatians might have conveniently "forgotten" or covered over.

The synoptic tradtion is also familiar with the problem of discernment:

> Beware of false prophets, who come to you in sheep's clothing, but inwardly are ravenous wolves. You will know them by their fruits. Are grapes gathered from thorns, or figs from thistles? So every sound tree bears good fruit, but the bad tree bears evil fruit. Every tree that does not bear good fruit is cut down and thrown into the fire. Thus you will know them by their fruits. (Mt. 7: 15-20)

In fact, the entire Christian tradition, from apostolic times to the present day can be considered a conversation in which Christians argue over who is following the tradition more faithfully, what ideas best express it today, and so forth, a conversation which takes for granted a much greater range of agreement than most Christians realize between the various components of the tradition, between the Baptists and the Greek Orthodox, the Lutherans and the Tridentine Catholics.

But the issue of discernment within the general framework of the Christian tradition, vital as that may be, is not the same issue as whether the Christian community itself is *right*, whether the cross and resurrection really do provide us with an authentic way of being in the world. This is not the questions of discernment but of conversion. Christian language, like all authentic religious language, brings the framework itself into view, if only dimly. But there is no denying that the cross is a difficult thing. If the cross can form the basis of religious life, it's difficult to see how it can be done. Comedian Dick Gregory's comment that, if Jesus Christ had come into the world today, rather than 2000 years ago, and been executed, Christians would now be wearing tiny gold electric chairs around their necks, captures as well as any one sentence could, the shocking character of the cross, a quality which Paul, of course, insisted on emphasizing to his hearers every chance he got.

What the story of the cross does, then, is to bring us into the *question* of faith, in all its radicality and terror. Recent studies on the parables of Jesus by such writers as C. H. Dodd, Paul Ricoeur and John Dominic Crossan emphasize the topsy-turvy, challenging nature of these Christian *koans*. If "myth" is in some sense analogous to what we have been calling "framework"--the general story within which we operate--within which conversation makes sense, then Crossan's comment is off-putting: "You have built a lovely home, myth assures us: but, whispers parable, you are right above an earthquake fault."[47]

As Sallie McFague puts it:

A parable is, in this analysis, an assault on the accepted, conventional way of viewing reality. It is an assault on the social, economic and mythic structures people build for their own comfort and security. A parable is a story meant to invert and subvert these structures and to suggest that the way of the kingdom is not the way of the world. Or, as Crossan says, a parable asks the question: "Why things might not be just as well some other way rather than the way we expected and presumed?" If we review in our minds the central relational parables of Jesus, we see again and again expectations being reversed: an older son who does not get what "deserves"; late workers who are paid the same as early ones; a feast that is given for the poor and "unworthy" when the prominent guests decline; a Samaritan who comes to the aid of a Jew while "religious people" walk by on the other side.[48]

Perhaps it's not so much that the conventions are "assaulted" as brought to light and relativized. And though McFague approvingly quotes Paul Ricoeur's suggesting that the parables lead the listener through a process of orientation, disorientation, reorientation, the result is not an "end product":

> a parable begins in the ordinary world with its conventional standards and expectations, but in the course of the story a radically different perspective is introduced that disorients the listener, and finally, through the interaction of the two competing viewpoints, tension is created that results in a redescription of life in the world.[49]

But this new description is not like the old one: "Reorientation in a parable is of an open-ended and relative sort, which does not allow us to remake our world according to a new set of rules and standards."[50] This would be to fall back into the problem rather than the solution. Rather, "what the parables stand for is opposition to *all* forms of idolatry and absolutism, *even* the new orientation to reality brought about through the parables' redescription of reality."[51] Thus the parabolic form-- and what must count as the ultimate parable--the cross and resurrection of Jesus--radically cuts off idolatry at the root. The continuing task of parables as a language form within the Christian tradition is "to enhance consciousness of the radical relativity of human models of reality, even when these models are 'divinely inspired', that is, based on the new way of the kingdom."[52]

But we are left with our question, if in heightened form. If the parables, if the cross of Jesus Christ, effectively shock us into the recognition that life is by no means as tidy as we had hoped, that all our images of reality are images and not reality, why bother at all? A generation obsessed by meaninglessness and a sense of vertigo has already learned about relativity. What it fears is that there is no center at all. Is there no truth? McFague puts it this way:

> Here and now there is no certainty, no "closure"; hence, we live intellectually as we live personally, on the "edge of the raft," knowing that our models are *only* models, and while we advance evidence energetically to support them over against other models, we should do so in the spirit of passionate nonchalance, that is, in the spirit of prayer.[53]

This is one sort-of-answer, with clear affinities to the Protestant tradition, but it seems to be one-sided, at least to an observer standing within the Catholic tradition. And it is at least questionable whether "passionate nonchalance" describes anybody at all we've come to regard as normative in the Christian community: Jesus in the garden, Jesus on the cross, Luther, Dorothy Day--passion, yes, but nonchalance?

Inevitably we are led back to the resurrection, the new life present in the community. To argue that the experience within the community of resurrection is not *certain* is misleading, for it all depends on what one means by "certain." If "certain" has to mean "established by technical means", then, obviously the experience of resurrection is not "certain." But if there is anything the New Testament wants to tell us, it is that the new way of being let loose in the world, the new creation, is true, and that we possess the Spirit to "prove" it.[54]

That there is a logical problem here is obvious. If the "proof" is available only to those who have already made a commitment, then how do we justify making the initial commitment? We have seen this as a classic conundrum in all forms of knowing, whether it is admitted or not. All knowledge is in some way circular; all knowledge is in some way based on trust. *What the Christian writings seem to do is to radicalize and explicitize human trust.* More than anything, the Christian invitation is to make a conscious choice to affirm unconscious faith, and to do this in the light of the "worst- case scenario": death. This choice is only possible within a community whose lifestyle is founded and formed by that choice. This is the nature of the invitation.

Within the Christian scriptures the problem of how some could accept this invitation and others refuse it is answered by attributing the decision to God, a theme most clearly stated by Paul, though by no means absent from the rest of the tradition:

> We know that in everything God works for good with those who love him, who are called according to his purpose. For those whom he foreknew he also predestined to be conformed to the image of his Son, in order that he might be the first-born among many brethren. And those whom he predestined he also called; and those whom he called he also justified; and those whom he justified he also glorified. (Rom. 8: 28-31)

This is by no means a casual passage in Romans. It is rhetorically and conceptually rich. God's condemna|tion had been the theme of Paul's first chapter, with the reason for the condemnation being the corruption of knowledge. Idolatry is the key symptom of the perversion of mind. Classical culture is accused of exchanging "the glory of the immortal God for images resembling mortal man or birds or animals or reptiles.' (1:23) The key concepts of knowledge (*gnosis*) image (*eikonos*) and glory (*doxa*) are introduced in the first chapter so that Paul can contrast their perversion with their proper use. In a world where human beings glorify perverted images and call that knowledge, God's truth appears. Those who have wandered in death and darkness are now saved through true knowledge, which involves the recognition of the true image of the human race, that of Christ, an image which is the very glory of God.

This is a magnificent vision, and there are certainly elements of universalism in it which prevent us from simply assuming that the whole non-Christian world will be lost. But the point we make here is the point of pre-destination: lost in error and darkness, the human race can only be saved by an action of God.

The issue of predestination waxes and wanes in the Christian scriptures. Judas, for example, is presented as fulfilling a pre-ordained plan, and is even urged on, as it were, by Jesus: "Jesus said to him, 'What you are going to do, do quickly' (Jn13:27)." Jesus later prays: "I have guarded them and none of them is lost but the son of perdition, that the scripture might be fulfilled." (16:12) But Judas receives no sympathy for playing an apparently essential but thankless role in the drama of salvation. As the fact that election is the grace of God, preventing any boasting on our own part, nevertheless does not preclude moral exhortation. The seeming contradiction here was not lost upon the early Christians, least of all Paul:

So then he has mercy upon whomever he wills, and he hardens the heart of whomever he wills. You will say to me then, "Why does he still find fault? For who can resist his will? " But who are you, a man, to answer back to God? Will what is molded say to its molder, "Why have you made me thus?" Has the potter no right over the clay, to make out of the same lump one vessel for beauty and another for menial use? (Rom. 9: 19-21)

The problematic nature of this language is obvious. The contradictions and conflicts in the New Testament under the rubric grace/freedom would erupt into total war more than once in the long history of the Christian tradition, and the story is not yet ended. But if we do not wish to take these words literally and accept that there are certain races, nations, sexes, who are condemned by God, then we must either reject them outright or find another, more adequate way of looking at them. It is not hard to find.

Surely no interpretation of this passage and others like it in Paul can ignore that for Paul the *chief issue is always the relationship between the Jews and the Gentiles*, and that exclusionary language is, often as not, part of the dialectical argument in which, soon enough, the opposite side will get heard. The exclusion of the Jews turns out to be a temporary measure:

So I ask, have they stumbled so as to fall? By no means! But through their trespass salvation has come to the Gentiles, so as to make Israel jealous. Now is their trespass means riches for the world, and if their failure means riches for the Gentiles, how much more will their full inclusion mean! (11:11-12)

What we keep coming back to is the inescapable historicity of salvation. The community which lives out of the resurrection of Jesus finds itself at once in a tense relationship with the community which lives out of the Law of Moses. Vindication of the truth of the Jesus community seems inevitably to require the condemnation of the Mosaic community. Being human seems always to involve taking sides, being here rather than there. One easy--too easy--solution to historicity is simply to take one's own side as the only one. Another easy--too easy--solution is to assume that all are equally true and that there need be no conflict. What the scriptural record really shows is a tragic failure on the part of two communities, the Jewish and the Christian, to continue the conversation, to realize that there could be an alternative between giving up the truth which undoubtedly appeared in their midst, and totally rejecting the truth which appeared among those others who were so close in training and heritage. We are only now, with faltering and frightened steps, rebuilding a dialogue which should never have stopped.

But have we strayed hopelessly from the question which generated this discussion? That question was justifying the *initial* commitment to Christianity. We have seen that the passages which most strongly condemn those who do not make that commitment are really best understood as part of a Jewish-Christian polemic, complicated a great deal, of course, by the fact that the boundaries between the two communities were at first quite flexible, and by the fact that the Christians themselves were subject to factions. We are left with the bare insistence that the movement toward the Christian community is of God and not of man. Can we make sense of the questions and answers now? In other words, once we have established that the community regards the act of faith as a "gift of God" is it possible to see this language as anything more than mythological thinking? Having pared away the peripheral issues, and concentrated on the core--is there anything left?

We could content ourselves with the assertion that there is fundamental trust as the basis of all life, a trust which grounds but is not grounded, and that the Christian community is the place where this trust is brought to light and lived out radically in the face of death. Language like "God acts" is useful as a way of pointing to this basic trust, but is certainly not to be taken literally, i.e., that a supernatural being chooses to do something. The problem is hardly a new one. Any system which manages to make the concept of "God" moderately intelligible (for example, and classically, Thomas' God as *actus purus*) leaves itself open to the charge that it is incompatible with any kind of language imputing activity to God (as the process critique of classical theism shows quite well[55]. The notion of "God acting in history" dies a death of a thousand qualifications.

We seem to have reached a dead end. It might be possible to salvage the concept of "God" as the pointer to the infinite abyss which surrounds us; we may be able to say that the inescapable fact of our trusting ultimately rests upon this abyss, that our trusting is justified, and that the abyss is called God. In fact, we do affirm all these things. But the scriptures suggest more than this. Resurrection, whatever else it is, is a surprise and an event. Nor did Jesus raise himself from the dead; he was raised, says the tradition, *by God*. What is signified by that prepositional phrase?

The answer is not far to seek. If our analysis of knowing in precedeing chapters has been correct, *language and experience go together*; language is not a receptical into which our experience is poured; rather language forms and makes experience possible. Let us put it bluntly: *language like "God saves" only makes sense within a particular language-tradition. It cannot be perfectly translated outside that tradition. In this it is like all other language.*

Our brief survey of the Christian scriptures has shown us that "faith" is by no means a univocal concept. It seemed in Mark to be that quality by which all things were made possible, a basic trust which, nevertheless, had to be reactivated. We saw that the cross and resurrection of Jesus brought faith to its radical test by facing it with death, death for others. The faith which made all things possible was now transformed into a darker reality: a faith which survives in the face of seeming impossibility. The community which continues the cross/resurrection experience of Jesus is the Christian community, the "body of Christ." Here basic faith is made explicit, here faith is lived radically unto death, here love is revealed as the fulfillment of faith. The community has as its task the dissemination of the gift of faith/hope/love which it possesses, a gift which is by definition the gift of life in the community of the followers of Jesus. We asked ourselves about the reception of the gift of explicit faith in Jesus' lordship. How does it happen? We found that the Christian community was unequivocal in its assertion that it was *God* who made possible the new life in Christ and it was *God* who drew people to join it.

Throughout, the Gadamerian analysis of our earlier chapters functioned as a framework, sometimes explicitly, more often implicitly. As we moved from Mark and the synoptics through John and Paul (glancing at the language of the parables of Jesus) we found ourselves stressing community, the language of community, the always-already quality of knowledge, the refusal to rest in any objectivized formulation of truth, the willingness to live by the life of the Spirit rather than by the written code, and so on. What we found was that the Gadamerian themes illuminated the reflection on the scriptures, and vice versa. This was all we were attempting to do in this chapter.

Notes

1. For summaries of the scholarship on Mark, cf. Sean P. Kealy, <u>Mark's Gospel, A History of Its Interpretation</u> (New York: Paulist Press, 1982), and Howeard Clark Kee, "Mark's Gospel in Recent Research," Interpretation 32 (October, 1978), p. 353-368.

2. W.D. Davies, <u>Invitation to the New Testament</u> (Garden City: Doubleday Anchor Book, 1969), p. 208.

3. All Scripture quotations are from the Revised Standard Version.

4. Eduard Schweizer, "The Portrayal of the Life of Faith in the Gospel of Mark," in James Luther Mays, ed., <u>Interpreting the Gospels</u> (Philadelphia: Fortress Press, 1981), p. 168.

5. James D.G. Dunn, <u>Jesus and the Spirit: A Study of the Religious and Charismatic Experience of Jesus and the First Christians as Reflected in the New Testament</u> (Philadelphia: Westminster Press, 1975), p. 75.

6. Jurgen Moltmann, <u>The Crucified God</u> (New York: Harper and Row, 1973), p. 63.

7. Moltmann, p. 38.

8. Moltmann, p. 123.

9. Moltmann, p. 151.

10. Moltmann, p. 146.

11. Moltmann, p. 153.

12. Cf. Edward J. Mally, S.J., "The Gospel According to Mark," in Raymond E. Brown, Joseph A. Fitzmeyer, and

Roland E. Murphy, eds., The Jerome Biblical Commentary (Englewood Cliffs: Prentice hall, 1968), section 42:96 (p. 60).

13. Dermot Lane, The Reality of Jesus (New York: Paulist Press, 1975), pp. 51-52.

14. Soren Kierkegaard, Fear and Trembling and The Sickness Unto Death, translated by Walter Lowrie, (Princeton, NJ: Princeton University Press, 1954), pp. 173-174).

15. John Knox, The Early Church (New York: Abingdon Press, 1955), p. 47.

16. Robert W. Funk, Language, Hermeneutic and the Word of God (New York: Harper and Row), p. 56.

17. Knox, p. 61.

18. J. Louis Martyn, History and Theology of the Fourth Gospel (New York: Harper and Row, 1968). Cf. Raymond Brown's Community of the Beloved Disciple (New York: Paulist Press, 1979).

19. M. Lowe, "Who Were the Ioudaioi?", New Testament Studies 18, 1976, 101- 130.

20. Edward Schillebeeckx, Christ, The Experience of Jesus as Lord, (New York: Crossroad, 11983), p. 382.

21. Lester J. Kuyper, "Grace and Truth," Interpretation 18, 1964, pp.15-16.

22. Krister Stendahl, "Paul and the Introspective Conscience of the West," in Paul Among Jews and Gentiles and Other Essays (Philadelphia: Fortress Press, 1976).

23. Jerome Murphy-O'Connor, Becoming Human Together (Wilmington: Michael Glazier, 1977, 1977), p. 202.

24. Murphy-O'Connor, pp. 202-203.

25. Ingo Hermann, The Experience of Faith (New York; P.J. Kennedy & Sons, 1966), p. 91.

26. Hermann, p. 92.

27. Cf. C.K. Barrett, The First Epistle to the Corinthians (New York: Harper and Row, 1968.).

28. Murphy-O'Connor, p. 229.

29. Murphy-O'Connor, p. 229.

30. Bornkamm, pp. 73-74.

31. On Galatians, cf. hans Dieter Betz's commentary, Galatians (Philadelphia: Fortress Press, 1979).

32. Dunn, p. 262.

33. Herbert Muhlen, "The Person of the Holy Spirit," in Killian McDonnell, ed., The Holy Spirit and Power: The Catholic Charismatic Renewal (New York: Doubleday, 1975), pp. 11-12.

34. Dunn, pp. 302-307.

35. Peter Berger and Thomas Luckmann, The Social Construction of Reality (Garden City, NY: Doubleday, 1966), p. 158. The quote continues: "The real thing is to be able to keep on taking it seriously, to retain a sense of its plausibility. This is where religious community comes in."

36. John C. Bennett, Witness (Tucson: Omen Press, 1974), pp. 331-332.

37. Bennett, p. 350.

38. Ernst Becker, The Denial of Death (New York: Free Press, 1973), p. 26.

39. Becker, p. 27.

40. James Reese, "The Event of Jesus--Power in the Flesh," in Franz Bockle and Jacques-marie Pohier, eds., <u>Power and the Word of God</u>, Concilium 90, (New York: Herder and Herder, 1973), p. 44.

41. John Howard Yoder, <u>The Politics of Jesus</u> (Grand Rapids: Eerdemans, 1972), p. 242.

42. Yoder, p. 243.

43. Yoder, p. 245.

44. Yoder, p. 250.

45. Yoder, p. 244.

46. Yoder, p. 86.

47. John Dominic Crossan, <u>The Dark Interval: Towards a Theology of Story</u> (Niles, IL: Argus Communications, 1975), pp. 56-57, quoted in Sallie McFague, Metaphorical Theology (Philadelphia: Fortress Press, 1983), p. 47.

48. McFague, p. 47.

49. McFague, p. 46-47.

50. McFague, p. 47.

51. McFague, p. 47.

52. McFague, p. 47.

53. McFague, p. 144.

54. McFague, p. 131.

55. Cf. Charles Hartshorne, <u>The Divine Relativity</u> (New Haven: Yale University Press, 1948).

Chapter Five
Some Reflections on Tradition

Anyone who stresses the importance of tradition cannot end a discussion of the tradition with the scriptural witness. Though the scriptures are the privileged expressions of the tradition, the life and reflection of the community did not end with the death of the last apostle. Certainly, there can be no question of doing here a detailed and exhaustive analysis of the history of the question of faith in the Christian tradition. Not only is there not room in this study, the writer of such a history would have to be competent in a bewildering variety of sub-fields. What we can do however, is to reflect, on some high points of the tradition and see, as we have done with the scriptures, whether some light can emerge from the encounter between our own emerging point of view and traditional formulations. Inevitably the Catholic Christian tradition will be emphasized, though not exclusively and not, it is to be hoped, insensitively.

Early reflections on the act of faith tended to be not very memorable, and it was not until Augustine that the problem emerged as such. Augustine, the controversialist, found himself justifying the rationality of faith to the pagan world and, more importantly, arguing with Pelagius over its gratuity. This last conflict was to mark Christian theology for all time and provide arguing positions for the great divisions of Christianity. Precisely because it is this latter Augustine who is so well-known, it might be helpful to turn our attention first to the Augustine who insisted that it was a very human and natural thing to believe.

I. Augustine: Faith, Natural and Supernatural

In his Liber de Fide Rerum Quae Non Videntur[1] (written about 400 AD) Augustine sets out to defend the Christian faith against "those who think that the Christian religion ought to be ridiculed rather than embraced for this reason, that in it, not the thing which may be seen is set forth, but faith in things which are not seen is imposed upon men."[2] Augustine's first line of argumentation is that we believe many things which we do not see; Christian faith is not unique in this regard. With a literalism which is disarming, Augustine points to the obvious fact that we not only believe, but even *know* things which cannot physically be seen, e.g., the very mental state of belief or unbelief. Augustine is quite aware that this is not a strong argument, but he seems to regard it as obvious that probing beyond the physical toward deeper realities, even those difficult to grasp, is a sort of preparation for faith: "Surely, therefore, we ought to believe also some temporal things which we do not see, that we may deserve to see also the eternal things which we believe."[3]

These abstract and general comments take on life when Augustine moves toward examples nearer to our common experience. Those who insist on having visible proof for something before they believe it, says Augustine, do not really live out their skepticism. "Tell me, please," he asks, "with what eyes do you see your friend's disposition toward you?"[4] The obvious answer of the skeptic is that he grasps the disposition of the friend through his physical words, gestures and deeds. The even more obvious reply is that these words, gestures and deeds are by no means the actual disposition of the friend:

> For that disposition is not color or figure that may be impressed upon the eyes; nor is it a sound or chant that may strike upon the ears; nor is it even yours to be felt through the impulse of your own heart. The conclusion is clear: for fear that your life would be barren of any friendship, and that love bestowed upon you would fail of payment in return, you do believe your friend's disposition though it is unseen, unheard and unperceived by you internally.[5]

This is a lovely passage, and the point, of course, is that a demand for proof in the most vital matters of our lives would be most silly, and, worse than silly, self-defeating. Augustine's Latin rises to exceptional loveliness as he insists that we already always believe. He tells the one who claims to need proof before he will believe:

Ecce ex corde tuo, credis cordi non tuo; et quo nec
carnis nec mentis dirigis aciem, accommodas fidem
...Amici vere non abs te amatur fides, si in te mutuo
nulla sit fides, qua credas quod in illo non vides.[6]

(Literally: "Behold, out of your own heart, you believe
in a heart not your own; and where neither by mind
nor flesh you direct your insight, you rely
on faith...The faith of your friend is loved by you not
at all, unless in you there is a corresponding faith, by
which you believe in what in him you do not see.)

Friendship would be impossible without faith, and
friendship, for Augustine, is not the rather limited and pale
reality which the word seems to connote in English, but the
basis of all human relationships, without which society would
simply crumble. If this is the case, says Augustine, if faith
is so necessary for human life, then it stands to reason that
faith must be necessary for the deeper life revealed by religion:

Since, therefore, merely human society, through the
destruction of concord, will not remain stable, if we
do not believe what we do not see, how much
more ought faith to be placed in divine things, even if
they are not seen! If this faith is not exercised, it is
not the friendship of certain men that is violated, but
the highest religious obligation itself, and the deepest
misery will necessarily follow.[7]

Thus is drawn the familiar analogy between human things and
things divine; if human faith is good, then so must divine faith
be, but much more. Despite the Platonism which causes
Augustine to denigrate the physical in a spontaneous and only
semi-conscious fashion, the basic argument here is quite
congenial and has a "modern" sound to a generation which
sometimes thinks it invented human relationships. But
Augustine is not concerned with simply validating religious-
faith-in-general. If that were his only interest, then he
could allow his listeners to remain pagans or join a new

Eastern cult. What must be justified is *Christian* faith, and Augustine is quite up to the task.

How, then, does Augustine take upon himself the task of convincing his hearers of the truth of the *Christian* faith? Interestingly, he does it by dropping his own personal voice and taking upon himself the persona of the Christian church: "The church herself addresses you with the voice of maternal affection."[8] Granted, says the voice of the church, that people now living did not see the events of the life of Jesus, how the ancient prophecies of the Jews were fulfilled in him, how he worked miracles and rose from the dead. Granted, then, that you do not believe what you do not see. But there *is* something for you to see: the church herself:

> Therefore, look at these things before you; gaze upon them intently; consider these things which you behold, which are not narrated to you as past, not foretold to you as future, but clearly demonstrated to you as present. Now does this seem vain or trivial to you, or do you think that it is not a divine miracle or merely one of little significance that the whole human race runs its course in the name of the One Crucified?[9]

Though a large part of the argument uses the fulfillment of predictions as a strong warrant for faith, it is clear that such predictions and their fulfillment are a stronger argument for those already in the fold than those on the outside. The roll call of fulfilled prophecies goes on, but Augustine knows where the Achilles heel of his pagan listeners really is: the decline of paganism and the rise of Christianity: "This, indeed, you do behold, whether you will or no, even if you still think that there is or has been some usefulness in idols."[10] That which amazes the entire human race is not the resurrection of Christ, which it did not see, but the growth of Christ's church: "All those things hitherto done and accomplished concerning Christ you did not see, but you cannot deny that you can see the present condition of His church."[11]

Indeed, the church as she now is, advancing in the world, is the fulfillment of prophecy, and by that very fact evidence for the future fulfillment of other prophecies: "Why, then, should we not believe the first and last things which we do not see, when we have, as witnesses for both, the things occupying a middle position which we do see?"[12] It might appear that Augustine's avid quotations of prophecies are a sure sign of a mentality with little link to our own. But surely there is a sense in which such interest is a cousin, at least, to modern empiricism. It takes a hard look at the "theories" and it takes a hard look at the "evidence" and attempts to show a correlation between them. And if more sophisitacted literary studies of the ancient prophets have convinced many of us that they were rarely interested in "foretelling the future" in any obvious sense, nevertheless, some of them certainly were, and the entire enterprise need not be swept away in embarrassment.

Still, as we have already suggested, the basis of Augustine's position is not prophecy, but the existence of the church:

> Even if no testimonies concerning Christ and the church had appeared in advance, should not the fact that a divine brilliance had unexpectedly illuminated the human race move anyone to believe, especially when, now that the false gods have been abandoned, their images everywhere dashed to pieces, their temples razed or converted to other uses, and so many vain rites rooted out from the most stubborn human customs, he sees the one true God called upon by all, and that this was brought about by one Man, a Man who was by men derided, seized, bound scourged, buffeted, reproached, crucified, and put to death?[13]

The church, then, this *magnum pietatis sacramentum* ("great sacrament of love")[14] is a movement, a force in the world which is so striking, so illuminative of divine truth, that those who refuse to submit to her authority are surely foolish.

Summarizing Augustine's teaching, then, we can say that faith, "belief in what we cannot see", is a human reality, in fact, the basis of all human community. Without it all societies would crumble. By such faith we entrust ouselves to others, and they to us, and thus allow the joy of love to have a place and a chance to appear. If this is the case with ordinary human life, then, all the more are we justified in having faith in that community known as the church of Christ. Its rise to prominence in the ancient world from the status of despised sect founded by a crucified outlaw, the virtues of its members, the purity of its teaching about the one true God, the obvious superiority of its practices--even the fact of its triumph over the heretics within it--all make it clear that we should confidently entrust ourselves to its authority.

But this giving over of ourselves to the authority of Christ as mediated by the church, while a rational action (Augustine gives reasons for it), is not simply rational in a calculative sense. Etienne Gilson expresses the Augustinian teaching rather nicely:

> In its essence, Augustinian faith is both an adherence of the mind to supernatural truth and a humble surrender of the whole man to the grace of Christ. After all, how could these two things be separated? The adherence of the mind to God's authority implies humility, but humility in turn presupposes a confidence in God, and this in itself is an act of love and charity. If then, the actual complexity of the life of the Spirit is borne in mind, we see that the man who adheres to God by faith not only submits his mind to the letter of the formulas but yields his soul and his whole being to the authority of Christ, Who is our model of wisdom and Who grants us the means of attaining it.[15]

One does not simply sit down at a desk, then, and calmly weigh up the arguments for or against giving oneself over to the Christian way of life. One might indeed do just that, as some converts have done, but by the time one has gotten to that stage, a great deal else has already gone on. One does not seek God unless one has already been sought, and the stage of

185

calculative rationality is reached after a great deal of the journey has already been made.

The problem we thus point to is that of the *initium fidei*, the origin of faith. Pelagius and the later semi-Pelagians had placed the emphasis on the conscious will. There are many unfortunate aspects of the debate between Augustine and Pelagius, including a denigration of human nature which the church has been paying for ever since, but from our point of view, the issue was that of calculative reason vs. the giftedness of faith. Faith is always already there. It precedes our awareness of it.

Augustine explores this point in his great commentary on the gospel of John, most clearly in the discussion of John 6:41-59, especially v. 44: "No one can come to me unless the Father who sent me draws him; and I will raise him up at the last day." How is it, asks Augustine, that the Father draws us to Christ? If we are drawn, after all, then we are doing something against our wills, and yet faith is supposed to be free:

> "How can I believe with the will if I am drawn?" I say it is not enough to be drawn by the will; thou art drawn even by delight. What is it to be drawn by delight?...There is a pleasure of the heart to which that bread from heaven is sent. Moreover, if it was right in the poet to say, "Every man is drawn by his own pleasure," not necessity, but pleasure; not obligation, but delight,--how much more boldly ought we to say that a man is drawn to Christ when he delights in the truth, when he delights in blessedness, delights in righteousness, delights in everlasting life, all of which Christ is?[16]

Reason has its place, but its place is to help us achieve the goal which has already been set for us by the good which we seek and desire. As Gilson showed us, for Augustine, faith is already a kind of love, and love is already a kind of faith. How can you give yourself over to that which you don't trust? And how can you give yourself over to that which you don't perceive as good? Nor can we really claim credit for our faith and love, for how can we *not* give ourselves over to that which we trust? How can we not give ourselves over to that which we perceive as good? Nor are we unfree, for we are doing exactly what we desire: loving the delectable, trusting the solid foundation.

If this is difficult to accept, Augustine, characteristically, says, "Give me a man that loves, and he feels what I say...But if I speak to the cold and indifferent, he knows not what I say."[17] This may seem like demanding assent before the conversation begins:

> Rational speculation, as conceived by St. Augustine, always makes faith its point of departure. This fact has often been used as a basis for denying that there is an Augustinian philosophy. The last act of that long inner crisis described in the Confessions ends with a twofold surrender: Augustine submits his mind once and for all to the authority of Plato and Scripture, and we are left in doubt as to whether "this vigorous genius ceased to be a philosopher in the fullest sense of the term on the very day he seems to have bound himself to philosophy forever." Moreover, it is unfortunate that this double authority is self-contradictory because one appeals to reason, the other to faith. It is as though reason's original decision to recognize an irrational datum were not the very negation of all rationality, and hence, of all philosophy.[18]

Recall Michael Polanyi's remark in Personal Knowledge that he is doing for this generation what Augustine did for his: institute a post-critical philosophy.[19] Of course, Augustine's focus on *religious* truth, the truth which leads to happiness, caused him to be uninterested in speculation about the *structural* relationship between faith and truth apart from a specifically religious context. He does *see* the relationship between human faith and human society, and he notes the necessity of human faith as a helpful pointer toward the necessity of divine faith, but that faith and reason are reciprocal ideas *in general* seems not to have been an issue for Augustine.

And so there is a sense in which Augustine does indeed demand assent before the conversation begins. (From our point of view, of course, there can be no conversation without assent.) But where does this primary assent come from? As we have seen, for Augustine, the *initium fidei* can be located in the movement of delight and pleasure which we cannot help but feel in the presence of that which is good. But how to account for the obvious fact that some are capable of feeling this delight and others are not? Why are some cold and some hot? The answer, for Augustine, is hidden in the inscrutable will of God, which is not our task to understand:

> What then did the Lord answer to such murmurers? "Murmur not among yourselves." As if He said, I know why ye are not hungry and do not understand nor seek after this bread. "Murmur not among yourselves: no man can some unto me, except the Father that sent me draw him." Noble excellence of grace! No man comes unless drawn . There is whom He draws, and there is whom He draws not; why He draws one and draws not another, do not desire to judge, if thou desirest not to err. Accept it at once and then understand; thou art not yet drawn? Pray that thou mayest be drawn.[20]

Finally we do not really know why we are drawn, except that we are drawn by God, and even that explanation is not helpful, for why God draws us and not others is not only mysterious, but Augustine tells us not to ask, only to accept. Though the language is different in Aristotle, Augustine, and our modern writers (Heidegger, Gadamer, etc.), we are confronted with what is really the same issue. *The issue is whether there can be knowledge without preconceptions and without faith; the answer is no.* We cannot get underneath our own foundations and examine them, for without some sort of foundation we can not stand at all.

But preconceptions are not the same as a strait jacket, and predestination, mysterious as it is in Augustine, is not as rigid as it later became in the Christian tradition. Even if one has not yet felt the pull, one can still pray that one might. Of course, this is paradoxical advice, probably recognized as such by Augustine. If one does not yet feel the desire to possess God, the need for delight in his presence, but still wants to pray for it, one clearly already feels *some* sort of desire, e.g., the desire for desire for God and this is really the same thing as the desire for God regarded simply. To pray that one might be drawn is already to be drawn.

Augustine's insistence on the mystery and gratuity of the *initium fidei* was to carry the day; the Pelagians were routed. The Council of Carthage, (418) for example, roundly condemned the teachings of Pelagius on the question of grace, sin, and freedom. But it was the second Council of Orange (529), actually a local gathering of bishops in Southern France, later affirmed by Pope Boniface II and accepted by the general tradition of the Christian church as authoritative, which stated most clearly what had become the orthodox position on the *initium fidei*. Augustine's spirit surely hovered over the proceedings, for the canons of the Council were in large part borrowed from his writings and in every part borrowed from his point of view:

> If anyone says that, as the increase, so also the beginning of faith, indeed even the pious readiness to believe, whereby we believe what justifies the impious and attain to the regeneration of holy baptism, is not in us by a gift of grace, that is , by inspiration of the Holy Spirit changing our will from unbelief to belief, from impiety to piety, but occurs naturally, shows himself to be an enemy of the apostolic teaching of St. Paul...(There follow quotations from the Apostle.) For those who say that the faith by which we believe in God is natural, define as faithful also all those who are strangers to the Church. (D698)[21]

Notice that the argument against the "natural" character of faith in God rests on the necessity of safeguarding the primacy of the Christian community's grasp of saving truth. If faith were "natural", i.e., obtainable apart from the community of Christ, then the whole point of evangelization would be lost. Why preach salvation to those already saved? Why preach faith to those already faithful? And, most importantly, why preach adherence to the Church to those who have no need for her?

Common sense and simple humanity, however, require that the negative corollary of the positive teaching, i.e., that if some are predestined to salvation in the Church, then others must be predestined to perdition outside of her walls, be explicitly condemned. This would obviously make of God a monster, and the Council shrinks in horror at the idea:

> Not only do we not believe that some by divine power are destined for evil, but if any there be who wish to believe so much evil, we anathematize them with all detestation. But this we salutarily profess and believe, that in every good work it is not we who begin and are afterwards helped by God's mercy, but that he first inspires us with belief and love for himself without any previous merits (of ours). (D702)[22]

Thus do the Fathers attempt to deal with a delicate question which would recur with frequency in the history of Christianity and which is very much discussed today: how can we trust our own tradition without regarding other traditions as worthless? Conversely, how can we respect other traditions without (even subtly) denigrating our own? The answer of the Fathers in this case is, in the absence of a really comprehensive and satisfying theory, a product of what we could call Christian common sense. It stresses what needs to be stressed, namely, the necessity of trusting in the truth which the community does possess, and trusting it in some absolute sense. Thus the community is entitled at this most solemn point to use the heaviest weapon in its linguistic arsenal: explicit God language.

God himself has acted to give us this gift of faith, and any other position must be that of enemies of the community.

How, indeed, could it be otherwise? To admit that the *initium fidei* could be *ours* would be to admit that it could be wrong, for the fallibility of human nature is as sure as anything about human nature. But to entertain the notion that the faith itself could be mistaken would be the end, quite literally, of the community. That this position (i.e., that the faith is of God, not man) can be perverted goes without saying. It can be used to buttress the most heinous of crimes, the most blatant oppression. Nevertheless, it is hard to see how one could be a Christian and not *in some sense* believe it to be true.

Having said this, Christian common sense must also say something which seems to be logically contradictory. If we agree that faith is a gift, then nothing is clearer than that the gift is not given to all. Even if we attempt to save God's goodness by claiming that he gives his gifts to all, but some refuse, then we are back in the problem of trusting in our own human fallibility again: we, the chosen, are chosen by ourselves! To argue that we are better than those who have rejected God's gift would surely be to run counter to the deepest intuitions of the faith itself. The Council's answer, as we have seen, was to stress the positive. God does indeed give his gift freely, and in this we rejoice. Nor does he destine some to perdition, for this would be a detestable opinion. The untidiness is instructive. Better to remain in a certain ignorance than be certainly wrong. Practically speaking, the ambiguity about those outside the fold saves them from being looked at exclusively as divided up between only two possible groups: the lost and the not-yet converted. On the tenuous foundation of this ambiguity, conversation might even, someday, be possible, though it has not often worked out that way in the history of Christianity.

II. Anselm: The Faith Seeking Understanding

Even a brief sketch of the tradition must mention the name of Anselm of Canterbury (d.1109). It is true that Anselm's ontological argument for the existence of God has few takers these days, most philosophers following the example of Thomas Aquinas, who explicitly rejected it.[23] But if Karl Barth is even *partially* correct in his retrieval of Anselm, Anselm's ontological argument is by no means an attempt to reason to the reality of God apart from faith.[24] Indeed, the phrase which has become so familiar, *fides quaerens,* is as crucial to Anselm as it has become well-known to the tradition. For Anselm, faith, by its nature, moves us out toward the delight of knowledge. As Barth puts it: "*Credo ut intelligam* means: It is my very faith itself that summons me to knowledge."[25] Starting on the firm foundation of faith, the mind reaches out to a clearer grasp of the truth, and this grasp, once it has been achieved, brings us great pleasure and joy. But faith does not cease to be faith, and the failure of an intellectual investigation does not destroy it : "Nulla difficultas aut impossibilitas intelligendi valeat illum a veritate, quem per fidem adhaesit, ecxutere." (Ep. de incarn. I: II 10, 15f)[26]

But if we reach back and ask where this faith itself comes from, then Anselm has only the answer that is familiar to us: it comes from God, mediated by the church. Indeed, so clear is the role of the church in mediating the Word of God that Anselm "declared that in the end the 'surest' way to refute an error theologically within the church is to refer it (*ostendere*) to the Pope at Rome, *ut eius prudentia examinetur.*"[27] The highest court for Anselm is not his own reason, not even his own faith, but the prudence of the church, as represented by the Pope. (Needless to say, this position has its own problems, but they need not concern us now.) Barth goes on: "Anselm's subjective *credo* has an objective *Credo* of the church as its unimpeachable point of reference...The 'Word of Christ' is the truth that faith believes it to be, in that it is identical with the 'Word of those who preach Christ.'"[28] And those who preach Christ are, of course, the officers of the Catholic Church.

And since the Credo of the church is indeed the truth, the advance from *credere* to *intelligere* is possible:

> It is just this relationship between *credo* and *Credo* that determined how far a Christian can advance from *credere* to *intelligere*, how far theology is possible: As *credere* of the *Credo*, faith is itself, so to speak, *intelligere*, distinguished from the *intelligere* which it 'desires' only in degree and not in kind.[29]

Barth refers here in a footnote to Anselm's <u>Proslogion</u> (IX): "Adiuva me, iuste et misericors deus, cuius lucem quaero, adiuva me, *ut intelligam quod dico*."[30] (Italics mine.)

Anselm here is asking to understand what he already is saying. For Anselm, the truth is always already there for the one who has faith. The reason for this is that the image of God is in each of us, and it is God, truth itself, which we seek, Thus we seek what we already have, in a sense. In a preliminary prayer in the <u>Proslogion</u>, Anselm makes this clear:

> Fateor, domine, et gratias ago, quia creasti in me hanc imaginem tuam, ut tui memor te cogitem, te amem. Sed sic est abolita attritione vitiorum, sic est offuscata fumo peccatorum, ut non possit facere ad quod facta est, nisi tu renoves et reformes eam. Non tento, domine, penetrare altitudinem tuam, quia nullatenus comparo illi intellectum meum; sed desidero aliquatenus intelligere veritatem tuam, quam credit et amat cor meum. Neque enim quaero intelligere ut credam, sed credo ut intelligam. Nam et hoc credo: quia 'nisi credidero, non intelligam'. (<u>Proslogion</u> I)[31]

The relationship between love and belief, belief and knowledge, are Augustinian to the core in this passage. Note that even the *proposition* that "unless I believe I shall not know" is itself an object of belief: "Nam et hoc credo." It is confidence in God, openness to God's truth, and desire for God's goodness which motivate Anselm in his philosophical journey.

Having said all this, is it not still true that Anselm's "proof" for the existence of God is meant as a rigorous philosophical proof? The answer is yes, of course, but it all depends on what you mean by philosophy. Anselm's familiar ontological argument for the existence of God uses as a definition for God the famous *quo maius cogitari nequit* (than which nothing greater can be conceived). He proceeds to show that a thing existing is greater than one not existing, or existing only in the mind. Thus, if God is truly the being greater than which nothing can be conceived, then he must exist; otherwise we could conceive of a being greater than God, i.e., a being actually existing. Whatever the merits of the argument, which tends to gain rather than lose interest as one wrestles with it, is it not an attempt to ground the existence of God in sheer human reason?

Barth's commentary here is, as usual, helpful in lifting up the important point. Recall that Anselm's opponent in the discussion is Guanilo, by no means a modern day atheist, but a Christian like Anselm who takes upon himself the role of the biblical fool (*insipiens*) who says in his heart there is no God.

> Notice how the formula is introduced--*et quidem credimus te esse aliquid quo maius* ...What is said here is confirmed by the conclusive statement in which Anselm later guarded against the possible rejection of this Name of God, that is against the fact that it is unknown to the Christian: *quod quam falsum sit, fide et conscientia tua pro firmissima utor argumento.* In this statement the *fides* of Guanilo, who is being addressed, is itself to confirm his acquaintance with this Name of God and his *conscientia* is to confirm his acquaintance with the Person whose name this is: as a believing Christian Guanilo knows very well the *quo maius cogitari nequit is.*[32]

Thus, the formula "than which nothing greater can be conceived" is not a formula at all, but is the actual Name of God. The corollary here is obvious: if the *quo maius* is the *Name of God*, and not simply a clever formula, then it must have been revealed. Where *did* Anselm get this phrase? It is surely not from scripture. In the Preface to the <u>Proslogion</u> Anselm himself gives us a personal account of how he found the phrase; how he had been thinking about the possibility of finding one, simple, cogent proof for God's existence ever since he had written his little tract on the nature of faith (<u>Monologion</u>), had spent many hours seeking it, to no avail, and had finally given up:

> Cum igitur quadam die vehementer eius importunitati resistendo fatigarer, in ipso cogitationum conflictu sic se obtulit quod desperavam, ut studiose cogitationem amplecterer, quam sollicitus repel‖lebam. (<u>Proslogion, Prooemium</u>)[3]

This may sound to us like a typical example of the creative process at work: one ponders a problem to the point of satiety, puts it away, and suddenly it is there, solved.

Barth, however, sees more than this: "Is this a scientific report on an investigation or is it not rather--a perhaps quite typical--account of an experience of prophetic insight?"[34] This may seem far-fetched at first, since Anselm does not mention prayer at this point. But this may be to simply assume a contemporary semi-skeptical attitude where it is not appropriate. Anselm himself gives us the clue:

> Aestimans igitur quod me gaudebam invenisse, si scriptum esset, alicui legenti placiturum: de hoc ipso et de quibusdam aliis sub persona conantis erigere mentem suam ad contemplandum deum et quaerentis intelligere quod credit, subditum scripsi opusculum. (<u>Prooemium</u>)[35]

As Anselm had spoken of his despair (*desperaveram*), now he speaks of joy (*gaudebam*), and anyone with a sensitivity to the Augustinian tenor of the proceedings should be aware of what the words "despair" and "joy" mean to such a monk as Anselm. Besides, Anselm makes it clear that he is writing " in the person" of someone who wishes to understand what he already believes, not for someone who does not yet believe. Therefore, there is textual evidence for Barth's conclusion:

> Thus in no sense is he of the opinion that he produced this formula out of his own head but he declared quite explicitly the source from which he considers it to have come to him: when he gives God a Name, it is not like one person forming a concept of another person; rather it is as a creature standing before his Creator. In this relationship which is actualized by virtue of God's revelation, as he thinks of God he knows that he is under this prohibition; he can conceive of nothing greater, to be precise, 'better', beyond God without lapsing into absurdity, excluded for faith, of placing himself above God in attempting to conceive of this greater. *Quo maius cogitari* only appears to be a concept that he formed for himself; it is in fact as far as he is concerned a revealed Name of God.[36]

Barth is surely right to this extent: when Anselm speaks of rationality he is not speaking of what we could call today technical reason, and, if we look at the proof in that light, we will miss its beauties (whatever our final opinion of its merits might be).

For our purposes, we only have to demonstrate a modest and easy proposition. It is clear, that is, that for Anselm the philosophical search for a rational proof for the existence of God is motivated by faith, not by doubt, and is not intended to shore up faith or to displace faith, but to fulfill it (as much as is possible here on earth), to bring it to its natural and logical conclusion: a deeper understanding of God, an understanding which brings joy. The question of whether Anselm intended his proof to be "objectively" valid for the unbeliever as well as the believer is one which most Anselm scholars would answer in the affirmative, disagreeing with Karl Barth's emphasis. Nevertheless, all would agree that the "knowledge" of God which could be achieved by purely rational means is not saving knowledge, but what Newman called "notional" knowledge. Jasper Hopkins puts it in this way:

Believing that God exists is only a necessary
precondition for believing in God. And perhaps this
distinction epitomizes the heart of Barth's
point: Anselm recognizes that even if a rational
argument brings the Fool to understanding, it can
never by itself bring him to saving faith--*fides
qua fiducia.* Nevertheless (and Barth does not
sufficiently emphasize this) the intelligent Fool will
never come to faith in the absence of
preparatory understanding. And for this reason
Anselm appeals directly to the intellect-- setting forth,
as best he can, what seem to him simple and
straightforward demonstrations. If these demonstrations succeed in leading the Fool to understanding,
then they may be instrumental in leading him also to
belief *in* God. But the commitment of faith involves a
deliberate choice of the will; and in fallen man there is
a pervasive discrepancy between what intellect
apprehends and will chooses. In this light, then,
Anselm discerns man's need for grace in understanding and for grace in order to will what one comes
to understand. Barth's unassailable service to the
history of theology has been to emphasize afresh
Anselm's awareness of this need.[37]

But Hopkins goes on to say that Barth's error is to fail to
recognize that, for Anselm, there is some common ground
between believer and unbeliever, and that common ground is
reason. But, even if we agree with Hopkins, this is a
fairly empty assertion. To agree, in an abstract way, that a
logical proposition is apparently true, but without issue in life,
without application, is a fairly unimportant enterprise. And as
soon as one moves from the notional to what we could call the
existential, we are, by everyone's account, already in the
realm of saving faith.

The point of our discussion of Anselm, and our use of
Barth's retrieval of Anselm, was to show that for Anselm,
rationality builds on faith; Anselm's entire context, his
psychology and his sociology, is ecclesial; his aim is the joy

which comes from the knowledge of the God revealed in his tradition. Barth saw this clearly, because Barth saw with the eyes of a theologian, not an academic commentator on ancient texts. What Karl Rahner said of his own study of Aquinas applies equally to Barth's study of Anselm: "If what matters is to grasp the really philosophical in a philosopher, this can only be done if one joins him in looking at the matter itself. It is only then that you can understand what he means."[38]

III. Thomas: The Several Sides of Faith

Our next task is to turn now to that same Thomas Aquinas, whose influence on subsequent theology is unsurpassed. In many ways, Aquinas' discussion of faith summarizes the results of the traditional discussions, though his emphasis on the intellectual (as opposed to the voluntaristic) side of faith will be the seed ground for the subsequent divisions in Christendom. But Aquinas is not usually easily categorized; his use of concepts in different ways throughout his works has been the despair of commentators. And so the one who would say something intelligent about Aquinas' teaching on the subject must be content with something other than a rigorous proof. And since we now enter an area which has generated a vast amount of secondary literature, and which is complex enough in Aquinas, we must resign ourselves for the purposes of this study of making some broad statements on the texts in the Summa, and trying to avoid the pitfalls of technical arguments bwteen commentators.

In our reflections on the tradition up to this point, we have seen that faith, even faith in the community known as church, appeared as the presupposition for the appearance of saving truth. This was true for Augustine, and, as we saw, it was also true for Anselm, despite the different intellectual interests and perspectives of the two men. But Aquinas may seem to some to offer us little help for our discussion of faith, knowledge and community. Luther's dismissal of Aquinas as the man who quoted the scriptures but wound up with Aristotle, is a well-known comment, and Aquinas is

sometimes dismissed these days by Catholics as well, and for
the same reasons as Luther (and with as little justice). As we
shall see, it is Aquinas' perspective which largely grounds our
own.

Categorization is revealing; where one decides to deal with
a question is often as important as what one says about it. In
Thomas' threefold Summa (God, Man, Christ), for example,
Thomas is sometimes criticized for putting the God-Man only
after the discussion of God and Man. Thomas discusses knowledge in the section of his Summa devoted to God. Where
does Thomas put his discussion of *faith*? Significantly,
Thomas discusses faith in the second part of the Summa. It
begins his discussion of the specific virtues (the
three supernatural virtues: faith, hope, and charity; the four
cardinal virtues: prudence, temperance, justice, fortitude--
forming the whole picture of the moral life), those habits or
dipositions which inhere in the human soul and enable the
person to do what has to be done. He discusses first the object
of faith, then, the act of faith, and thirdly, the habit, or virtue
itself *qua* virtue. Let us look briefly at each of these
discussions.

Thomas is quite clear as to the *object* of the act of faith.
It is *veritas prima*, first truth. That this is God goes without
saying, and the God of Christians, not the God of
philosophers. Thomas wants to insist that the term of the act
of faith is really and truly the *first truth* itself. Nevertheless,
from the point of view of the one who has faith, what is
grasped is a *proposition*, not the substance of God. By
making a distinction between what we would call today the
subjective and objective aspects of the act of faith, Thomas is
able (characteristically) to agree with everyone who
went before him, subsuming their positions into a larger
perpsective:

Sic ergo objectum fidei dupliciter considerari potest.
Uno modo, ex parte ipsius rei creditae, et sic
objectum fidei est aliquid incomplexum, scilicet res
ipsa de qua fides habetur. Alio modo, ex parte
credentis, et secundum hoc objectum fidei est aliquid

> complexum per modum enuntiabilis. Et ideo
> utrumque vere opinatum fuit apud antiquos, et
> secundum aliquid utrumque est verum. (2a2ae. 1,2)[39]

Thus the ancients who held that faith was simple are right; so are they who held that faith was complex. This distinction between the simple object-in- itself (*prima veritas*) and the complex object of the human act of faith enables Thomas to explain a bit later why faith cannot be mistaken, despite the obvious fact that people have believed false things. The deductions and (we might stress) practical applications of faith are very fallible, even though the actual articles of faith proposed by the church are inerrant (and few in number), and even *they* are not the ultimate, simple object of faith, God himself as *prima veritas*. (2a2ae, 1,3).

The distinction comes into play again in Article 7 (*Utrum articuli fidei secundum successionem temporum creverint*). Thomas can affirm both the unchanging character of the substance of the faith while affirming also the obvious fact that the *number* of articles of faith has increased over the centuries. The later articles arose as the result of controversies, and made explicit what was implicit in the earlier articles. That these derivations are legitimate, and to be trusted, is certain because they are made by the church, which is infallible, because guided by the Holy Spirit, i.e., God Himself. Thus *"confessio fidei traditur in symbolo quasi ex persona totius Ecclesiae, quae per fidem unitur. Fides autem Ecclesiae est fides formata; talis enim fides inventur in omnibus illis qui sunt numero et merito de Ecclesia."* (2a2ae, 1,9, ad 3) Thus, the members of the church are formed into one person, as it were, by their very faith, and as such have the special assistance of God. Yet, significantly, faith is not for Thomas faith *in* the church itself. The article of the Creed, "I believe in the Holy Catholic Church" is a bit misleading, one may infer from Thomas' discussion of it. What it really says is *"credo in Spiritum Sanctum sanctificantem Ecclesiam."* ("I believe in the Spirit of holiness making holy the Church.") Thus, despite his immense respect for the Church, Thomas never confuses the Church with God. The Church is that body of people

whose faith directs them to the first truth, not a body of people
which believes in itself. (2a2ae 1,9, ad 5)

Having settled to his own satisfaction the outstanding
questions pertaining to the object of faith, Aquinas now turns
to the actual, inward act of faith, and the first order of business
is to define the term "to believe" (*credere*). Thomas turns at
this point to Augustine and tells us that believing is *cum
assensione cogitare.* (2a2ae 2,1). To believe is to "think with
assent", then. Aquinas notoriously takes over traditional
formulations and translates them into his own perspective. In
this case Aquinas wants to point out that *cogitare* has
imperfection in its very etymology, "to turn over (in the
mind)." If one has certain knowledge, one need not ponder in
this way. God, of course, does not ponder; God *knows* in a
simple act. Aquinas makes the distinctions with typical
precision:

> Actuum enim intellectum pertinentium quidam habent
> firmam assensionem absque tali cogitatione, sicut cum
> aliquis considerat ea quae scit vel intelligit; talis enim
> consideratio jam est formata. Quidam vero actus
> intellectus habent quidem cogitationem informem
> absque firma assensione sive in neutram
> partem declinent, sicut accidit dubitanti; sive in unam
> partem magis declinent sed tenentur aliquo levi signo,
> sicut accidit picanti; sive uni parti adhaereant, tamen
> cum formidine alterius, quod accidit opinanti. Sed
> actus iste qui est credere habet firmam adhaesionem
> ad unam partem , in quo convenit credens cum sciente
> et intelligente; et tamen ejus cognitio non est perfecta
> per manifestam visionem, in quo convenit cum
> dubitante, suspicante et opinante. Et sic proprium est
> credentis ut cum assensu cogitet; et propter hoc
> distinguitur iste actus qui est credere ab omnibus
> actibus intellectus qui sunt circa verum vel falsum.
> (2a2ae 2,1)[40]

Aquinas quite boldly (and typically) takes both sides of the
argument. He agrees that faith is like certain knowledge in one
way, and that faith is like doubt and opinion in another way.

Insofar as faith firmly (and rightly) adheres to one position, it is like science; insofar as it does not achieve the clear vision of, say, geometric proofs, it is like opinion. It is *sui generis*.

As an intellectual act, faith is looking very mysterious at this point. It seems to have no more *data*, as it were, than opinion, and yet it possesses strict adhesion to one alternative. How can this be? The key to the issue of the act of faith for Aquinas is that, oddly enough, *it is an intellectual act which is motivated, not by the intellect, but by the will.* In Thomas' faculty psychology, the human person is composed of these two elements: intellect and will; desiring and knowing are two distinct functions of the human soul. But in this case it is the will which takes the initiative, as it were, influencing the intellect to make an act which, on strictly intellectual grounds, it need not make.

That there are problems in this conception from a strictly logical point of view, is obvious. How can the will be moved toward the good (its proper object) unless it knows the good as *true* (the proper object of intellect)? There *must* be, in a conception which divides knowing and desiring into compartments, some interpenetration between them to explain the phenomenon of faith. T.C. O'Brien's gloss on this point is helpful:

> The genesis of faith (*initium fidei*), however, offers...a problem, in the Thomistic presupposition that "nothing is willed except it be first known"; seemingly believing presupposes willing, yet willing presupposes knowing (believing)...The problem can be solved in detail only by a careful study of 1a2ae III, 2, on "operating grace" (a text that is often neglected or misunderstood by those who consider the genesis of belief). There is a *cogitatio*, an intellectual awareness of the truths of the faith and of the possibility of assenting, a kind of call to faith that is prior to any response of will. That a person apprehend this call as a good, and so appealing to will, cannot be explained either by the will as natural orientation to the human good or by some

previous, specific intention of will to pursue the human good. The anterior *cogitatio* becomes a proposal of good, with the quality of appeal to the person, only because of grace moving; and because of grace that proposal excercises attraction (becomes *exercitans*) on the will...(O'Brien concludes) All is under grace and does not issue from the natural resources of mind and will.[41]

What is absolutely clear, then, is that *faith is an action of both intellect and will which is explainable by neither faculty working alone nor by both of them working together, but by God's grace*, that unexplainable free gift.

This may seem unsatisfying. When we push the discussion as far as it will go, we are left with the fact that we do not have an explanation for this thing called faith; all we have is a word ("grace") which points to the fact that faith is always already there, that by the time we are in a position to reflect on what faith is, its origin is obscure. It is simply *there*, as a ground of our Christian way of life. Nevertheless, Thomas insists that faith is *meritorious*, and so is to some extent a product of our own free will; it is a virtuous act, in other words, albeit a supernaturally virtuous one. But here one must distinguish. For, while *all* faith is a gift of God for Thomas, not all faith is meritorious. How this is possible is made clear in Thomas' discussion of the faith of devils. It is customary to belittle the medievals' discussion of such matters as angelic intellect or the faith of devils, but, apart from the question of whether such beings exist (a matter by no means settled), angels and devils served the medieval philosophers as what we might call thought experiments and thus enabled them to explore the workings of human psychology by isolating elements within it in a purer state. Be that as it may, how do the devils clarify our own faith?

By discussing the faith of devils, Thomas can point out that there are two kinds of faith, "formed faith" and "unformed faith"; the former is both caused by grace and cooperated with by the human will; the latter, while remaining in a sense a gift of God, is not a result of the cooperation of grace and free will, but as it were of the natural light of intellect and natural movement of will. The word "formed" here reminds us that for Aquinas *love is the form of all the virtues, including faith*. Thus a faith which does not come from that movement toward the good which we call love is at best a deformed faith, a privation of what faith really should be. As he says,

> Quod autem voluntas moveat intellectum ad assen-tiendum potest contingere ex duobus. Uno modo, ex ordine voluntatis ad bonum, et sic credere est actus laudabilis. Alio modo, quia intellectus convincitur ad hoc quod judicet esse credendum his quae dicuntur, licet non convincatur per evidentiam rei. Sicut si aliquis propheta praenuntiaret in sermone Domini aliquid futurum, et adhiberet signum mortuum suscitando, ex hoc signo convinceretur intellectus videntis ut cognosceret manifeste hoc dici a Deo, qui non mentitur; licet illud futurum quod praedicitur in se evidens non esset, unde per hoc ratio fidei non tolleretur. (2a2ae. 5,2)[42]

Thus one can be moved to believe by force, as it were. If someone raises a man from the dead, and then predicts an earthquake, one had better believe that there will be an earthquake! Yet one can so believe without having the virtue of faith, and thus without merit. This is the faith which St. James referred to as dead. *Living faith* , on the other hand, the faith which saves, *is motivated by love*. It believes because it is drawn toward the good.

All of which is to say that to speak of living faith apart from the other two supernatural virtues, hope and charity, is to indulge in an abstraction, though no doubt a necessary one. But *in concreto* we are faced with a reality known as faith-hope-charity which forms the foundation of the Christian life, or, rather, which *is* the Christian life. Of course, if our previous investigations have any validity at all, the Christian discovery of faith reveals for us not so much a special, *sui generis* way of being and knowing, as Thomas suggests, but the paradigm for *all* being and

204

knowing. Struggling with the paradoxical and at times maddening reality of their own Christian faith and the difficulty of fitting it into Greek thought forms, Christian philosophers, willingly or not, knowingly or not, were actually exploring the deepest questions of all human knowing under the rubric of the special case known as faith.

In the example quoted above, for example, of "dead" faith, (*fides non formata*), the fondness of Aquinas (and the Fathers, as we have seen in Augustine) for the category of prediction should not obscure the bedrock fact: faith is a human act of trusting in the word of someone because of the evidence of his trustworthiness. It is reliable precisely to the extent that the one in whom we trust is reliable. As in everything else, one can err in this regard in the direction of the two extremes; one can refuse to believe anything at all unless it is proven, and this is the vice of defect; or one can believe anything at all without proper investigation, and this is the vice of excess. But human faith is an inevitable part of human life.

Such human faith is meritorious and virtuous, only insofar as its *motivation* is meritorious. If one believes on account of love (justified love, of course) for the one who speaks, then faith is virtuous. If one believes on account of love for the God who reveals his truth, then the action is *supernaturally* meritorious and virtuous, and, strictly speaking, is not to be attributed to the human being's unaided intellect or will but to grace.

An illuminating connection between human and divine faith occurs in Thomas' discussion of the question of whether it is possible to please God without faith. Aquinas wants to say that no one can attain to the knowledge of God unless God gives him that knowledge, and, of course, we are required to believe the knowledge which God gives through revelation. This is all not very surprising, but Aquinas goes on to use the metaphor of teacher and learner:

> Ad quam quidem visionem homo pertingere non potest
> nisi per modum addiscentis a Deo doctore, secundum
> illud Joann, "Omnis qui audit a Patre et didicit venit

ad me." Hujus autem disciplinae fit homo particeps non statim, sed successive secundum modum suae naturae. Omnis autem talis addiscens oportet quod credat ad hoc quod ad perfectam scientiam perveniat, sicut etiam Philosophus dicit quod opertet addiscentam credere. Unde ad hoc quod homo perveniat ad perfectam visionem beatitudinis praeexigitur quod credat Deo tanquam discipulus magistro docenti. (2a2ae, 2,3)[43]

Here Aquinas, following his own guide, Aristotle, tells us that, *even with regard to human knowledge, faith must come before vision.* One must trust the master before one can go on to know anything for oneself. This is a position which would be congenial to Michael Polanyi or Stephen Toulmin! But the metaphor of student and teacher brings up the fact that, as Thomas says quite clearly, we learn step-by-step, as befits our nature, and not all at once as might be appropriate to an angel (or devil). There must, then be a certain training of the intellect and will (always assuming grace) so that we can become, little by little, the kind of people who can more and more give ourselves trustingly to the one who deserves trust. We must go through a purification of the heart and mind, both caused by and a condition of faith. (Cf. 2a2ae. 7,2)

What we are pointing to here is that at the heart of faith is a kind of judgment, a kind of prudence by which we are enabled to grasp just who should be trusted (in whom we should place our faith), and that this aspect of the complete act of faith can only be developed in that school which we call the Christian community and by listening to that teacher we call the church. Trust, like everything else, is something you learn how to do, and you learn how to do it from the people around you.

For Thomas this was really so obvious that it didn't need to be spelled out in detail. It surfaces now and then, in matter of fact discussions of the question of whether heretics should be allowed to fall away from the church, or whether pagans should be compelled to the faith. Public witness to the faith is of immense importance, and public disaffection from the faith is extremely dangerous:

> Dicendum quod infidelium quidam sunt qui nunquam susceperunt fidem, sicut gentiles et Judaei; et tales nullo modo sunt ad fidem compellendi ut ipsi credant, quia credere voluntatis est. Sunt tamen compellendi a fidelibus, si adsit facultas, ut fidem non impediant vel blasphemis, vel malis persuasionibus, vel etiam apertis persecutionibus. Et propter hoc fideles Christi frequenter contra infideles bellum movent non quidem ut eos ad credendum cogant, quia si etiam eos vicissent et captivos haberent, in eorum libertate relinquerent an credere vellent; sed propter hoc ut eos compellant ne fidem Christi impediant. (2a2ae. 10,8)[44]

Thus the point is not to force into belief those who are outside the faith, but rather to guard and protect the faith of those within the church. This justifies stern measures, including physical complusion. This is not pleasing to contemporary ears. But it is the negative side of the positive need for good example. The only solution that seemed plausible for Aquinas was to remove the bad example. The point we wish to make is that, despite the strong emphasis in Aquinas on the inner illumination from God which supports the act of faith, he was by no means unaware of the fact that faith (especially, as he is fond to say, the faith of the simple and unlettered) is heavily dependent on the social-cultural surroundings. He needn't always say this explicitly for it to be obvious.

IV. Martin Luther: The Gratuity of Faith

Thomas Aquinas is, of course, a world unto himself, a world which we must now leave to touch upon the relevance of the Reformation for our present inquiry. Luther's prolific pen produced works which fill several long shelves and a Catholic may well be daunted by the attempt to say anything. Nevertheless, if anything is obvious, it is obvious that Martin Luther felt that he was saying something important on the subject of faith, something which was at once deeply Christian

207

and ignored by the church of his day. The man whose *sola fides* echoes down the corridors of the Christian tradition must be carefully listened to in a study such as this.

The problem of misunderstanding is still present on both sides of the division. Hendrikus Berkhof, for example, speaking for the Reformers at Catholic Maynooth Seminary in 1970 quoted John Calvin's definition of faith: "the firm and certain knowledge of God's goodness to us which is revealed to our minds and sealed on our hearts through the Holy Spirit."[45] Whereupon he, Berkhof, went on to say: "Insights and utterances like this had a revolutionary effect on the first decades of the sixteenth century. They meant a radical break with an age-long tradition."[46] Calvin's "radically new doctrine of faith" as Berkhof calls it, doesn't sound like something Aquinas would have had problems identifying as Christian, at least. The key divergence, however, is going to be in the relationship between faith and charity and on the difference between *fides formata* (living faith, for Aquinas, a faith moved by charity, the only faith which is justifying) and *fides informata* (the faith, as we saw, of the devils).

For the reformers, it is faith, and not charity, which will be the decisive act. Before I can love God, I must trust him. For Aquinas, before I can be moved to believe in God's words, I must find God trustworthy, attractive, in a word, good, in another word, lovable. Love comes before adherence to God's word. But let us look at what Luther himself actually says.

In his early essay, "The Freedom of a Christian", Luther had spoken eloquently about faith and had underlined his opposition to the notion that a person is saved by his own works, an obviously Pelagian point of view which Luther saw everywhere about him in the church of his time. For Luther, then,

> A Christian has all that he needs in faith and needs no works to justify him; and if he has no need of works, he has no need of the law; and if he has no need of the law, surely he is free from the law...This is that Christian liberty, our faith, which does not induce us

to live in idleness or wickedness but makes the law
and works unnecessary for any man's righteousness
and salvation. This is the first power of faith.[47]

Faith *is* freedom, then, for once one is able to trust in the
promises of God, one needs nothing more; one does not "have
to" perform works of charity to merit salvation. The only
work which God seems to demand of us is to rely on him and
not ourselves. This leads Luther naturally to a discussion of
what he calls the "second" power of faith.

> It is a further function of faith that it honors him whom
> it trusts with the most reverent and highest regard
> since it considers him truthful and trustworthy. There
> is no other honor equal to the estimate of truthfulness
> and righteousness with which we honor him whom
> we trust.[48]

And so, while faith is freedom from our point of view, faith is
also the highest worship which we can offer. We can, after
all, do nothing for God; all we can *do* is to humbly trust in his
mercy. This is not unrewarded:

> When, however, God sees that we consider him
> truthful and by the faith of our heart pay him the great
> honor which is due him, he does us that great honor
> of considering us truthful and righteous for the sake
> of faith. Faith works truth and righteousness by
> giving God what belongs to him. Therefore, God in
> turn glorifies our righteousness. It is true and just
> that *God is truthful and just, and to consider and
> confess him to be so is the same as being truthful and
> just.*[49] (Italics mine.)

This is a remarkable sentence, and it is probably as mysterious
to the average Protestant as to the average Catholic today. And
yet it conveys something at the very heart of Luther's teaching,
if we can only manage to put our finger on it. It is
understandable that if we trust in God's mercy God will come
to our aid. It is another thing to say that confessing God's
justice makes *us just,* but that is what Luther is saying here.

Luther's keen awareness of the essential sinfulness of the human condition makes him suspicious of any teaching which would proclaim that here and now human beings have been made just. There is an infinite variety of ways in which we can fool ourselves into thinking that we are good people, and there is no way to avoid a falling away from our trust in God and not in ourselves if we do start thinking of ourselves as good people. The only way, absolutely the only way, to avoid this trap is to give up the dream of ourselves being good and holy and just, and to realize that being just *means* nothing more or less than honoring God for *his* justice.

That this is possible comes about solely because of the cross and resurrection of Jesus Christ. Christ has taken upon himself the sin and perfidy of the human race, including every sin of my own. By uniting with Christ through the act of faith, I am enabled to share in the mercy of God, even though I have absolutely no claim on it. Thus there is a third aspect of faith which Luther wants to stress:

> The third incomparable benefit of faith is that it unites the soul with Christ as a bride is united with her bridegroom. By this mystery, as the Apostle teaches, Christ and the soul become one flesh. And if they are one flesh and there is between them a true marriage...it follows that everything they have they hold in common, the good as well as the evil.[50]

And so, there is a strange kind of exchange, in which all the good is on one side and all the evil on the other:

> Christ is full of grace, life, and salvation. The soul is full of sins, death, and damnation. Now let faith come between them and sins, death, and damnation will be Christ's, while grace, life and salvation will be the soul's; for if Christ is a bridgroom, he must take upon himself the things which are his bride's and bestow upon her the things which are his.[51]

Of course, our union with Christ on this earth does not make us righteous in a way which would enable us to glory in ourselves. Luther presents the soul as a bride who can say, "If I have sinned, yet my Christ, in whom I believe, has not sinned, and all his is mine and all mine is his."[51]

But just how is this union with Christ achieved? In a very interesting passage (from our point of view) Luther criticizes those who preach about Christ in such a way as to cause the congregation to feel sympathy for his sufferings, a traditional form of piety in the Germany of Luther's day, and one which continues today in what Catholics (at least) call devotion to the Passion, often connected with the cult of the Sacred Heart popularized by the Jesuits. For Luther, this is a mistake, and one can almost hear in this passage a hint of the Gadamerian critique of Schleiermachian Romanticism with which we are familiar:

> Now there are not a few who preach Christ and read about him that they may move men's affections to sympathy with Christ, to anger against the Jews, and such childish and effeminate nonsense. Rather ought Christ to be preached to the end that faith in him may be established that he may not only be Christ, but be Christ for you and me, and that what is said of him and is denoted in his name may be effectual in us. Such faith is produced and preserved in us by preaching why Christ came, what he brought and bestowed, what benefit it is to us to accept him. This is done when that Christian liberty which he bestows is rightly taught and we are told in what way we Christian are all kings and priests and therefore lords of all and may firmly believe that whatever we have done is pleasing and acceptable in the sight of God.[53]

In this passage Luther makes it clear that simple notional acceptance of the lordship of Christ is useless for salvation. (In this he would be joined, as we have seen, by Aquinas, who would call such faith "dead", the faith of the devils.) Nor should we be overly concerned with knowing the inner personality of Jesus of Nazareth, feeling his pain and understanding his sorrow. Gadamer has shown us how this can be a self-indulgent aestheticism, and experience confirms that often enough people who are drawn to emotional devotions can avoid the harsher claims of religious commitment quite easily.

What *is* important, Luther says, is the "Christ for you and me." We do not simply contemplate Christ, we find ourselves involved in a reality of ultimate importance for us, a reality provoking a decision. (Aquinas would use different language, but would also insist that "living" faith is moved by the vision of the good--good "for us" understood--toward an adherence to the truth.)

The decision which we are called to make is very much a decision to ratify the reality of what we always-already are. As is clear in this passage, the job of the Christian preacher is to reveal to people who they are, who they have always been, to interpret the meaning of their lives to them. Luther, somewhat differently from Aquinas, wants to put the arousal of love *after* the act of faith, while for Aquinas, charity motivates true, living faith. But, as we have seen, Luther does mention the "benefits" as a motive for faith, and benefits are objects of one's desire and love. Perhaps the important difference here between Thomas and Luther is that Luther emphasizes much more than Aquinas the issue of *fear* and the corresponding fear-assuaging quality of faith. The problematic is different. Indeed, for Aquinas, fear is a *gift* of faith (how can one fear to lose that which one never heard of? to be afraid of hell is a good thing),[54] as long as it is not excessive, in which case it is a sin against hope.

It is quite clear, then, that Luther is stressing an authentic aspect of biblical teaching, recovering the trust-character of the act of faith, the mutually exclusive character of fear and faith which we saw so sharply etched in the gospel of Mark. "Recovering" here does not mean, however, "rediscovering", but, as Gadamer had shown us, *emphasis is a means of interpretation*, and to stress as Luther did the fiducial character of faith is indeed to say something new, but that new thing which Luther said about faith was always there, albeit obscured in the tradition (and not simply the scriptural tradition), waiting to be lifted up at the right moment.

What *we* want to stress as well about the passage quoted from Luther is that the Word of God by no means comes crashing down from heaven upon a wondering populace who come to examine the crater it formed and stay to become Christians. Rather, the Word seems to make clear, out of the resources of the community's tradition, just what the purpose, the reality, the goal of the community's existence really is. The Word, we might say, relying on this passage, tells the *story* which the people recognize as their own, and to accept that story is to be faithful. Thus, even for Luther, what we might call the intellectual element of faith is not missing. Though faith is trust, it is also belief that certain things are so (i.e., both belief *in* and belief *that* makes up faith). Perhaps the problem is not the cognitive character of faith, but just what one means by the terms "cognitive" and "intellectual". Aquinas' distinction between "living faith" and its opposite, Luther's insistence on knowing Christ's benefits and not Christ as historical personage, Heidegger's distinction between *zuhandenheit* and *vorhandenheit*--all these distinctions underscore the same truth: that knowledge is contextual, that knowledge's context includes situation, purpose and community.

Faith, then, is what justifies, for by faith one unites oneself to Christ, and such a union *is* justification, for Christ is justice. But what of the objection that such a conception of faith leads to idleness? Having been justified through faith, what need have we of works? Having been justified by faith, why do anything at all? Luther rejects such a criticism. (Actually, this is a criticism of the entire Christian notion of salvation as grace, of God as gracious giver.) But it is not all that easy to reply to it:

Since by faith the soul is cleansed and made to love God, it desires that all things and especially its own body, shall be purified so that all things may join with it in loving and praising God. Hence a man cannot be idle, for the need of his body drives him and he is compelled to do many good works to reduce it to subjection. Nevertheless the works themselves do not justify him before God, but he does the works out of spontaneous love in obedience to God and considers nothing except the approval of God, whom he would most scrupulously obey in all things.[55]

Luther illustrates that the good man does good works but good works do not make a man good by pointing to homely examples:

Illustrations of the same truth can be seen in all trades. A good or a bad house does not make a good or a bad builder; but a good or a bad builder makes a good or a bad house. And in general, the work never makes the workman like itself, but the workman makes the work like himself. So it is with the work of man. As the man is, whether believer or unbeliever, so also is his work--good if it was done in faith, wicked if it was done in unbelief.[56]

Perhaps the relationship between being and doing is more complex than this. How does a workman become a good workman if not by doing work, at first poorly, then a little better? Luther's strong emphasis on faith can lead him into difficulty. To get over the very evident problem of Pelagianism and pride in human doing, he places the emphasis, quite rightly, on God's gift of faith. But that gift seems to remain external to the individual, with the result that good works must be done, as it were, with the eyes closed, "spontaneously", without human advertance. For the Lutheran tradition, the *fides formata* of the scholastics is dangerous because it seems to place good works before faith and thus leave the door open to self-congratulation. As we have seen, this is a caricature of Thomas' teaching, but it is perhaps a keen critique of the kind of thinking present in later scholasticism. At any rate, the point is not to defend either Thomas or Luther, but to point out the insights in their teachings which can help us as we struggle to construct our own retrieval of the tradition.

And for us there *is* a way out of this dilemma, and it is to move the focus *away* from the individual human will *to* the movement of the Spirit within the community. This doesn't completely solve the problem of course, but it does at least locate it in the right place and avoid an overemphasis on individual psychology.

To sum up: we resist the notion that Luther reinvented or rediscovered Christian faith, and there are problems with his teaching. But, as we have said, emphasis is a form of interpretation, and Luther's emphases provide the Christian community with a definite "language gain" (if not an entirely new language). Where is this language gain located? For us, Luther's emphasis on the relationship between fear and faith brings something into the discussion which is genuinely dominical, and by no means totally absent from the tradition, but which had not been used, as it were. The Northern European temper of the Middle Ages, and perhaps to this day, is more likely to experience life as anxiety, more likely to focus on the *fearful* character of our human fragility than are other temperaments. One looks in vain in Paul, Augustine, Anselm, Aquinas for this strain; it is absent in classical literature in general. The monks knew *acedia* and Horace knew world-weariness; Aeneas knew about the *lachrimae rerum* and Aeschylus knew about the wisdom which comes only from suffering. But the terror of existence, and the way in which it paralyzed human life--these, if not completely new as themes, nevertheless found new emphasis in Germany and in the young Augustinian monk. A culture which had known the Black Death and the *danse macabre* has touched realities which go deeper, perhaps, than could be expressed by an Italian like Aquinas.

But Luther's retrieval of the connection between fear/faith was by no means an imposition on the Christian symbol system, an alien intrusion which did not fit. Rather, Luther's anguished struggle with anxiety made him open to something which others were unable to see. Avoiding cheap psycho-analysis of Luther, we can nevertheless state as fact that Luther's life was dominated by anxiety even before his entry into the monastery, of the strictest order he could find. The famous story of his decision to enter the monastery, and what had precipitated it--the promise extracted in a thunderstorm--make that abundantly clear. Luther's experience in the tower, the experience which changed his life, was sharp and decisive, but it was by no means a sudden bolt from the blue without preparation or context. His anxiety led him to search for certainty of salvation in strict observance of the Augustinian rule.

Notice that Luther's problem was not terror at the meaningless void, but at the exceedingly concrete hell of medieval piety. Those who have spent time in Roman Catholic novitiates know that in every group there is someone obsessed with detailed fidelity to the letter of the rule, an obsession which is made worse by the general *ethos* of such communities. In Luther's case, the relatively easy route of rote obedience was closed, for whatever reasons. His powerful mind broke through finally to the answer that had been there all along: the just man lives by faith, not works. Paul's struggle with the idolatry of legalism exploded into meaning for Luther in his own struggle with fear. The burden of trying to do the right thing, the burden, really, of saving oneself, is now lifted.

> I frankly confess that, for myself, even if it could be, I should not want 'free-will' to be given me, nor anything to be left in my own hands to enable me to endeavor after salvation; not merely because in the face of so many dangers, and adversities, and assaults of devils, I could not stand my ground and hold fast my 'free-will' (for one devil is stronger than all men, and on these terms no man could be saved); but because, even were there no dangers, adversities, or devils, I should still be forced to labour with no guarantee of success, and to beat my fists at the air. If I lived and worked to all eternity, my conscience would never reach comfortable certainty as to how much it must do to satisfy God. Whatever work I had done, there would still be a nagging doubt as to whether it pleased God, or whether he required something more.

The experience of all who seek righteousness by works proves that; and I learned it well enough myself over a period of years, to my own great hurt. But now that God has taken my salvation out of the control of my own will, and put it under the control of His, and promised to save me, not according to my working or running, but according to His own grace and mercy, I have the comfortable certainty that He is faithful and will not lie to me, and that He is great and powerful, so that no devils or opposition can break Him or pluck Him from me.[57]

This may appear to be sheer irresponsibility: making my own decisions is too much to deal with, so I give myself over to someone stronger. This language certainly *could* be irresponsible, and many Catholics have found it such, but it is both more charitable and more accurate to see this passage as the acceptance of human finitude in serenity. We need not do what we cannot do, and what we cannot do is to be other than human, fallible, subject to death and imperfection and disease. With this acceptance, the controlling personality is freed, as Gadamer might say, to play the game, to give oneself over to the flow of events confident that one will not be overwhelmed. The heavy burden of ego may be laid down.

Thus we are turning Luther's individualistic language into an argument for a communal interpretation of faith, and we feel justified in doing this seemingly paradoxical (even perverse) sleight of hand trick because in Luther we see the individual brought into full relief only to be revealed as the helpless thing it really is. The obsessive concern for one's own safety (as expressed in the fear of hell) gives way to a confidence which frees the individual for those spontaneous good works Luther mentions, frees the individual to take part in the life of the community without overcontrol, without excessive concern for planning either the details or the grand design. Both are in the hands of a power greater than that of the individual.

Through the movement which Luther aroused, the Catholic Church found itself under attack, at times justly, at times not. Leo X condemned several "errors" of Luther as early as 1520, but it was the great Council of Trent which went about formulating not only a reply to Luther (and the other Reformers) but summarizing the teaching of the Catholic Church on the general topics which had been controverted. In its sixth session, in 1547, the Council treated the central question of justification, attempting to defend itself against charges of Pelagianism while at the same time attacking what it saw as Luther's overdenigration of human nature and (as a consequence) free will. The teaching of the Council, then, finds both common ground and disagreement with the Reformers. The point of agreement is clear: that God is the absolute cause of justification. The point of disagreement centers around the role of human volition in the accomplishment of justification. Several of the key issues are expressed in Chapter VII of the Decree on Justification; in this chapter the Council fathers discuss the *causes* of justification, and in quasi- Aristotelian fashion they find instrumental, formal, final and efficient causes, while discovering a new one: the meritorious cause:

> The causes of this justification are: the *final cause* is the glory of God and of Christ and life everlasting; the *efficient cause* is the merciful God who washes and sanctifies gratuitously, signing and anointing 'with the Holy Spirit of promise who is the pledge of our inheritance' (Eph. 1:13f); the *meritorious cause* is his most beloved only-begotten, our Lord Jesus Christ, who, 'when we were enemies', for 'the exceeding charity wherewith he loved us' (Eph. 2:4) merited for us justification by his most holy passion on the wood of the Cross and made satisfaction for us to God, the Father; the *instrumental cause* is the sacrament of Baptism, which is the sacrament of faith, without which no man was ever justified; finally the single *formal cause* is the justice of God, not only that by which he himself is just but that by which he makes us just, that, namely, whereby being endowed with it by him, we are renewed in the spirit of our mind, and not only are we reputed but are truly called and are just, receiving justice within us, each one according to his own measure, which the Holy Spirit distributes to

everyone as he wills (1 Cor. 12:11), and according to each one's disposition and cooperation. For though no one can be just except him to whom the merits of the Passion of our Lord Jesus Christ are communicated, yet this takes place in that justification of the sinner when by the merit of the most holy Passion, 'the charity of God is poured forth by the Holy Ghost in the hearts' (Rom. 5:5) of those who are justified and inheres in them. Whence man, through Jesus Christ in whom he is grafted, receives in that justification, together with the remission of sins, all these infused at the same time, namely faith, hope and charity. For faith, unless hope and charity be added to it, neither unites a man perfectly with Christ nor makes him a living member of his body. (D1528-1530)[58]

The contrast with Luther will be apparent. The fathers reject the total loss of human free will without imputing the cause of justification to human beings. Human free will *cooperates* with grace; it is not simply given up. Human beings are not simply *called* just because of an almost extrinsic relationship to the just one (Jesus), but are *truly* just, receiving within them the gifts of faith, hope and charity at the same time. For without the latter two, faith by itself is dead and useless, albeit still a kind of faith. Echoing the teaching of Aquinas on the faith of devils, the fathers insist that one is still able to be called a Christian as long as one has the gift of faith, but is living in mortal sin, cut off from God: "It must be maintained that the grace of justification once received is lost not only by infidelity (unbelief) whereby also faith itself is lost, but also by every other mortal sin, though in this case faith is not lost." (D733)[59]

Thus the disagreement is not simply terminological, though it is partly that. Luther would not deny that it is possible to believe *that* as well as to believe *in*; he is actually accusing the church of his time of doing the former without doing the latter. So it might be possible to call what Aquinas terms "dead faith" by some other term acceptable to both sides, reserving the actual word faith for what Aquinas called *fides formata*, faith informed by love. But immediately we see the difference is not simply terminological. For Aquinas simply could not see that faith *in* is possible without a movement toward the good, i.e., hope and love. The confident giving-over-of-oneself to the promise of God occurs because one has sighted the *benefit* of those promises. I believe because I see that it is better to believe than not; in Aquinas' psychology, confidence that one will not be harmed, trust, is a logical correlate to hope in obtaining the good. For what we trust is precisely that we may obtain the good (be preserved from evil). To be preserved from evil is a kind of good in itself. And as soon as we talk about the good, we are in the realm of love, and, consequently, of will.

But talk of the will seems to deny, for Luther, the joyous fact that we are not saddled with the burden of saving ourselves. The act of faith is precisely giving up that burden of will, and not even by an act of permissive will, which we allow God to take over, for will is will, and as soon as there is will there is self justification.

That the language shared by both Luther and his opponents is itself inadequate is admitted by Luther himself:

> I could wish, indeed, that a better was available for our discussion than the accepted one, *necessity*, which cannot be accurately used of either man's will or God's. Its meaning is too harsh, and foreign to the subject; for it suggests some sort of complusion, and something that is against one's will, which is no part of the view under debate.[60]

This opens up the possibility that the debate could become more fruitful if cast into more adequate language. As we have seen, there are real differences between Trent and Luther, and not simply terminological ones. And yet, as we have shown previously, language is not simply terminology. If in this discussion we begin to search for the language of mutual respect, a language which searches for the truth in the other's words rather than for a way to put down the other, we may discover that our differences are complementary rather than contradictory. What sounds like language which shamefully degrades the human person may simply be an inadequate expression of a more primary religious language of total trust in God. What sounds like Pelagianism may turn out to be an inadequate expression of a more primary religious language about the need for human effort.

At any rate, one thing is undeniable: the conversation broke down, and people began to fight (literally) over objectified bits of language, language which had ceased to play a role in authentic conversation. The religious communities of Europe then paid the price. After a hundred years of war over inauthentic words, a large number of human beings came to the conclusion that the language spoken in the relgious communities of Christianity was bankrupt. The Enlightenment rejection of supernatural revelation, tradition, and faith set the stage for the contemporary debates.

V. Immanuel Kant: Faith Without Revelation

One thing became obvious to those who watched, sometimes with horror, sometimes with amusement, sometimes with pity, as Christians cut each other to shreds in the name of Christ: these people were fighting over something they could not prove, even to themselves. "Dogmatic faith", as Kant put it, "which proclaims itself as a form of *knowledge*, appears...dishonest or presumptuous"[61] to reason. Kant's Religion Within the Limits of Reason Alone states its theme in its title, and by so doing also states the attitude of the Enlightenment toward religion. Kant is interested in religious language only insofar as it makes moral behavior easier. His deconstruction (as it were) of the word *grace* is a good example of his general attitude:

The concept of a supernatural accession to our moral, though deficient capacity and even to our not wholly purified and certainly weak disposition to perform our entire duty, is a transcendent concept, and is a bare idea, of whose reality no experience can assure us. Even when accepted as an idea in nothing but a

practical context it is very hazardous, and hard to
reconcile with reason, since that which is to be
accredited to us as morally good conduct must take
place not through foreign influence but solely through
the best possible use of our own powers...Hence,
apart from the general assumption that grace will
effect in us what nature cannot, provided only we have
made the maximum use of our own powers, we will
not be able to make any further use of this idea.[62]

One can imagine what Luther would think of such ideas coming
from the mouth of a German Protestant. But the dirty little
secret was out. The entire edifice of Christianity was based on
a shaky, historical foundation. Separated from the cultural
supports which had sustained it, and which had, indeed, made
it impossible to question, Christianity was now revealed as
being based on assumptions which were not only difficult to
support, but, more that that, were not even necessary, and
more than *that*, were sometimes harmful to moral behavior.

But there is good news. And the good news is that the
essence of the Christian faith is quite rational, being a
collection of moral precepts which could be derived from
reason itself, but which, in the lively form in which they are
found in the scriptures and in preaching, are conducive to
true religion, i.e., the establishment of the moral
commonwealth, the kingdom of God (here on earth, of
course). To conceive of religion as having something to
do with our relatonship to God apart from service to our
fellows is sheer superstition:

Every initiatory step in the realm of religion, which we
do not take in a purely moral manner but rather have
recourse to as *in itself* a means of making us well-
pleasing to God and thus, through him, of satisfying
our wishes, is a *fetish-faith*.[63]

Kant takes four traditional pillars of religion (prayer,
church-going, the sacraments of baptism and communion) and
shows that, rightly understood, they are rational, i.e., moral.
Thus prayer, if understood *not* as converse with a supernatural

deity, but as a way of inciting moral sentiments in the heart, is
rightly done; church-going, baptism and communion can be
interpreted along the same lines, with the added advantage of
mutual support in the ongoing attempt to lead a moral life.[64]

Where this leaves the traditional notion of faith should be
clear by now. If faith is the assent to certain propositions on
the basis of trust in the truthfulness of God who speaks these
propositions through the mouth of certain messengers, then
such faith is useful only to those who need to be coerced into
doing good by external means:

> We have noted that a church dispenses with the most
> important mark of truth, namely, a rightful claim to
> universality, when it bases itself upon a
> revealed faith. For such a faith, being historically
> (even though it be far more widely disseminated and
> more completely secured for remotest posterity
> through the agency of scripture) can never be
> universally communicated so as to produce conviction.
> Yet, because of the natural need and desire of all men
> for something *sensibly tenable*, and for a confirmation
> of some sort from experience of the highest concepts
> and grounds of reason (a need which must be taken
> into account when the universal *dissemination* of a
> faith is contemplated), some historical ecclesiastical
> faith or other, usually to be found at hand, must
> be utilized.[65]

Most people, whether through moral weakness or lack of
education or some other lack, need the sound and light show
which is ecclesiastical religion, and it will be denied them only
at the risk of deadening their moral sensitivities altogether.
Naturally, however, our task is to raise the general level of
the ecclesiastical faith, bringing it more and more into
conformity with the principles of reason and of rational
morality:

> When, therefore, (in conformity with the unavoidable
> limitations of human reason) an historical faith
> attached itself to pure religion, as its vehicle, but with

the consciousness that it is only a vehicle, and when this faith, having become ecclesiastical, embraces the principle of a continual approach to pure religious faith, in order finally to be able to dispense with the historical vehicle, a church thus characterized can at any time be called the *true* church.[66]

Note that "pure religious faith" for Kant is based wholly on reason, though he continues to use the term faith. Thus the doctrines of the Christian church which are based on certain saving events which must be believed are eventually to be transcended, as we move closer and closer to "pure" faith in a world come of age. Doctrines, for example, like the Atonement, if they ever had any utility, are certainly not helpful for rational people. Kant's analysis of the psychology of Atonement would be shocking indeed for traditional theologians, but possesses a cogency of its own nevertheless:

> It is quite impossible to see how a reasonable man, who knows himself to merit punishment, can in all seriousness believe that he needs only to credit the news of an atonement rendered for him, and to accept this atonement...in order to regard his guilt as annihilated...No thoughtful person can bring himself to believe this, even though self-love often does transform the bare wish for a good, for which man does nothing and can do nothing, into a hope, as though one's object were to come of itself, elicited by a mere longing. Such a persuasion can be regarded as possible only if the individual regards this belief as itself instilled in him by heaven and hence as something concerning which he needs render no further account to his reason.[67]

Again, Kant is ruthless in pushing over the very foundation stones of evangelical faith. And in so doing Kant pushes over also the foundation stones of any revealed religion. In a revealed religion, one finally accepts what God says *on the authority of God*. The logical dishonesty into which this leads us is now forever exposed by Kant and will have to be dealt with.

224

Flushed with the excitement of having knocked over its idols, the human race is at last on the road to enlightenment: "We have good reason to believe...that 'the kingdom of God is come unto us' once the principle of the gradual transition of ecclesiastical faith to the universal religion of reason...has become general."[68]

It is customary for Christian theologians to criticize Kant for his "uncritical individualism...lack of historical imagination, and...exaggerated reliance upon reason as the cure of human ills and the guide to all truth."[69] Nevertheless, as we assess Kant's contribution to the continuing discussion of faith, we must pay tribute to the fact that *he saw the obvious*. He saw the inauthenticity at the heart of traditional theological language. In other words, what Kant saw was that the classical use of God language made God into the god-of-the-machine, the deus-ex-machina of classical stagecraft, into an object within the world of objects. Like the later "masters of suspicion", he interpreted theological doctrines as covered up inauthenticity. He interpreted the doctrine of the Atonement, as we saw, as an attempt on the part of humans to avoid responsibility.

But his contribution was hardly all negative. While demolishing traditional language and practices, or rather, the traditional justifications for them, he replaced the traditional justifications with new ones. Thus, as we saw, if prayer to Father in the sky was clearly not suitable for a race come of age, nevertheless prayer could be reinterpreted as inciting in oneself the sentiments of duty and self-sacrifice which could make the world a better place. If coming together in public worship made no sense as the attempt to propitiate an angry God or ask him for favors, nevertheless, it could be retained for other reasons. If Kant's reconstruction of these practices did not match his deconstruction, nevertheless, his attempt to recover and reinterpret the tradition was not entirely misguided. It is true that his use of the practices was utilitarian in the narrowest possible sense, that Kant was not alive to the conscious and unconscious effect on us of symbols and ritual behavior, but for that matter, neither were the orthodox

Protestant theologians of his time. But Kant's attempt to understand the *meaning* of religious language and practice, his insistence that the meaning had in some way to be *practical*, is an attempt with which we are sympathetic, even if we think of practice in a broader sense than Kant might have.

But what, finally, of faith? It is interesting that, while destroying the traditional notion of faith, Kant continued to use the word for a religion based wholly on reason. Why bother with the word at all? Why not just talk about natural religion and avoid the use of the word faith? Towards the end of the <u>Religion</u> Kant discusses the notion of *mystery*:

> Investigation into the inner nature of all kinds of faith which concern religion invariably encounters a *mystery*, i.e., something *holy* which may indeed be *known* by each single individual but cannot be *made* known publicly, that is, shared universally...It is impossible to settle, *a priori* and objectively, whether there are such mysteries or not. We must therefore, search directly in the inner, the subjective, part of our moral predispositon to see whether any such thing is to be found among us...Freedom...is no mystery, because the knowledge of it can be *shared* with everyone; but the ground, inscrutable to us, of this attribute is a mystery because this ground is *not given* us as an object of knowledge. Yet it is this very freedom which, when applied to the final object of practical reason (the realization of the idea of the moral end), alone leads us inevitably to holy mysteries.[70]

In language which at times sounds (not so coincidentally) like Rahner or Tillich, Kant points to the ultimate incommunicability of the mystery of our own freedom, a freedom which leads the individual to what Kant calls "the abyss of a mystery regarding what God may do"[71] in relationship to the achievement of that good which we experience ourselves as free to work for or not, and yet bound to in duty. To such an incomprehensible mystery an attitude of reverence is appropriate, and the word faith is also appropriate, as expressing the reality that "it may well be expedient for us merely to know and understand that there is such a mystery, not to comprehend it."[72]

Thus Kant offers us here and there glimpses of profound reverence in the face of the mystery of God, and it might be possible to work out their logical consequences in an interesting way, a way which might lead us to see that Kant was by no means the narrow rationalist he sometimes appears to be. And yet, for our purposes, it remains true that the greatest mind of the 18th century offers us little or no explicit or useable reflection on Christian faith. In this he was, of course, representative of his age, an age when Christian theologians spent their time proving that Christian revelation was not mysterious at all. Edward Shils describes that age very well:

> Rationality and scientific knowledge on the one side and traditionality and ignorance on the other were set against each other as antitheses. The party of progress, which believed that mankind must move forward toward emancipation from arbitrary and oppressive authority and towards the conduct of human affairs by scientifically illuminated reason, abominated the condition of superstition and ignorance in which most human beings lived. It associated that condition with ecclesiastically imposed dogma. It was in the nature of dogmas that they were to be accepted without rational relfection and empirical observation. The substance of most dogmas was often of long duration; it was part of tradition. Dogmas and the coercion of belief were coupled with each other. Tradition acquired the bad name which had become attached to dogma.[73]

The ascendency of reason was by no means all of a piece among the nations of Europe. In England, for example, rationality and conservatism joined hands to perpetuate the perfect order of Newtonian physics and the traditions of monarchy and parliamentary government. Nevertheless, with that oversimplification which is the inevitable companion of broad historical judgments, we must say that the Enlightenment understood Christian faith poorly; that it understood Christian faith poorly because it understood knowledge narrowly; that the narrowness of its understanding of knowledge resulted from its suspicion of tradition, community, and history (a suspicion not without motive, as we have seen). It has been our constructive task elsewhere in this project to point to the possibility of an understanding of knowledge which makes the understanding of faith possible because it understands the role of tradition, community and history in every act of knowledge.

VI. Schleiermacher:
Faith as Experience of Dependence

The publication at the turn of the century of Wordsworth and Coleridge's Lyrical Ballads marked the beginning of the British phase of a reaction to Enlightenment overrationality which had already been stirring for some time in Germany. Friedrich Schleiermacher, with youthful exuberance, recast the terms of the discussion. Religion, he says in his Speeches, is not to be reduced to ethics (Kant), nor is it to be reduced to metaphysics either. It is not simply a way of looking at the world. Rather, it is something deeper than knowing and doing, something previous to their split. It is:

> ...the immediate consciousness of the universal existence of all finite things, in and through the Infinite, and of all temporal things in and through the Eternal. Religion is to seek this and find it in all that lives and moves, in all growth and change, in all doing and suffering. It is to have life and to know life in immediate feeling, only as such an existence in the Infinite and the Eternal. Where this is found religion is satisfied, where it hides itself there is for her unrest and anguish, extremity and death. Wherefore it is a life in the infinite nature of the Whole, in the One and in the All, God, having and possessing all things in God and God in all.[74]

For Schleiermacher, religion is an awareness (<u>Gefuhl</u>, feeling) rather than objective knowledge. By placing it before the rise of propositional statements Schleiermacher removes it from the danger of being associated with any one such statement. By placing it before the rise of acts of will, he removes it from the danger of being reduced to ethics. At one stroke Schleiermacher sets the terms for a large part of the modern debate on religion, a debate which could be placed under the general heading "religious experience." On the one hand, Schleiermacher gives religion (and, consequently, Christianity) an honored place. It is not a poor version of something else, destined to be outgrown someday. He makes it possible for people of different religious backgrounds to speak to one another without either contempt or surrender, for he makes it possible for them to see their own doctrines as relatively adequate expressions of a deeper ineffable experience. He helps us to see why the piety of a washerwoman may be just as profound as that of a philosopher without denigrating the honor due to propositional knowledge. His grasp of the way in which his <u>Gefuhl</u> seems to be transmitted from one to the other seems to give proper respect to the role of the community (and for that reason he has often been admired by some Catholic writers).

But there is another hand. One does not have to be a confirmed follower of Karl Barth to appreciate Barth's criticism: where is *faith*? Is there in Schleiermacher's conception an assent to truths on the basis of the authority of God revealing them? If the term "revelation" for Schleiermacher can refer to any religious experience of an individual[75] it seems that there is neither intellectual content (intellect) nor risk (will) involved in religious experience, where traditionally, faith did not escape from the problems involved in being both act of intellect *and* act of will.

It is true that, although Schleiermacher's magnificent <u>Glaubenslehre</u>, his systematic theology, is precisely "doctrine about *faith*", the actual discussion of faith takes little space in the book. Nevertheless, what he does say is instructive:

The term "faith in Christ" relates the state of redemption, as effect, to Christ as cause. That is how John describes it. And so from the beginning only those people have attached themselves to Christ in his new community whose religious self-consciousness had taken the form of a need of redemption, and who now became assured in themselves of Christ's redeeming power. So that the more strongly those two phases appeared in any individual, the more able was he, by representation of the fact (which includes description of Christ and His work) to elicit this inward experience in others. Those in whom this took place became believers, and the rest did not. This, moreover, is what has ever since constituted the essence of Christian preaching. Such preaching must always take the form of testimony; testimony as to one's own experience, which shall arouse in others the desire to have the same experience. But the impression which all later believers received in this way from the influence of Christ, i.e., from the common Spirit communicated by Him and from the whole communion of Christians, supported by the historical representation of His life and character, was just the same impression which His contemporaries received from Him directly. Hence those who remained unbelieving were not blamed because they had not let themselves be persuaded by reasons, but simply because of their lack of self-knowledge, which must always be the explanation when the Redeemer is truly and correctly presented and people show themselves unable to recognize him as such. But even Christ represented this lack of self-knowledge, i.e., of the consciousness of needing redemption, as the limit to his activity. And so the ground of unbelief is the same in all ages, as is also the ground of belief or faith.[76]

In the Glaubenslehre Schleiermacher had clarified some of the conceptions of the Speeches, which had gotten genuinely murky in parts of that volume. Now religion is defined as the "state of absolute dependence", with God defined as the *whence* of that state. (1,4) Sin is anything which hinders the development of this feeling of dependence on God, and in the state of sin, if we are aware at all of that feeling, we tend to be aware of it as irksome. The state of sin is pervasive and cannot be overcome by our own unaided efforts. Thus the need for the redemption offered in Christ and communicated through the body of believers known as the church. The church is the continuation on earth of the work and the person of Jesus Christ, the continuation of the perfection of his own God-consciousness, his awareness of total dependence on God and his joyous acceptance of that dependence.

Of course, we must not assume, simplistically, that one walks around in some obvious "state of needing redemption" and then finds that need fulfilled in Christ. Rather, the satisfaction of the need and the clear awareness of it may arrive simultaneously. Not until the need has been satisfied do we become conscious that we had the need in the first place. After the fact, of course, we can quite rightly interpret the experience as one of being lost and now being found. As Schleiermacher puts it:

> Faith is nothing other than the incipient experience of the satisfaction of that spiritual need by Christ: There can still be very diverse ways of experiencing the need and the succour, and yet they will all be faith. Moreover, the consciousness of need may be present for a long time in advance, or it may, as is often the case, be fully awakened only by the contrast which the perfection of Christ forms with our own condition, so that the two things come into existence simultaneously, the supreme consciousness of need and the beginning of its satisfaction.[77]

Faith is therefore by no means some kind of deduction from evidence, even deduction assisted by the grace of God:

> Our proposition says nothing of any intermediate link between faith and participation in the Christian communion, and is accordingly to be taken as directly combining the two, so that faith of itself carries with it

that perticipation; and not only as depending on the spontaneous activity of the man who has become a believer, but also as depending on the spontaneous activity of the communion (church), as the source from which the testimony proceeded for the awakening of faith. At the same time, in shutting up the whole process between these two points, the witness of testimony and its effect, our propsition is intended to make an end of everything which, in the form of demonstration, is usually brought to the aid of the proper witness or even substituted for it.[78]

As we have seen, the Fathers of the church tended to favor arguments based on miracles and prophecy, but Schleiermacher dismisses these facts as possible grounds of faith: "The efficacy of these things somehow always presupposes faith, and therefore cannot produce it."[79]

Thus, for Schleiermacher, unlike Kant, the essence of religion is the participation in a particular kind of community, a community which prolongs on earth a particular kind of God-awareness, a God-consciousness first experienced by Jesus of Nazareth and now available to us through the community which is called the Christian church. Faith is the experience one has of beginning to become a part of this community. Listening to the Christian preacher, the potential Christian realizes that the new life of which the preacher speaks is just what he has been longing for, and accepts it, not because of external evidence, but because of the feeling of joy which has possessed his heart.

This is in some ways a very traditional conception, and Schleiermacher's well known predilection for the gospel of John brings to our minds the fact that for Schleiermacher, as for John, the important thing is the new *life*, the new way of being in the community. What is new about Schleiermacher's understanding is that he has dispensed with objective language about God as the essence of faith. Faith is not the belief *that* certain promises of God will be kept in the future, nor is faith the belief *in* the trustworthiness of God grounding those promises. Faith is not about promises at all, not about propositions at all, and is therefore not an act of the intellect properly understood. It is the beginning of the new life, the moment when the new life of Christ--the God-consciousness which is his and which only his church can communicate-- begins to be appropriated.

Though faith is not intellectual, it is nevertheless certain, for there is nothing more certain than one's own experience, in this case the satisfaction of one's need for redemption. And it is voluntary, in that it can be refused--one is free to accept or reject it. Thus the traditional Protestant emphasis on faith as voluntary rather than intellectual is carried through by Schleiermacher.

Schleiermacher's view of faith will be attacked on very different, even contradictory, grounds. Catholics, for example, would be disappointed that the essential *knowledge* component of faith is practically eliminated. Does Schleiermacher not run the risk of dissolving faith into sheer subjectivism? Can statements about God's objective reality so easily be dispensed with? And from the neo-Orthodox school comes the criticism that Schleiermacher has lost the confrontative aspect of the Word of God. The preacher does not only offer new life, but he demands a revolution of heart and mind. If Christian faith is the modification of the religious self-consciousness in a particular fashion, then it is not the affront to the way of the world which the cross was for St. Paul.

That there is truth to this criticism can be seen most clearly by looking at Schleiermacher's <u>Christmas Eve,</u> in which he reflects on the mystery of the incarnation while reflecting on the education of the young girl Sophie. This little dialogue, with its Victorian trappings, tells us as much about the spirit of Schleiermacher, or more, as his more scholarly writings. And what we discover as we read through this family conversation is a strong sense of connectedness, community, and continuity.[80] If in his systematic theology Schleiermacher sees faith as the beginning of the satisfaction of one's own need for redemption upon the encounter with the community, in <u>Christmas Eve</u> we see the beloved community in the flesh. It is the joy which these friends share which leads them to reflect upon its source. Their conclusion is that it must be traced back to the introduction upon this earth of the possibility of a new kind of consciousness; traced back, in other words, to the birth of the savior, whose feast it is. There is a kind of transcendental proof for the existence of Jesus as savior given here: he is the only possible condition capable of explaining the present state of blessing of the community.

There is sorrow, and need for repentance in Schleiermacher's world. It seems that men (though perhaps not women) need to go through a period of asserting their independence before they return to the embrace of the community. But the emphasis, surely, is on the communal and familial experience of the new life made possible by Christ. The discussion of Sophie's religious education envisions a gradual growth and deepening of the God-consciousness in her, a consciousness of which the child already shows many precocious (it seems to us) signs. There need be no shock for Sophie, no moment when everything she has learned will be put into question. Rather, there will be for her a steady progress in the awareness of dependence on God a dependence which she will experience as joyous and not burdensome. Indeed, sin *is* the experience of our dependence as irksome, grace the experience of our dependence as joyous.

In many ways Schleiermacher's conception is indis-pensible. Just as in his pioneering hermeneutical studies, Schleiermacher had emphasized (though not invented) the circularity of hermeneutical understanding, that in order to understand the sentence's parts one had to understand the sentence as a whole, that one could not separate the understanding of part from whole but rather "always already" understood the sentence, parts and whole together, so in the understanding of faith, the experience of being in the community does not consciously follow one's decision to join it, but the two are "always already" together. The act of faith is not some clear, naked, presuppositionless moment of titanic will, but a process, and by the time we realize what has happened, we are unable to distinguish a before and after.

The problem with all this is that it tends toward a certain smugness, as can clearly be seen by a reading of <u>Christmas Eve.</u> Schleiermacher has, as it were, solved the problem of God as external object, as *deus ex machina,* by focusing attention on the community's experience of new life, but at the cost, perhaps, of a certain dynamic quality which seems indispensable to Christian living. The positive side of objective God langauge is that it allows something to happen *to* the community as well as within it, something which is not brute facticity but has the feel of agency about it. Schleiermacher's theology tends to downplay the Jewish roots of Christianity, and perhaps as a consequence, to downplay the Jewish notion of a God actively involved in securing justice for the oppressed, or sending down commands which have to be obeyed whether we understand them or not, simply because they are his commands. It is hard to imagine the middle-class comfort of the family in <u>Christmas Eve</u> being shattered by the cry for repentence. We repented, they might say, a long time ago, thank you.

VIII. The Constitution on Faith of Vatican I

It requires no great effort of imagination to see that the emphasis on the will has remained a Protestant emphasis, the emphasis on the intellect a Catholic one. And as we turn from the middle-European Protestant world of Luther, Kant, and Schleiermacher to the somewhat Meditearranean world of Catholicism we see that the concern for the intellectual nature of faith dominates the Catholic discussion (though by no means exclusively: Roman Cathlic Fideism was one response to 18th century over-rationality).[81] And the emphasis on faith as intellectual act thus is obvious in the last solemn pronouncement of the Roman Catholic magisterium on the nature of the act of faith, the <u>Constitution on Faith</u> of the First Vatican Council.

The Council has no difficulty in affirming that natural reason can show us the existence of God. (D3004) The paradoxical character of proposing as an article of faith the proposition that God can be known by natural reason alone never seemed to occur to the Fathers. Nevertheless, the sheer notional acceptance of the existence of God is all that is argued for here, and even at that, what is affirmed is the bare possibility that it can happen, not that it must happen or even that it has happened. Nor is this natural knowledge to be identified with faith. Faith is, just as the tradition has always asserted it to be, an act of supernature, not nature:

> Faith, which is the beginning of man's salvation, is a supernatural virtue whereby, inspired and assisted by the grace of God, we believe the things which he had revealed are true; not because of the intrinsic truth of the things, viewed by the natural light of reason, but because of the authority of God himself who reveals them, and who neither can be deceived nor deceive. (D3008)[82]

We believe, therefore, on the authority of God revealing, and not because of the intrinsic rationality of the truths of faith. Nevertheless, the traditional emphasis on the proofs of the faith is not neglected. Miracles and prophecies are mentioned as giving evidence for the assent of faith, thus preserving faith from being a blind assent without any evidence at all. (D3009) Nevertheless, these so-called proofs are by no means sufficient, even for what we have called "dead" faith, *fides non formata*, the faith of the devils:

> But though the assent of faith is by no means a blind action of the mind, still no man can 'assent to the Gospel teaching', as is necessary to obtain salvation, 'without the illumination and inspiration of the Holy Spirit, who gives to all men sweetness in assenting to and believing in truth' (Can. 7 of the II Council of Orange). Wherefore, faith itself, even when it does not work by charity is in itself a gift of God, and the act of faith is a work appertaining to salvation, by which man yields voluntary obedience to God himself by assenting to and cooperating with his grace, which he is able to resist. (D3010)[83]

Thus the 19th century council makes clearer than Trent did the ability of the human person to *resist* the grace of God, which distances the Catholic teaching from that of Luther, who, as we have seen, regarded God's grace as a sort of re-creation of the will. Further, the council insists that we do not simply believe in God; we also believe *that* certain definite things are so precisely because we believe *in* God who tells us about them. Faith, for this council, is very much a matter of belief in certain propositions. It is by no means a blind leap into an irrational abyss. For these propositions of faith are in no way *opposed* to intellect and reason, even if they *are* above them; they are not simply impenetrable mysteries, or opaque algebraic notations standing for something unknown. They have a content, a content which, despite its being in one sense beyond us, is nevertheless meaningful to us:

> Reason indeed, enlightened by faith, when it seeks earnestly, piously and calmly, attains by a gift from God some understanding, and that very fruitful, of mysteries; partly from the analogy of those things which it naturally knows, partly from the relations the mysteries bear to each other and to the last end of man; but reason never becomes capable of apprehending mysteries as it does those truths which constitute its proper object. (D3016)[84]

Here the council sets forth the conditions which make theology possible. Human reason (aided, of course, by grace) is able to achieve what the council calls an understanding which is "fruitful." "Fruitful" here can only mean "helpful toward salvation." And the fact that this fruitful understanding is achieved partly from analogy with ordinary human realities means, of course, that there is some taken for granted similarity between nature and supernature, between the world we know and the world revealed by God. Thus, far from there being any inherent *conflict* between the two worlds of faith and reason, there is an inherent *harmony* between the two realities.

The Council puts it quite clearly:

And not only can faith and reason never be opposed to one another, but they are of mutual aid to the other; for right reason demonstrates the foundations of faith and, enlightened by its light, cultivates the science of things divine; while faith frees and guards reason from errors, and furnishes it with manifoldknowledge. (D3019)[85]

Thus, once one knows a proposition by faith, one can combine it with propositions known from reason and advance both in theology and in philosophy. For example, if one is unable, because of whatever reason, to prove the existence of God by one's reason, one can nevertheless, once one learns from faith that there is such a being, go on to build a natural philosophy around him. For if something is true, it is true; faith and reason complement and never contradict each other. Similarly, if one knows from reason that things are composed of substance and accidents, then one can use that fact to throw light on what happens in the mystery of the Eucharist. Paradox is possible on this account only in the (inadequate) subjective awareness of the human being trying to fathom the supernatural mysteries; *per se* they are contradictory neither to themselves nor to reason.

And if we ask ouselves, as we must, the question of how we are to know about these propositions of faith, how we are to find out about the word of God, the answer comes back unambiguously from this council that it is only through the church, and only the Roman Catholic Church, that one finds the truth for which one seeks:

So that we may be able to satisfy the obligation of embracing the true faith and of consistently persevering in it, God has instituted the Church through his only begotten Son, and has bestowed on it manifest marks of that institution, so that it may be recognized by all men as the guardian and teacher of the revealed Word; for to the Catholic Church alone belongs all those many and admirable tokens which have been divinely established for the evident credibility of the Christian faith. Nay more, the

Church by itself, with its marvelous extension, its eminent holiness, and its inexhaustible fruitfulness in every good thing, with its Catholic unity and its invincible stability, is a great and perpetual motive of credibility and an irrefutable witness of its own divine mission. And thus, like a standard set up unto the nations (Is. 11:12), it both invites to itself those who do not yet believe, and assures its children that the faith which they profess rests on the most firm foundation. (D3012, 3013)[86]

Note how the church here begins to take on an importance which, at least in one sense, it did not have for Thomas Aquinas: it is a motive for belief by its very existence. The argument is not novel (we saw it in Augustine) but it is now pushed hard in the face of loss of belief in the claims of Catholicism to be the one true church, or, even more ominous, the general loss of belief in any supernatural revelation at all.

What this passage lacks (from a contemporary point of view, at any rate, looking back at the First Vatican Council from the vantage point of the Second) is any honest recognition that the church, far from always being a motive for belief, in its unity, holiness, universality and apostolic zeal, is often enough a disincentive to belief, because of its disunity, hypocrisy, narrowness, selfishness, and sheer laziness in the face of the tasks of modernity. Undeniably, then, the council is one-sided, lacking a sense of the dialectic between sinfulness and holiness which is the lot of the church on earth, lacking a sense that the very tension between good and evil in the life of the church might be, rightly understood, a kind of motivation for faith in itself, along the lines of Paul's claim that "when I am weak, then I am strong."

By speaking of the "credibility" of the church, i.e., the notion that certain visible qualities adhering to the church of Christ can move people to admiration and (ultimately) to faith, we find ourselves once again entering the difficult waters of the *preambula fidei*. Is the council saying that a fair- minded person, *without grace*, would be moved to faith by the sight of the glory of the Catholic Church? Not really. But if faith is a sheer gift of God (as the Council undoubtedly says it is), then why bother with such external marks of credibility? We have seen this problem before, of course, and can recall that St. Augustine wrestled with it. We tried to suggest before, and will point out again at this point, that the rubric "grace of God" is not simply objectified language but the description of an experience. The experience which it points to is that of finding oneself (suddenly or gradually) in the middle of a process which one had not (at least consciously) initiated. We find ourselves moved by trains of thought which never seemed quite as cogent to us before. Connections force themselves into our awareness. And yet, they *are* connections, they *are* trains of thought, i.e., rational in some sense. One wants to hold onto two apparently contradictory truths. On the one hand, all is grace, new creation. On the other hand, the new creation is just what was there all along. The same external facts which we have always known now suggest something new. Has someone caused us to look at things differently? Has God's grace suddenly taken hold of us? It seems that all these propositions are inadequate to describe the reality, which seems to be quite human and yet quite mysterious.

At any rate, it is undeniable that the First Vatican Council regards the church as central to the virtue of faith. The church, by its qualities, excites faith, by its practices nurtures faith, by its magisterium guards faith's purity, by its apostolicity guarantees faith's authenticity. Everything moves, then, towards the crowning pronouncement of the council, the statements on papal infallibility. No less a light than John Henry Newman insisted that "The word of the Church is the word of revelation. That the Church is the infallible oracle of truth is the fundamental dogma of the Catholic religion."[87]

It should be clear that we are both sympathetic toward and suspicious of this position. It speaks the truth--there is no place to go, really, outside of the community--but it speaks it with a kind of security which is impossible. But let us be clear (as clear as possible) about what the Council actually taught about infallibility, papal or otherwise. Every Catholic schoolchild used to be taught the "three conditions" for the exercise of papal infallibility, but conditioned or not, papal infallibility has always appeared, to Protestants and Catholics alike, as a kind of magical thing, separated from the rest of the experience of Christians. But the Council's language, though by no means free of the kind of triumphalism already noted, makes some important distinctions not often enough noted:

> We teach and define that it is a dogma divinely revealed: that the Roman Pontiff, when he speaks *ex cathedra*, that is, when in discharge of the office of Pastor and Doctor of all Christians, by virtue of his supreme apostolic authority he defines a doctrine regarding faith or morals to be held by the Universal Church, by the divine assistance promised him in Blessed Peter, is possessed of that infallibility with which the Divine Redeemer willed that his Church should be endowed for defining doctrine regarding faith or morals: and that therefore such definitions are irreformable of themselves, and not from the consent of the Church. (D3073, 3074)[88]

Note first that the purpose of the gift is eminently practical. The Pope through the gift of infallibility is serving as Pastor and Doctor. Thus there is no question of the enunciation of propositions for the purpose of curiosity or theological system building, but for "the salvation of Christian peoples," (D3073) as the council stated a sentence earlier. Thus, *ex cathedra* is not simply a description of the universal *intent* of a papal statement, but of its *purpose* as well.

Note next that the Pope is said to be endowed with "that infallibility with which the Divine Redeemer willed that his church should be endowed." It has not escaped notice that this sentence is remarkably ambiguous. It can be taken to mean that there are kinds of infallibility, and the kind of infallibility with which the pope is endowed is "that with which," etc. And what kind is that? Obviously, that is unclear. But what is clear is that the gift is given to the church, by Christ, not to the person of the Pope, and that the Pope thus functions in this regard as representative of the church, not above it, even though the "consent of the church" is not required for his definitions. Nevertheless, even this is ambiguous, for it is the church which the Council claims has the infallibility. Besides, is not the Pope, after all, *part* of the church? The word *ecclesia* seems to function in different senses in the same definition.

That there are other difficulties, including logical ones, with the definition, is well known. There is, for example, the difficulty that the doctrine of the Pope's infallibility is proclaimed by a Council and ratified by him. Does the infallibility of the Pope rest then on the infallibility of the Council? If not, why did the Pope need to ratify it? If the doctrine rests on the authority of the Pope it seems to be a strange case of a person declaring himself to be infallible, and that his statement of infallibility is therefore infallible too. These are interesting questions, but their pursuit would take us far afield. Suffice it to say that the problem of infallibility's grounds should be quite familiar to us, for we have seen it in various guises throughout our study. It is the problem of founding knowledge upon an unassailable rock. We have seen that the desire to do this is a temptation which, if given in to, will result in an ossification of the conversation, the triumph of technique over truth. Thus the dogma of the infallibility of the Pope, from our perspective, can quite easily be fitted under the category of inauthenticity: an attempt to control the uncontrollable.

But perhaps this is too harsh. Undoubtedly infallibility lends itself to this use, but it may be that there is something positive to retrieve from the teaching. What the doctrine is saying, perhaps, is that there is no better place to look for truth than here, in the community; what the doctrine is saying is that we must trust, finally in the community, and not in particular statements of doctrine or even particular people, but in the community as a whole. This may seem a perverse reading of a dogma which seems to place so much emphasis on both propositional truth and the authority of the bishop of Rome, but, finally, individual statements and individual Popes are instruments in the hands of the church, whose purpose in wielding these tools is the salvation of the race and the glory of God, not the enunciation of abstractions. Whether the dogma can be freed from triumphalism and narrowness and brought into the conversation of twentieth century Christians remains to be seen. It just may be that retrieval of this doctrine will prove impossible. But it may also just be that a way might be found for Christians in general to see that the dogmas might be a helpful alternative to a fundamentalism which grounds the faith in a *book* rather than a people's trust.

At this point we may end our reflections on tradition. The last official conciliar pronouncements of the Catholic church on faith have been examined; the "classical" Protestant theologian of the 19th century has been commented upon (albeit inadequately). We find ourselves already involved in the contemporary discussion when we consider Schleiermacher. But what have we, at last, learned from what may appear to be a digression of some length? Has an encounter with the tradition confirmed or made perilous our own tentative insights into the notion of faith?

First of all, *the tradition does not speak with one voice about faith.* That is obvious. Not only are there traditions in the use of the word, but the word is by no means univocal. It can mean many different things. On the other hand, though it can mean many different things, it can not mean *any* thing. The word is intelligible through its many contexts and uses; *it has a "family resemblance" throughout its several forms.* As soon as we speak of family resemblance rather than essence we commit ourselves, not to finding the Archimedean point from which all statements about faith in the tradition can be moved, but rather to making some general comments which, it is hoped, will illumine the resemblances between usages and point the way to a deeper and more fruitful understanding.

One thing which is very much common to all uses of the word is that *faith is a gift of God.* There seems to be no one who wants to deny this who is in the main stream of the tradition, either Protestant or Catholic. All agree, as well, that faith has something to do with the *will*, by which the gift of God is somehow appropriated. Thomas' use of the language of virtue underscores this fact for the Catholic tradition, while Luther's discussion of the will and its bondage points the way for the Protestant tradition. What happens to the will may be a point of debate, but that the will is in some sense involved in the process of faith, is agreed to.

There is strong, though not universal, warrant in the tradition for some other generalizations. Though faith has to do with an act of will by which we believe--assent to--God himself as saving faith, it is also an act by which we believe the things which God has said, and not simply *that* God speaks. Thus we can speak of believing *that* as well as believing *in*. When questioned as to how this act of faith comes about, the tradition tends to reply, as did Augustine, Anselm, Aquinas, and the First Vatican Council, that one is *attracted* by those who have already believed, the community of Christians: the church, in other words. That we are not the first to believe is truly central to most notions of faith in the Christian tradition; *faith is indeed "handed on"* and is not received from some special, personal encounter with God.[89] Thus believing *in* and believing *that* both seem to be mediated by the community.

Believing *that*, i.e., assent to particular statements on the word of God as revealer, as mediated through the church, is not to be regarded as what we have previously called "present-at-hand" knowledge. Even the most "intellectualist" interpreta|tions of the act of faith do not regard the individual propositions to which Christians adhere as being revealed for the sake of philosophical curiosity. Rather, *truths* are revealed by *the* truth (God) in the community (church) for a *practical purpose*: the salvation of the human race. Even theology itself, the rational reflection on the faith, retains its *practical* character for theologians from Aquinas to Barth, to Rahner (to skip to the modern period for a moment). The tradition is not always clear on the practical application of particular propositions, but that they are of practical and not simply theoretical value, is without question, even if some writers may from time to time show more interest in technical matters than in developing a "useful" understanding of the faith.

That faith is absolutely necessary and the beginning of everything else in the Christian life is universally held. Since faith is handed down through the ministrations of those who have gone before "in the sign of faith," the absolute necessity of the church is a logical corollary. Thus, it seems undeniable that "outside the church there is no salvation." This is rarely held to with a rigor which would positively exclude from salvation those who through no fault of their own find themselves outside the visible community of believers; ingenious solutions, accordingly, are found in the tradition to account for the apparent discrepancy.

The major fault-line which runs through the later tradition, is the one, of course, which divides Protestant from Catholic (the division between East and West was not over the question of faith), and the reason for the division is very much the question of faith, as we have seen. If faith is an act with an intellectual and communal component and a volitional and individual one, then the Catholic tradition has tended to emphasize the former, the Protestant tradition the latter, aspects of faith. Except for the "evangelical" group in this country, the ancient disagreement is being increasingly attenuated by the following (and other) considerations:

First, there is general admission that the received *language* is relatively inadequate to convey the complexities of religious experience. Thus we are somewhat humbler than we might have been in centuries past about our ability to describe the act of faith.

Second, the revival of biblical studies among Catholics has made it clear that the Protestant version of faith is supported by scripture.

Third, ecumenism has provided a non-argumentative framework for theologians of various traditions to work out their disagreements, and remarkable joint statements have come forth on subjects like Eucharist, ministry, authority, etc.

If these considerations have validity, then it may be hoped that the future will see a common exploration of the mystery of faith rather than continued narrow defensiveness over particular denominational vocabulary. This study, of course, is an attempt to be part of that exploration. But any such exploration, we have contended, will have to build upon the tradition rather than avoid it. What these last two chapters have shown is that there is a large measure of agreement within the tradition on this topic, though there are differences, sometimes significant ones. Is it possible that these differences may be overcome in the common exploration, or will we have to accept that we will forever disagree? The future cannot, of course, be predicted, but perhaps the following consideration might be helpful.

The two polarities around which the disagreements swirl are intellect/will and community/individual, with Catholicism emphasizing the former, Protestantism the latter. If we could develop a richer understanding of the interplay of these four elements we could, perhaps, remain faithful to the tradition while transcending some of its contradictions, which could now be seen as struggles over fidelity to parts of the truth. If we could show, for example, that individualism is a product of a particular world-view, and is thus relative to community, we would not have to *choose* between community and individual, but see these terms as mutually defining. Similarly, if we could show that *every* act of so-called intellect is part of a context and a purpose, we would be on our way to transcending sterile dichotomies between these two terms which, it turns out, are as mutually necessary as the terms "community" and "individual."

But this is precisely what we have been about, as should be quite obvious. A contemporary post-Heideggerian grasp of understanding enables us to lift up (almost in the Hegelian sense of *aufheben*) the elements of the tradition into a higher synthesis. But it works the other way, as well. That is, while a richer understanding of understanding enables us to see things about faith which might not have occurred to us before, it is just as true that it is precisely the millenia of discussion about faith which made possible a richer notion of knowledge. Christian theologians, forced to deal with the necessity of belief for theological knowledge, were actually working out issues which were not narrowly Christian (or even narrowly religious) but which were common to all human acts of knowing, just as, perhaps, reflection on the nature of Christ made possible reflection on the nature of human personality in general. Fortunately, there is no need to trace what Gadamer calls the "effective history" of Christian concepts like *faith* and *truth* and their relationship to the continuing philosophical discussion of concepts like *knowledge* and *understanding*. It would be an impossible task. But what was possible for us in this chapter was to show that the post-Heideggerian phenomenology of understanding which we have been developing, so far from being alien to the tradition of Christian faith, is in some ways an heir of it. Thus it is not a question of applying to Christianity philosophical terms derived from a source outside of it, but of using one part of the tradition to illuminate another part. If, for example, Gadamer's (and Heidegger's) rehabilitation of prejudice makes it clear that every act of knowledge depends on a previous set of background assumptions and questions, then we are enabled to see why the Christain tradition, quite rightly, insisted that the "grace of God" went before any conscious act of faith. One can, with difficulty, trace back the act of faith to a conscious act, can divide it up into its components, but its true origin is shrouded in mystery. The point is not to reduce the religious phrase "grace of God" to Heidegger's "pre-understanding" without remainder--that would be an arrogant reductionism. But what is undeniable is that the two terms, in their respective contexts, illuminate each other.

We will end our explicit reflection on the tradition at this point. So far we have, in this study, suggested that a renewed grasp of human knowing might illuminate what we mean by faith. We tried to show just what a renewed, non-objectivistic understanding of knowledge might look like. We showed the inadequacy of its opposite. And we looked at the Christian scriptures and traditions to see if the phenomenology of knowing which we had developed was at all congenial to the Christian reality. The task now is to pass toward a more constructive phase of this study.

Notes

1. Augustinus, <u>De Fide Rerum Quae Non Videntur: A Critical Text and| Translation with Introduction and Commentary by Mary Francis McDonald</u> (Washington, DC: Catholic University Press, 1950).

2. Augustinus, p. 81.

3. Augustinus, p. 83.

4. Augustinus, p. 83.

5. Augustinus, p. 83.

6. Augustinus, pp. 82-84.

7. Augustinus, p. 89.

8. Augustinus, p. 91.

9. Augustinus, p. 99.

10. Augustinus, p. 103.

11. Augustinus, p. 105.

12. Augustinus, p. 105.

13. Augustinus, pp. 109-111.

14. Augustinus, p. 112.

15. Etienne Gilson, <u>The Christian Philosophy of Saint Augustine</u> (London: Victor Gollancz, Ltd., 1961), p.31. (Contains a helpful bibliography on Augustine.)

16. Augustine, <u>Lectures or Tractates on the Gospel According to St. John</u>, Vol.I, Translated by John Gibb. (Edinburgh: T. and T.Clark, 1873), p.370.

17. Augustine, p. 370.

18. Gilson, p. 34.

19. Michael Polanyi, <u>Personal Knowledge</u> (Chicago: University of Chicago, p. 265-268.

20. Augustine, p. 368.

21.Josef Neuner and Heinrich Roos, <u>The Teaching of the Catholic Church as Contained in Her Documents</u>. Translated by Geoffrey Stevens. (Staten Island: Alba house, 1967), pp. 378-379. (Original numbers are given in the text.)

22. Neuner-Roos, p. 381.

23. But see Charles Hartshorne, <u>Anselm's Discovery</u> (LaSalle, IL: Open Court Press, 1965). For bibliography and background on Anselm, cf. Jasper Hopkins, <u>A Companion to the Study of St. Anselm</u> (Minneapolis: University of Minnesota Press, 1972).

24. Karl Barth, <u>Fides Quaerens Intellectum</u> (London: SCM Press Ltd., 1960).

25. Barth, p. 18.

26. Quoted in Barth, p. 18, footnote #2.

27. Barth, p. 23.

28. Barth, p. 24.

29. Barth, p. 24.

30. Anselm, <u>St. Anselm's Proslogion.</u> (Oxford: Clarendon Press, 1965), p. 128.

31. "I acknowledge, Lord and I give thanks that You have created Your image in me, so that I may remember You, think

of You, love You. But this image is so effaced and worn away
by vice, so darkened by the smoke of sin, that it cannot do
unless you renew and reform it. I do not try, Lord, to attain
Your lofty heights, because my understanding is in no way
equal to it. But I do desire to understand your truth a little, that
truth that my heart believes and loves. For I do not seek to
understand so that I may believe; but i believe so that i may
understand. For I believe this also, that 'unless I believe, I
shall not understand.'" (Is. vii, 9). 32. Barth, p. 76.

33. "So it was that one day when I was quite worn out with
resisting its importunacy, there came to me, in the very conflict
of my thoughts, what I had despaired of finding, so that I
eagerly grasped the notion which in my distraction I had been
rejecting." Anselm, pp. 102-103.

34. Barth, p. 76.

35. Anselm, pp. 102-103: "Judging, then, that what had given
me such joy to discover would pleasure if it were written
down, to anyone who might read it, I have written the
following short tract dealing with this question as well
as several others, from the point of view of one trying to raise
his mind and to contemplate God and seeking to understand
what he believes."

36. Barth, p. 77.

37. Hopkins, pp. 60-61.

38. Karl Rahner, Spirit in the World, Translated by William
Dych. (New York: Herder and Herder, 1968), p. xix.

39. Latin text and translations of longer passages are taken
from St. Thomas Aquinas, Summa Theologiae (New York:
McGraw Hill, 1972), the edition and translation of the
Dominican Fathers at Blackfriars. References to the Latin text
will use the notation, i.e., 2a2ae, 1,3 means "the second part of
the second part of the Summa, question one, article 3" etc.
English translations will be provided with a page number in the

Blackfriars translation. Translation which follows is of the Latin quoted in my text:

> To apply this: consider the object of faith from its two perspectives. First, from the perspective of the reality believed in, and then the object of faith is something non-composite, i.e., the very reality about which one has faith. Second, from the perspective of the one believing, and then the object of faith is something composite in the form of a proposition. This explains why earlier theologians were correct in maintaining either alternative; there is a sense in which each is true. (<u>Summa</u>, Vol. XXXI, p. 13.).

40. Among acts of the intellect, some include a firm assent without pondering--thus when someone things about what he knows scientifically or intuitively; thinking of that kind reaches a finished term. Other mental acts are marked by a pondering that is inconclusive, lacking firm assent, either because the act leans toward neither of the alternatives--the case with doubt; or because it leans to one alternative, but only tentatively--the case with suspicion; or because it decides for the one side but with fear of the opposite--the case with opinion. The act of believing, however, is firmly attached to one alternative and in this respect the believer is in the same state of mind as one who has science or understanding. Yet the believer is in the same state of mind as one who has science or understanding. Yet the believer's knowledge is not completed by clear vision, and in this respect is like one having a doubt, a suspicion, or an opinion. To ponder with assent, is, then, distinctive of the believer; this is how his act of belief is set off from all other acts of the mind concerned with the true or false. (<u>Summa</u>, Vol. XXXI, p. 63).

41. T.C. O'Brien in St. Thomas Aquinas, <u>Summa Theologia</u>, Vol. XXXI, p. 64, footnote m.

42. Now the will's influencing the intellect towards assent can come about from either of two sources. The first is the will's own relationship toward the good, and it is on this basis that belief is a praiseworthy act. The second source is the mind's being convinced, even though not on the basis of internal

evidence, to the point of judging that what is proposed ought to be believed. For example: raising of a dead man to life; the mind of one seeing this is convinced by the sign to the point that he clearly knows that it is God speaking, who does not lie; the future event, however, would still not be intrinsically evident and so cause for faith to be eliminated. (<u>Summa</u>, Vol. XXXI, p. 155.).

43. No one can attain to this vision of God except by being a learner with God as his teacher; everyone that had heard of the Father and hath learned cometh to me. Now a person becomes a sharer in this learning not all at once but step-by-step, in keeping with human nature. Even Aristotle says that every learner must first be a believer in order that he may come to full knowledge. Thus, in order that a person come to the full, beatific vision, the first requisite is that he believe God, as a learner believing the master teaching him. (<u>Summa</u>, Vol. XXXI, p. 73-75).

44. Among unbelievers there are some who have never received the faith, such as heathens and Jews. These are by no means to be compelled, for belief is voluntary. Nevertheless, the faithful, if they are able, should compel them not to hinder the faith whether by their blasphemies or evil persuasions or even open persecutions. It is for this reason that Christ's faithful often wage war on infidels, not indeed for the purpose of enforcing them to believe, because even were they to conquer them and take them captive, they should still leave them free to believe or not, but for the purpose of stopping them obstructing the faith of Christ. (<u>Summa</u>, Vol. XXXI, p. 63.).

45. John Calvin, <u>Institutes of the Christian Religion</u> III, 2, 7: Nunc justa fidei definitio nobis constabit si dicamus esse divinae erga nos benevolentiae firmam certamque cognitionem, quae gratuitae in Christo promissionis Veritate fundata, per Spiritum Sanctum et revelatur mentibus nostris et cordis obsignatur.

46. Hendrikus Berkhof, "The Act of Faith in the Reformed Tradition," in Paul Surlis, ed., <u>Faith: Its Nature and Meaning</u>

(Westminster, Maryland: Christian Classics, 1972), p. 99. For the classic short biography of Luther in English, see Roland Bainton, Here I Stand (Nashville: Abingdon, 1978). For an interesting comparison of Luther and Aquinas on the subject of faith and justification, see Stephen Pfurtner, Luther and Aquinas on Salvation. Translated by Edward Quinn. (New York: Sheed and Ward, 1964).

47. Martin Luther, Selections from His Writings. Edited and with an Introduction by John Dillenberger. (Garden City, NY: Doubleday Anchor Books, 1961), pp. 58-59.

48. Luther, p. 59.

49. Luther, p. 60.

50. Luther, p. 60.

51. Luther, p. 60.

52. Luther, p. 61.

53. Luther, p. 66.

54. See Aquinas, Summa, 2a2ae.

55. Luther, p. 68.

56. Luther, p. 70.

57. Luther, p. 199.

58. Neuner-Roos, p. 388.

59. Neuner-Roos, p. 395.

60. Luther, p. 182.

61. Immanuel Kant, Religion within the Limits of Reason Alone. Translated by Theodore M. Greene and Hoyt M. Hudson. (New York: Harper and Row, 1960), p. 48.

62. Kant, p. 179.

63. Kant, p. 181.

64. Kant, p. 181.

65. Kant, p. 100.

66. Kant, p. 106.

67. Kant, p. 107.

68. Kant, p. 113.

69. Theodore M. Green, in his introduction to Kant, p. lxxiv.

70. Kant, p. 129.

71. Kant, p. 130.

72. Kant, p. 130, footnote.

73. Edward Shils, Tradition (Chicago: University of Chicago Press, 1981), p. 5.

74. Friedrich Schleiermacher, On Religion. Translated by John Oman. (New York: Harper and Row, 1958), p. 36.

75. Schleiermacher, p. 36.

76. Friedrich Schleiermacher, The Christian Faith. Edited by H.R. Mackintosh and J.S. Stewart. (Philadelphia: Fortress Press, 1928), pp. 68-69.

77. Schleiermacher, p. 70.

78. Schleiermacher, p. 70-71.

79. Schleiermacher, p. 71.

80. Friedrich Schleiermacher, <u>Christmas Eve.</u> Trans- lated by Terence Tice.

81. See: Gustavo Weigel, <u>Summarium Doctrinale de Actu Fidei</u> (Woodstock, Athenaeum Pontificium, 1952), p. 94.

82. Neuner-Roos, pp. 33-34.

83. Neuner-Roos, pp. 33-34.

84. Neuner-Roos, p. 36.

85. Neuner-Roos, p. 37.

86. Neuner-Roos, p. 210.

87. John Henry Newman, <u>The Grammar of Assent</u> (New York: Longmans, Green & Co., 1947), p. 113.

88. Neuner-Roos, p. 229.

89. The one who comes closes to denying this is, of course, Kierkegaard, who reduces tradition to a bare statement of the fact of the God-Man's existence. Presumably, if one leafletted a primitive tribe with Kierkegaard's bare statement, Christianity would be possible for someone living there.

Chapter Six
Renewing the Concept of Faith

Having surveyed the tradition of the community on the subject of faith, we must now turn to the contemporary scene and see if we can find there resources with which to construct a renewed understanding of faith, based on the principles set forth in our earlier chapters.   In some ways the range of possibility is bewilderingly large: hermeneutics has become a popular and self-conscious enterprise in the Christian community, and our concerns for a non-objectivist theology are shared by many. By choosing the Catholic Tracy and the Protestant Hauerwas we do not claim to be choosing the only possible (or even the most likely) resource people, but they have credentials which are significant.   Tracy, more than anyone else, has consciously made use of Gadamerian insights in constructing a foundational theology.   Hauerwas never explicitly mentions Gadamer, but in many ways his style of doing theology is exactly what we think theology's style should be. And, as we have suggested earlier, the two are so different that they can shed light on each other's weaknesses when we compare them, or at least that is the prejudice with which we begin this chapter.

I. David Tracy and Faith's Disclosure

David Tracy has addressed the problem of how (and whether) it is possible to do theology today in a number of articles and in two books, <u>Blessed Rage for Order</u>, and <u>The Analogical Imagination</u>. We will concentrate our attention on the latter book, which tends to include the better insights of the earlier effort, while subtly admitting some of its weaknesses. Tracy's concern in that book (<u>The Analogical Imagination</u>) is one with which we can sympathize. It is the problem of pluralism and how true community can survive within a culture of many communities.   As he puts it: "Must each religious tradition finally either dissolve into some lowest common denominator or accept a marginal existence as one interesting but purely private option?"[1]

To set the question in our own context: we have been assuming that knowledge is possible on the basis of a ("communal" in some sense) pre- understanding. Faith, knowledge and community are terms which cannot be understood apart from each other. This remains our position. But the situation is not so simple. We seem to live in more than one community at the same time; the communities within which we live and those against which we rub shoulders tend to be (at times) contradictory in their beliefs and goals; and the very possibility of community has been questioned on the grounds that contemporary individualism has robbed it of its traditional force. One way out of this problem is, as we have seen, to break out of it entirely, i.e., to set up a *universal* situation (a universal community as it were). This universalism is precisely what we have rejected, and we need not rehearse the argument here. But there is the other side to consider. Is it possible to converse *within* a community and yet not to deny the validity of *other* conversations, other communities? Is it possible, in other words, to conceive of knowledge as something which occurs in this *particular* conversation without succumbing to narrowness, without looking at other conversations as the mutterings of barbarians? Are we caught between a bloodless (and finally impossible) universalism and a narrow and dangerous (if vital) tribalism?

Tracy rarely rises to eloquence, but his description of the temptations of contemporary theology is telling and eloquent:

> A relaxed if not lazy pluralism contenting itself with sharing private stories while both the authentically public character of every good story and the real needs of the wider society go unremarked; a passionate intensity masked as authentic prophecy that resists necessary pleas for empirical evidence while demanding compliance to a particular ideology; a rush to the right for the false security of yet another restoration--too often a restoration which, like that of the Bourbons, has forgotten nothing and learned nothing; a reigning pathos among those who still

demand argument and evidence (in a word, publicness) and whose inability to cut through the swamp of privateness may finally force them to become those who lack all conviction.[2]

We are looking for a community which in its very basis is open and not closed. So is Tracy, and it is important to understand what he is *not* saying as much as to understand what he *is* saying. For in this passage, we meet two of Tracy's favorite words--public, and private--and his use of them can create problems in our appreciation of Tracy's achievement. Tracy insists repeatedly on the public character of theology. In <u>Blessed Rage for Order</u> he had stated simply that, "...in principle, the fundamental loyalty of the theologian *qua* theologian is to that morality of scientific knowledge which he shares with his colleagues, the philosophers, historians, and social scientists."[3] Taking a position which caused controversy at the time, he argued that one could be a Christian theologian without being a Christian:

> The Christian theologian, by professional and, thereby, ethical commitment, has resolved to study that tradition's past and present claims to meaning and truth. Ordinarily he will choose to do so because he has committed himself to a Christian self-understanding. Yet, in principle, *such commitment need not be the case.*[4] (Italics mine.)

Tracy was criticized (quite rightly) because he was saying that one could be a Christian theologian *outside of the Christian community*. The reason he was moved to do this was his almost visceral fear that Christian theology will dissolve into a "private" enterprise: a handful of white men, perhaps, reading over each other's works while the world yawns. But those who felt that Tracy had "lost his faith" (in the traditional Catholic phrase) were not *quite* right. In <u>Blessed Rage</u> the basic "faith" of the Christian theologian turned out to be the same "faith" as the rest of the society, Christian or not. "Faith" here is defined by Tracy as "a basic orientation or attitude which determines one's cognitive beliefs and one's individual ethical actions."[5] There is a "faith" (so defined) which characterizes the "authentic" person in the world today, Christian or not. It is the "faith" of secularity,

> ...that fundamental attitude which affirms the ultimate significance and final worth of our lives, our thoughts, and actions, here and now, in nature and in history. An explicit and full recognition of this faith as, in fact, *the* common faith shared by secularist and modern Christian is perhaps the most important insight needed to understand the contemporary theological situation in its full dimensions and its real possibilities.[6]

Tracy's desire to break out of what we might call the melancholy privatism of Christian theology is understandable. Still, to argue that, after all, we all believe the same things, is an old ploy by now, and notably unsuccessful. People seem remarkably resistent to the argument that Christianity is what they have been believing all their lives, but better expressed.

Besides, one must question whether Tracy's mythical secular people would want to affirm the "ultimate" significance of anything at all, even their own work and lives. Perhaps the contemporary urban intellectual (like the rest of us) is hard put simply to cope with what goes on every day without needing to affirm its ultimate significance.

As we turn to The Analogical Imagination we see that Tracy's position has developed. He begins his book with "A Social Portrait of the Theologian" and notes that the theologian is a member of not one, but three "publics." There is the "public" of *society*, the "public" of the *academy* and the "public" of the *church*. Within the public of society there are *three realms*: the realm of *economics*, the realm of *politics*, and the realm of *culture* (art and religion). Economics seems to be the realm of technical reason. In the realm of politics we move from the instrumental rationality of economics to the demands of practical reason. The realm of politics is the place where society hammers out its value conflicts on the basis of rational discussion (though, again, we are speaking here of practical reason, not instrumental reason):

> In the Western tradition of ethical philosophy...one finds authentically public ways to discuss policy issues. Whether those ways be based upon teleological, deontological, axiological or responsibility models for ethical reasoning, or upon some "mixed theory", there seems to be little doubt that all ethical arguments are in principle open to intelligent, reasonable, and responsible persons. As grounded in comprehensive notions of practical reason, they are public, not private.[7]

The reference to Bernard Lonergan's transcendental precepts ("Be attentive! Be intelligent! Be reasonable! Be responsible!")[8] is no accident. David Tracy regards human reason as a transcendental characteristic of every human person, and feels that, in principle, any human person can work out any problem with any other human person, given enough time and good will. What becomes clear now is the way in which the escape from privatism will proceed: it will proceed in the traditional fashion of Western philosophy. It will point to what is universal in the human experience, and therefore obligatory upon all, regardless of their situation and heritage.

To put it bluntly: *Tracy can find no escape from "privacy" (relativism, isolationism, tribalism) but in foundationalism.*

But we have not yet reached the third realm of society, the realm where theology belongs, the realm of culture, the realm, for Tracy, of symbol and value. Again, the fundamental concern of Tracy is with avoiding privatism. He complains that religion, even more now than art, is "the single subject about which many intellectuals can feel free to be ignorant."[9] It is, after all, a "private consumer product that some people seem to need."[10] But the symbols of religion and art are *not* fundamentally private for Tracy, though they may appear (can only appear) within a particular culture:

> One need not (indeed, should not) absolutize the claims of any religion in order to realize that any

major religious tradition does disclose in its symbols
and in its reflections upon these symbols (i.e., its
theologies) some fundamental vision of the meaning
of individual and communal existence providing
disclosive and transformative possibil|ities for the
whole society. Both ethos and world-view are
disclosed in any religion. One need not minimize the
need for reasoned public discourse upon all claims to
truth in order to recognize the indispensible role that
cultural symbols, including the religious, can play in
the wider society.[11]

The basic move Tracy wants to make is implicit in this passage,
as is much of the language he will later use. He is going to
show that *particular religious traditions possess a particular
kind ot truth, the truth found in symbols*. The model for Tracy
here is, of course, a Heideggerian disclosure model for
truth. The flexibility of the disclosure model for truth (as
opposed to, say, the correspondence theory of truth found in
scholasticism) enables Tracy to have his cake and eat it too,
i.e., to argue that the religious symbol can disclose truth to the
whole society (and thus be public) and yet not be reduced
to manipulable, technical rationality, not be turned into
eternally true propositions.

Recall that Tracy had been speaking of the social portrait of
the theologian and had argued that the theologian spoke to three
"publics"-- society (consisting of the three realms of economy,
polity and culture), academy, and church, with the latter two,
of course, necessarily being included within the former larger
concept, especially in the realm of culture. Having sketched
out the notion of society, he now turns to the publics of
academy and church. By specifying the particular
characteristics of each of these publics and the appropriate
theological specialty relevant to each (i.e., practical theology
relates to society at large; fundamental theology to the
academy; systematic theology to the church[12]) Tracy hopes to
bring clarity to a muddled field. Let us briefly look at the
publics of academy and church.

In the world of *academia*, the theologian is, presumably, engaged in the search for the particular kind of truth appropriate to the scholar. Drawing upon the work of Stephen Toulmin, Tracy must admit that Toulmin's criteria for a discipline apply to theology only in hope. Theologians simply do not agree on what theology is, and thus the progress made in a "compact" field like physics (ever the shining example) is simply not possible in theology. Nevertheless, this does not mean that theologians will not agree in the future. In fact, the discussion over the appropriate paradigm for theology can be fruitful. Proposals like that of Bernard Lonergan may eventually lead us to agreement, at least enough agreement to constitute a "diffuse" discipline in Toulmin's vocabulary. But Tracy's fundamental concern, the concern for publicness, for a truth which all can accept, is what must always be kept in mind, he says, even in our present confused state in theology:

> Theology aids the public value of both academy and society when it remains faithful to its own internal demand--publicness. Without that demand for publicness--for criteria, evidence, warrants, disciplinary status--serious academic theology is dead. The academic setting of much of the best theology, precisely by its demands for public criteria in all disciplines, assures that announcements of that death remain premature.[13]

Notice Tracy's gloss on the meaning of the term "publicness." Publicness for Tracy means *giving reasons*. Its opposite would be talking to oneself alone, refusing to test one's understanding against that of others: a fundamental closedness to reality. But despite his admirable concern for the sociology of the theologian, Tracy's use of the term "public" sometimes ignores the fact that there are different kinds of publicness. Despite his detailing of the various publics of the theologian, Tracy still seems to regard "public" as referring, ultimately, to *any and all human beings in principle*. The image which comes to mind is standing in the market place.

What also inevitably comes to mind at this point is that the public for Tracy's book is in some sense the University of Chicago, with its own rich tradition of inter-disciplinary conversation and its Great Books heritage. In other words, what Tracy does *not* reveal in his sophisticated discussion of the various publics of the theologian is that the model for academia (and perhaps for rationality itself) is constituted for Tracy by his own particular experience in a particular place. The universalist tends to reveal his particularity to everybody but himself.

There is a third, final public for the theologian, a third aspect of the social portrait: *the church.* Tracy is keenly aware of the complexity of the theologian's relationship to church. What tends to get ignored, Tracy argues, quite rightly, is the *sociological* reality of the church. Concerned with the explicitly theological reality of church, many theologians seem frightened by what they would consider a reduction of the Christian community to the categories of secular understanding of people in groups. As Tracy says,

> The key concept here is reductionism. Indeed, so frightened by this reductionist prospect do some ecclesiologists seem that they are incapable of undertaking, or even appreciating, strictly sociological understandings of the reality of the church. For this reason, they become trapped in their own form of reductionism.[14]

What is needed, Tracy would argue, is an honest understanding of the fact that, in our own society, the Christian church is one (of several) voluntary associations which influence and are influenced by the rest of society in a complex, difficult-to-sort-out fashion. And while for any theologian, church is going to function as one important reference group, one public, there remain the two others, and the relationship between church, and the realms of economics and politics, and the rest of the realm of culture, is going to be one of the theologian's major concerns:

The theologian, like all others in a pluralist and denominational society, is involved, consciously or unconsciously, in an ongoing process of reflection upon one's voluntary commitment and loyalty to the Christian church and, ordinarily, to particular church tradition. The theologian must thereby relate that commitment and its attendant responsibilities to one's other commitments and responsibilities to the wider society and to the academy and thereby to their plausibility structures.[15]

By placing the theologian (and, by extension, the theologian's work) in the text of three publics, Tracy, more than any other theologian today, has addressed the social reality of the theologian, revealing its confusing complexity.

But what of the *theological* reality of church? Is not the Christian church something more than a sociological reality? Of course it is, says Tracy, but he adds an all-important proviso: so also is the rest of society more than a sociological reality. Looked at sociologically, the theologian's world breaks down into the three publics Tracy described. Looked at theologically, the world breaks down into the realities which the tradition has termed "world" and "church." These latter terms are dialectical realities, not abstract essences, and the proper relationship between them is one of the issues the community has struggled with over the centuries. Should church be totally (or as much as possible) a separate structure from the rest of society (the "sect" option)? Should it, strive as much as possible to be part of the rest of society (the "broad church" option)?

This seems to leave us in a confused state. The theologian lives in a world of the mutually interpenetrating realities known as economics, politics, culture, of which the voluntary associations known as the the academy and the church form sub-groupings (specifically, of the latter reality, culture). This is the sociological reality. But the theologian, precisely as such, is concerned with relating the Christian tradition to those within it and without it. And such a relationship falls under the explicitly theological label of church-world. There are those who have accepted the symbols and have begun to live the life of the followers of Christ, and they must always turn in some fashion to face those how have not (yet?) done so. But now that Tracy has given us sociological and theological descriptions of the world of the theologian, has he not left us with mutually exclusive languages for the (presumably) same reality?

Not really. "The theologian should in principle use a correlation model for relating sociological and theological understandings of the reality of the church in the same way one uses a correlation model for the more familiar relationship between philosophy and theology."[16] Theology's traditional dialogue partner has indeed been philosophy; what Tracy is suggesting here is that another dialogue partner must be sociology. Just as theology has at times regarded philosophy as useless worldly wisdom, more often as a source of insight, so can it now reject or engage in dialogue with the newer discipline.

Perhaps the key point for us is that *the recognition of the sociological reality of the church means that there is no archimedean point,* no place to stand from which the theologian can pass judgment, either philosophically or sociologically, on reality. He (or she) is already formed by a particular philosophical pre-understanding before he does theology; he is already formed by a particular theological pre-understanding before he does philosophy; he comes out of a particular sociological reality before he reflects on church; he is a Christian before he tries to understand what it means to live in a group. Recognition of this reality enables the theologian,not to transcend it surely, but to employ it as he strives for greater understanding:

Any theologian will necessarily interpret the tradition in critical relationship to some explicit or implicit contemporary self-understanding. Even if the theologian's self-understanding does not include an explicit recognition of the publics of society and academy (and thereby of the theological significance of the "world" as a theological locus) the

influences from those other two publics remains
potent. For the theologian, like any other human
being, has been socialized into a particular society and
a particular academic tradition and has been encultured
into one particular culture. Even when the
relationships to society or academy are negative
ones, the theologian will be internally related to the
plausibility structures of that society, especially as
those structures are formulated and refined
into plausibility arguments and criteria of adequacy by
the academy.[17]

Unfortunately, Tracy seems to abstract from his nuanced
understanding of the sociological reality of the theologian
whenever he talks about the academy, which is the public for
fundamental theology (also known as philosophical theology).
For the *ultimate* truth claim is that made by fundamental
theology, and that truth claim is *not* made from within a culture
or a tradition of interpretation, but from Olympus, the
mountaintop of universal reason: "the word 'public' here refers
to the articulation of fundamental questions and answers which
any attentive, intelligent, reasonable and responsible person
can understand and judge in keeping with fully public criteria
for argument."[18]

It turns out that there are different kinds of truth,
appropriate to each of the theological sub-disciplines and their
corresponding publics. There is the truth of the aacademy--
vaguely alluded to--which is employed by fundamental
theologians to adjudicate the truth claims of their (or
others') religious commitment. They "in principle will abstract
themselves from all religious 'faith commitments' for the
legitimate purposes of critical analysis of all religious and
theological claims."[19] Only after the fundamental theologians
have established the plausibility of the claims of truth of
a particular religious tradition does the systematic theologian
get to work. Having established the validity of the tradition's
symbols, the systematic theologian now has a hermeneutical
task to perform, i.e., the interpretation of that tradition for the
contemporary world. The model for truth here is
the disclosure model of Gadamer and Heidegger. (The third

266

sub-discipline, practical theology, uses a *praxis-oriented* paradigm for truth.)

What is bothersome about all this is that Tracy truly wants to have it *both* ways. He wants to give every truth-claim its due, and he is sensitive to the fact that they cannot all be reduced monistically to one paradigm. His solution is undoubtedly brilliant. Yes, the Marxist-oriented liberation theologians are right when they argue for a truth arising out of action. Yes, the hermeneutical theologians are right when they argue for the primacy of interpretation. And yes, the fundamental theologians are right when they claim that their enterprise is truly the foundation of all the others. *But the last claim is the operative one. The fundamental theologian gives the others permission to exist,* he adjudicates their truth claims, and, as judge, sits on the bench while the others must stand at attention. And so, though his claim is that every sub-discipline is "public", yet one is more public than others; though all are equal, one is definitely mor equal then the others.

For Tracy, then, as we have noted several times, the fundamental theologian need not be a Christian, but he is concerned with adjudicating truth-claims. (This distinguishes him from his colleague in religious studies.) But does anyone really believe that David Tracy, the fundamental theologian, is abstracting from his own Christian pre-understanding when he writes his own books? Does anyone really believe that the whole problematic of his books would *matter* to a Hindu or Buddhist? If the answer to these questions is obvious, why not admit the truth that (to put it in disciplinary terms) fundamental theology is a sub-heading of systematic (hermeneutical) theology and not the other way around? Why not admit that it is the concrete experience of the truth of a tradition which leads people to reflect at some point on the more theoretical aspects of their primary commitment?

Still, while it is fair to say that at bottom Tracy remains committed to a foundationalist reading of Bernard Lonergan as his basic philosophical position , it is also fair to say that his discussion of the hermeneutical task of systematic theology, and his use of Gadamer's notion of the *classic* in that discussion is genuinely illuminating for our own discussion. In fact, Tracy will argue that systematics is in some sense distinct from (though perhaps not completely independent of) fundamental theology.

Tracy views systematic theology as the interpretation of the "*classics of the Christian tradition*" in such a way that truth appears. Tracy defines "classics" as "those texts, events, images, person, rituals and symbols which are assumed to disclose permanent possibilities of meaning and truth."[20] Through his use of the term "classic" (borrowed, of course, from Gadamer), Tracy intends to show that systematic theology is the kind of hermeneutical enterprise described by Gadamer in Truth and Method. But here, instead of interpreting "secular" works of art, the theologian interprets the central symbols of the religious tradition out of which he comes. "Like every interpreter of every classic, the theologian will enter the risk of interpretation with the same basic moments."[21]

Following Gadamer, Tracy distinguishes three such basic moments. There is, first of all, the moment of *pre-understanding*. Before he ever gets to the text or event or person or symbol to be interpreted, the theologian already has an attitude to its subject matter, a problem with it, a question about it, a language which he uses to speak about it-- in a word, a tradition, a community of sorts. Next there is a moment of *claim*. The text is not read as one reads an encyclopedia article; rather, it seizes its reader, makes demands on him, shocks him with its power. Recall at this point Gadamer's rich phenomenology of the claim of one person on another in conversation. This insight leads us to the third moment, the moment of *conversation* with the *res*, the existential issue raised by the text. "Like all true dialogues, the theological dialogue will be marked by the bouyancy of both critical freedom and real appreciation in the face of the claim of the classic and its exertion of an unmistakable *fascinans et tremendum* power."[22]

For Tracy, of course, the advantage of the term "classic" is that it enables him (so he thinks) to satisfy his own deepest desire--the desire for publicness--while remaining a Christian theologian with intellectual respectability in the academy. If there is such a thing as a classic in a culture, argues Tracy, then the theological classic has just as much right to be so termed as Dante's <u>Divine Comedy</u>. One does not have to be Italian or Christian to understand Dante; one can still appreciate Dante's genius if one is a Jewish atheist from New York. Accordingly, Barth's <u>Church Dogmatics</u> should also be available to any and all in the culture, and for the same reasons. Reject this hypothesis, says Tracy, and you make of Chrisitanity "no more than a set of personal preferences and beliefs making no more claim to either publicness or univerality than the Elks Club".[23] Fortunately, the classic, while particular, and part of a concrete tradition, nevertheless reaches out to the world at large:

> Who can deny any classic's claim to a real, even sometimes a paradigmatic, public status? It is counterintuitive to suppose that Dante's <u>Divine Comedy</u> is disclosive and transformative only for a fourteenth century Florentine; that James Joyce's <u>Ulysses</u> is disclosive and transformative only for someone who may have personally experienced Dublin on Bloomsday. It is similarly counterintuitive to suppose that such candidates for theological classic status like Karl Barth's <u>Church Dogmatics</u> and Karl Rahner's <u>Theological Investigations</u> are disclosive and transformative only for a person commited to either the Swiss Reformed tradition or the German (indeed Swabian) Catholic Tradition.[24]

It is difficult to know how to respond to a man who can argue for the genuine publicness of Barth's <u>Church Dogmatics</u>! What is counterintuitive is to believe that Rahner's <u>Theological Investigations</u> will ever be of interest to any but a very few Christian theologians. Tracy's entire paragraph, in fact, is rhetorical overkill. Dante hardly limited even his original audience to Florence; Joyce in point of fact could not have limited his audience to Dubliners on Bloomsday, a moment in time long past when he wrote his book. But be that as it may, it is by no means clear that the genuine publicness of either of these great works of art will survive the collapse of traditional Catholic symbolism (notice that Tracy's two examples of genuine publicness are heavily Roman Catholic in imagery).

A classic is not simply a ship sealed in a bottle; it is more like a ship kept afloat by tradition, and where that tradition ebbs, so does the classic. And even the most secure classic can topple from its throne. It is hard for us today to recapture, for example, the veneration with which Vergil was read in the Middle Ages, possibly because we no longer believe he was a pre-Christian prophet.

There are other problems with Tracy's use of Gadamer's category. For Tracy, the classic is an attempt, as we have suggested, to finesse the issue of particularity and universality, to have the cake of concreteness and eat it too. As such, the classic is absolutely central to Tracy's enterprise, focused as it is on the struggle between private and public. But Gadamer's use of the term is firmly rooted in an understanding that what makes a classic is precisely its reception as such by a continuing culture, a tradition which continues to see in that classic, or, better, continues to *experience* in that classic, the disclosure of truth which is its reason for being. For Gadamer, the publicness of a classic is publicness within a community of interpretation. This is what Tracy is insufficiently sensitive to. The tragedy of Tracy's position is that is could have been at least partially rescued if he had simply agreed to limit himself to the Western culture derived from Europe which he is obviously talking about anyway.

Worse, Tracy uses the term so much that it begins to lose meaning. Throughout the book and in its footnotes, he labels recent theological literature "classic" with abandon. Everybody from the Niebuhrs to the "event" of liberation theology is classic. But if "classic" is to mean anything as a word, it must surely be restricted to relatively few examples of "permanent" meaning (as Tracy claims in his own definitions of the term).

By the writing of <u>The Analogical Imagination</u> (and after a deeper reading of Gadamer) Tracy began to employ the category of the classic more subtly in his description of the way in which religious language effects and affects us. In the presence of the religious classic, one finds oneself shaken to the roots in a way which is not possible in classics which do not make claims so profound. Already in "major" classics like Shakespeare, we find ourselves in a "world disclosive of a radical sense of both participation and nonparticipation in the comprehensible mystery that is our experience, the mystery which we can now feel, not merely affirm. That meaning cannot be stated with the same adequacy outside the form."[25] If this is the case, then the religious classic should have intrinsic problems with whatever form is used. "Indeed the surest clue to the reign of the subject matter by the religious classic can be witnessed by the relative inadequacy of any religious form for communicating its meaning."[26] Thus the religious classic will find itself using dialectical language, paradoxical language, sometimes contradictory language. It is surely a mark of the strength of the Jewish and Christian traditions that their classic writings are notoriously untidy.

How do we achieve some sort of unity in our understanding of the Christian religious classic? The classic of Christianity is fundamentally the event and person of Jesus of Nazareth, not a text or a set of texts. (Here Tracy departs from Gadamer, for whom only a text can be classic.) How do we contact this Jesus-event? "The tradition is the major constitutive mediating reality of the event of Jesus Christ."[27] Of course, this is the beginning of problems rather than the end of them. How does the tradition mediate the reality of the event of the Lord? The tradition mediates Jesus through "the classic words, sacraments and actions expressing the Christ event in the present community, in conformity with the original apostolic witness."[28]

Heavily influenced by Paul Ricoeur, but employing him for his own purposes, and adding his own creative analyses, Tracy offers an intriguing account of our appropriation of the New Testament. Rejecting arguments which propose that the

New Testament can be reduced to its most primitive parts or to a "canon within the canon", Tracy insists, with the Catholic tradition, that the *entire* New Testament is what has been preserved by the community, and with some reason. Thus "early Catholicism" is not to be eliminated from the corpus in favor of Romans, Galatians and Mark, for example, nor is James to be termed an "epistle of straw" and demoted to an appendage. This leaves us again with the problem of integration, and Tracy's proposal is suggestive:

> Let us assume that some major genres of the New Testament are as follows: apocalyptic, proclamation-confession, gospel (especially narrative), symbols-images, reflective theology and doctrine. Within that complex, a further proposal for relative adequacy seems to emerge: The basic unity and diversity of the New Testament expressions may be found not only in the earliest witnesses but in the later witnesses as well through the genres of proclamation-confession to narrative to symbol to reflective thought. The genres "apocalyptic" and the "doctrines" of early Catholicism may be employed as correctives upon this basic complex. Such is the proposal.[29]

This scheme allows Tracy to make use of the entire New Testament while distinguishing lesser and greater parts. By making the division on the basis of genre rather than date of composition, for example, or fidelity to some norm of orthodoxy, Tracy finesses a number of knotty questions. But is it fair to use what is basically literary-critical methodology as the basis of one' entire analysis of the New Testament? This answer is not hard to discover: why not? The proof of the usefulness of this approach will be if we can recognize some truth we haven't seen before through its employment. So we must wait to see.

Thus we have a "basic complex" of genres in the New Testament, organically interrelated, as we shall see, and two "corrective" genres, apocalyptic and doctrines. Let us turn to an examination of the "corrective" genres first. Tracy sees the key to apocalyptic in the notion of *intensification*. Apocalyptic serves as a constant challenge to complacency, as a reminder that all our images are inadequate, and that the future will overturn them. It is a reminder that a faith which is not passionate, which does not hope in history for the fulfillment of God's promises, is no faith at all, or rather, is not Christian faith. As Tracy puts it,

> Apocalyptic seems better observed in fidelity to the New Testament by allowing its contextual and pervasive role to act not as a central genre but as a central corrective to all other genres through its challenge of intensification, its disclosure of the pain and seriousness of the negative, its challenge towards any claims to more than relative adequacy in the realities of the *novum* and the future in the event of Jesus Christ.[30]

But the intensification which apocalyptic provides must be balanced by the patient acceptance of the everyday, the humdrum, the *cotidianum terribile,* lest it turn into fanaticism. Thus Tracy gives apocalyptic a twin, the genre of *doctrines.* If apocalyptic scandalized by its almost mad intensity, doctrines (and Tracy here refers chiefly to the Pastoral Epistles), scandalize by their boring sensibleness. To go from apocalyptic to doctrines is to go from the sound of the last trumpet to the sound of bingo. But Tracy's pairing of these two genres is extremely helpful, reminiscent of Aquinas' pairing of temperance and fortitude in his discussion of the cardinal virtues. They are not central, but without them, the major virtues would go astray, either through laziness and fear, on the one hand, or rashness and foolhardiness on the other. The genre of doctrine helps us to see that the ordinary, the run of the mill, the institutional, are themselves *extra*ordinary when seen rightly. "So the ordinary seems to any Christian consciousness that realizes that the extraordinary event of Jesus Christ discloses that all is grace, that the event happens everywhere, that we can clarify certain essential moments in the event as shared truths and doctrines."[31]

But if apocalyptic and doctrines form corrective genres, then we must look elsewhere for the heart of the New

Testament message, and it is in the complex of genres already referred to as proclamation- narrative- symbol- thought that Tracy finds the heart of the classic Christian writings. The placing of proclamation first in this complex is no accident, for "proclamation is, in fact the transformative presupposition of all further genres."[32] The reason for this is that there is a claim at the heart of all language, even the most prosaic. This we learned from Gadamer, among others. Conversation takes for granted that the partners are open to the claim of the others; otherwise there is no conversation, though there might be manipulation of words. And the claim of the religious classic, the claim of the Christian classic event of Jesus Christ, is a claim which reaches to the core of our lives. Thus *the paradigmatic genre of the New Testament is the kerygmatic address:*

> ...a word of address bearing a stark and disconcerting shock of recognition for the self; a word of address with the claim of a nonviolent appeal to listen and receive its gift and demand; a questioning, provocative, promising and liberating word that the event happens now; a judging, forgiving word. The proper Christian response to this word is called faith: a new self understanding elicited by the proclamation and eliciting both freedom and a sense of dependence, forgiveness and sin, radical acceptance of the gift and command to the hearer disclosed in the kerygmatic word of address.[33]

Here Tracy is obviously availing himself of what we might call a general Post-Heideggerian world-view, employing some of the language of Bultmann and more recent interpreters. Note that faith here is "a new self- understanding" which is stirred up by the claim made by the proclamation. But it is not clear how a claim could give me a new understanding of who I am. Just exactly what *is* the Christian proclamation? One's mind moves quickly to such phrases as "Jesus is Lord!" or "He is risen!" as candidates for the honor of being the most basic Christian word of address. The problem of what the primitive kerygma really is, is, of course, much controverted; but Tracy finds his archimedean point in the presence of Jesus at the moment of proclamation. Thus, says Tracy, what is common to the primitive preaching and the proclamations of Paul and John is "that the *present* reality of Jesus as the exalted one (as *Kyrios*, Risen Lord, Son of Man, Son of God, Messiah-Christ, etc.) is experienced *now* as the decisive disclosure of who God is and who we are."[34]

Thus, to say to a group of people that Jesus is their Lord is not to make a statement about a state of affairs presently obtaining and which might be of some interest; rather, that statement invites people to see themselves in a new way, a way which is challenging to their deepest self-understanding. Tracy quotes James D.G. Dunn, the renowned British scholar, to support the thesis that "the bedrock of the Christian faith confessed in the New Testament writings, is the unity between the earthly Jesus and the exalted one who is somehow involved in or part of our encounter with God in the here and now."[35]

But there are problems with an emphasis on proclamation. Stressing the *event* of the claim of God runs the danger of turning God's word into a magic trick, an infallible formula. We respond, as Christians, to the phrase "Jesus is Lord", but we do not respond to the phrase "John is Lord" or "Henry is master", and yet they have exactly the same grammatical form. As Charles Wood points out, "the confession 'Jesus is Lord' makes sense only within a story. Its value as a confession...depends upon its users' and hearers' acquaintance with some account of who Jesus is and what it means...that he is Lord."[36]

Thus, proclamation *cannot* stand by itself. And though Tracy seems to be somewhat aware of this fact, he does not seem to grasp the point that proclamation is not simply *helped* by the other genres, it *cannot exist without them.* As he puts it, "the other genres are also needed for relative adequacy. Without them proclamation is ever in danger of becoming either merely abstract content or violent and authoritarian act of address."[37] But this is not strong enough. As we have suggested, *proclamation is meaningless* (quite literally) *without a context.* Thus it might be more helpful not to regard proclamation as an independent genre but as a quality of the other genres, i.e., the narrative is a narrative which makes a claim, not simply a nice story. But isn't this true of any classic narrative?

As even Tracy says,

> It is not necessary to decide between proclamation and narrative as *the* primary (too often synonymous with sole or exclusive) New Testament genre. The New Testament includes and demands both. So, it would seem, does human experience. There is something intrinsic in experience which demands narrative.[38]

The story (whether that of the New Testament or not) says things which cannot be said any other way, reduced to any other genre, boiled down to propositions or painted in a picture: "The disclosive and transformative power and meaning of the story are grasped only in and through the narrative itself."[39]

In the gospels, then, we experience the authoritative life of a man whose stance toward reality was "that the final power is gracious, that the final power is love."[40]

And if the heart of the gospel story is the account of the passion, the very incompletion (as in Mark) and unresolved tension of the passion suggests to Tracy that the gospels reveal to us the very incompleteness and unresolved tensions of our own mortal lives. The *form*, in other words, of the gospels, is as important as the content. The story of the gospels will have its end, suggests Tracy, only at the real end of the human story, when the promises of the Jesus-story are radically fulfilled. The gospels, one might say, initiate us into a story more than they tell a story to us.

To be a Christian, then, is to find oneself living out the story of the gospels. It means:

276

to trust that, empowered, enabled, gifted and commanded by the Christ event of God, I can because I must attempt to risk a life like that disclosed in these gospel narratives. The gospel narratives of the message, actions and fate of Jesus of Nazareth are the primary story that the Christian learns to trust: to focus, confirm, correct, challenge, confront and transform my present questions, expectations, reflections on life and all my attempts to live a life worthy of the name "human."[41]

But Tracy's complex of New Testament genres includes more than proclamation and narrative. He suggests that there are two more: symbol and reflective thought. Along with the challenging word and the involving story, the New Testament also employs the symbol, and "the heart of the Christian symbol system is none other than the unbreakable dialectic of cross- resurrection-incarnation disclosing through its own internal tensions the fuller meanings of the event of Jesus Christ."[42] Whether incarnation is a symbol in the same sense as the other two is questionable, and Tracy spends no time defining what a symbol might be, so the utility of his discussion is limited. It is clear that his real concern is not with symbol, but with the reflective thought to which symbols (he says) give rise.

The two great theologians of the New Testament, Paul and John, are then examined, and their differences underlined. Paul's theology, his reflection on the Christ-event, is pure proclamation (using Ricoeur's distinction of proclamation/ Imanifestation to refer to the tension between the challenging/ comforting, not yet/but already here, word/Isacrament aspects of authentic religious experience), and Paul's dialectical and paradoxical mode of thought never ceases to rub the noses of his listeners in the folly of the cross.

John, on the other hand, "moves to a form of meditative thought appropriate to his emphasis on the manifestiation of the Logos. In John even the symbol "cross" is so united to the symbols of glorification..that cross itself now becomes the disclosure of that glorification."[43] Thus John is the theologian of manifestation, emphasizing a "realized eschatology", pointing to the fact that here and now we can experience the new life of the risen Christ.

And so, by looking at the New Testament as a complex of mutually interrelated genres, Tracy grounds the pluralism of the contemporary theological scene in the pluralism in unity of the original New Testament witness. Pluralism becomes, for Tracy, not the tired allowing of differences, but a recognition of the relativity of all expressions of the absolute event of Christ. Only the whole (which is not an undifferentiated mass) is finally relatively adequate. And this is because "only the whole of the New Testament expressions will disclose with relative adequacy the whole dialectical meaning of both our situation and the event of Jesus Christ."[44] Thus Tracy can call for a dialogue among those he calls modern classic theologians. "Each of these classical expressions needs self-exposure to the other: the act-of-proclamation orientation of Bultmann, for example, to the narrative-pattern orientation of Barth and the image-symbol-thought orientations of Tillich and Rahner--and vice-versa."[45]

The pluralism of theology is a reflection of a more important contemporary pluralism--that of the church. For the New Testament complex upon which the theologians reflect is part of the witness to the Christ-event kept alive only through the tradition. "Insofar as we trust in the present reality of that event, we also trust in its mediation to us via that tradition which is the church."[46] The classic texts of the New Testament are revelatory of Jesus Christ only in the context of the struggles, successes, hopes and dreams of this people out of which the texts came in the first place. Each saint, each outcast, each religious reformer and each organization within the church has left its mark on the common culture, has contributed to the "language gain" of the Christian community, and has thus expanded the possibilities of faithful witness to Jesus. To be a Christian means, dedication of an isolated consciousness to Jesus, learning to play a part in an ongoing enterprise, giving oneself over to something which then carries one along. When we do this, "we become consciously part of the tradition. We explicitly include an ecclesial faith in our primary faith in Jesus Christ. We live in the Christ event in and by the tradition, the community, the church."[47]

Inevitably the mention of faith in the church calls up its opposite: the problem of church's distortion of the truth and the consequent doubting of our faith in it. But this doubt does not paralyze us because within the very tradition of the church is the call for reform. "The tradition of *ecclesia semper reformanda* is one of the surest signs in the ecclesial tradition itself of the reality of a living tradition."[48] The tradition is self-correcting, not because of institutional safeguards, as in the U. S. Constitution, but because of the nature of the religious reality to which the tradition gives witness. The dangerous story of Jesus keeps reminding us that all our language (which is all we are) is inadequate to the mystery to which we can witness, but never control. Armed with this (traditional) insight, we realize that part of what it means to be church is the continuing argument over what it means to be church, what it means to be faithful to the unsettling memory of Jesus. This last sentence goes beyond Tracy and reflects the thought of Alasdair MacIntyre, but it is not unfaithful to what Tracy is saying.

Of course, for Tracy, the "argument" as we have called it, over the tradition, is carried on through the three basic methods of critique: the historical-critical, ideology-critique, and literary-critical paths. Thus, the "import of the historical critical recovery of the original apostolic witness is to provide a new and legitimate check upon any lack of fidelity to the Jesus remembered by the early church."[49] Less familiar but equally important is the check provided by ideology critique. Here Tracy is clearly pointing to the work of Jurgen Habermas and others of the Frankfurt school, who have alerted us to the domination sedimented into the very language. Finally, Tracy reveals that his genre approach (which we have been following) is part of the reformatory impulse:

> The import of the kind of literary-critical, hermen-
> eutical approach employed in this work is also to
> provide a legitimate, reformatory corrective of
> present ecclesial and societal praxis and thought by

means of a renewed sense of the disclosive and transformative need for such genres as proclamation and narrative, such symbols as the reign of God preached by the Jesus narrated in the gospels and the symbols, cross, resurrection, incarnation of Jesus Christ, such modes of liberating models for systematic theology as Paul's dialectical thought or John's meditative style, such liberating principles of intensification and negation as provided in apocalyptic, or principles of necessary clarificaltion as provided in the doctrines of early Catholicism.[50]

This passage reveals the correctness of our insight that Tracy's importance to us will be primarily in the how of the disclosure of what faith is. In other words, Tracy, through his discussion of the inter-relationship between the various genres of the New Testament, shows us how the faith is conveyed without unacceptable distortion to each new generation of Christians. This passage also makes it clear that Tracy himself regards this discussion of genre as central to his book, and therefore as central to systematic theology, which this book is supposed to be.

To summarize, then: Despite his tendencies toward foundationalism, deriving from a quite laudable desire to communicate the Christian message to a wide audience, Tracy is sensitive to the inadequacies of foundationalism. His solution is to incorporate into a higher synthesis the various competing models for truth, correlating them with the three major divisions of theology and its three "publics." Thus, fundamental, systematic, and practical theologies find themselves using respectively, a correspondence model, a hermeneutical disclosure model, and a praxis-oriented model for truth, and to be directed, respectively, to academy, church, and world. This attempt to satisfy everyone (typical of Tracy) will probably satisfy few. Nevertheless, one need not agree with all parts of Tracy's grand scheme to find its various parts helpful. Tracy's vision of a systematic theology which is an enterprise of hermeneutics, of interpretation of the classic Christian event (as mediated by the classic witnessing texts, symbols, rituals, persons, institutions, etc.) from within the community which is formed by those classics--that vision is indeed our own. And Tracy's analysis of how the classic texts of the tradition disclose meaning by their very unity-in-difference, their plurality without chaos, is a brilliant help to us in understanding how the community can be one in its witness to the truth and yet not monolithic or repressive. In the very heart of the Christian revelation, Tracy shows us, is freedom of interpretation.

Finally, as to the *what* of faith, as to what Christian faith is, Tracy finds it to be an explicitation of a basic human trust in the worthwhileness of life, an explicitation, a re-presentation, flowing out of the historical event of the resurrection of Jesus of Nazareth, embodied in the community which bears his name.

> In response to the Christ event as God's own self-manifestation the believer dares to trust: to trust in the God who is Love, now represented anew in the Christ event; to trust in the gift and command to the self to live in freedom and love; to trust in the ordinary and its extraordinariness; to trust in history and its struggle for justice, for authentic freedom, for the coming reign of love, for the future as God's own future enabling and commanding us to enter into that struggle in the present; to trust in nature and its manifestations and its yearnings for the whole; to trust *in* Jesus Christ as primal word and sacrament of God's own self.[51]

Is this particular faith of a particular people finally justified? Does it work? As Tracy says, "the final test of that vision will always be the risk of a life. The final test is the future...The Christian truly believes in Jesus Christ only by risking the kind of life narrated as Jesus' own."[52] And that life, we would add, is not the isolated project of an individual, but the shared enterprise of a community.

We leave our discussion of Tracy with admiration, but with some questions. At the center of our own project is an attempt to talk about Christian faith against the background of a theory of knowledge which is non- foundationalistic. But Tracy sees the (non-foundationalistic) disclosure model for truth as only one among several, and ultimately dependent on the foundation of universal reason. It is true that at times Tracy is aware, through his reading of Toulmin, that philosophy is a discipline (and therefore community of inquiry, methodology, and aims) within Western culture, but at other times he seems to assume that philosophy as practiced in the academy is simply identifiable with universal reason. Thus our *first question*: is it possible to do theology without resting it ultimately on philosophy? (The traditional theological question of faith and reason.)

What Tracy does show us most passionately is the danger of fideism, the danger of narrow-mindedness, what Lonergan calls *scotosis*, a refusal to be open to the truth. If we reject a theology which needs the support of a foundationalistic notion of truth, do we then lapse into sheer tribalism? Thus our *second question*: is it possible to reconcile the notion that knowledge is based on a community of faith with the fact that there are *several* communities of faith in the world, in our own environment, perhaps even in our selves? (The traditional theological question of church and world.)

Tracy brilliantly shows us the way in which the classic texts of the Christian tradition disclose a pluralistic truth within the community. By the diversity of their genres, they provide for a diversity of experiences and interpretations and make it impossible to ever arrive at a monistic account of Christian faith. Christian faith can never be reduced to a simple formula, in the same way and for the same reason that Shakespeare's "Hamlet" can never be reduced to a simple formula. But if such meanings cannot be reduced to simple formulas, they can at least be described. Tracy's own descriptions of the *what* of faith, reflecting the influence of Schubert Ogden, tend to the abstract. Christian faith tends to be described in terms with which any secular humanist would agree. Thus the *third question:* is it possible to describe faith more concretely than Tracy does? Is it possible, at last, to answer the question, what is faith? (The traditional theological question of the meaning of faith.) Armed with our three questions we can now proceed to a conversation with a contemporary theologian who may be able to answer them in a way at least supplementary to Tracy, and perhaps more than that.

II. Stanley Hauerwas and the Community of Faith

When Hauerwas says, in his most systematic monograph since his doctoral dissertation (in which he studied the topic of character and its relationship to theological ethics), that "if we have a 'foundation' it is the story of Christ"[53], he is not simply indulging in pious talk. He is disclosing an entire theological program, a program which will seek to avoid the twin schools of fideism and rationalism. Note how Hauerwas' language succinctly displays his rejection of foundationalism and his recognition of the contextual character of all human knowing.

Fideism may be defined as a foundationalism of revelation; rationalism may be defined as a foundationalism of reason; they are both attempts to find a firm ground upon which to build the house of certainty. Thus they are cousins. But these cousins are, to continue the metaphor, so much members of the same family that they would die outside of it. In other words, they are both products of a very inner-Christian discussion about a very inner-Christian problem. That problem is the problem of the Christian community's encounter with the world of non-Christian thought. The problem is as old as the New Testament (for Christians; obviously, it is present before Christianity in the issue of Jewish/Gentile relations). It led Paul to excoriate all philosophy as "worldly wisdom" which can never grasp the folly of the cross. But it also led Justin Martyr not long after to see Christianity in the philosophy of the Greeks (the same philosophy which Paul had rejected). It led to the regularly renewed battle within Christianity between philosphers and theologians, between those who wish to perfect human reason, like Aquinas, and those who wish to plow it under, like Martin Luther, right on up to the recent dialogue between von Balthasar and Karl Rahner, in which the latter is accused of giving up the gospel in favor of philosophy.

Clearly, if one sets up these two terms as opposites, any attempt to deal with the "problem" of their opposition will be forever frustrating. Hauerwas refuses to see the issue in such terms:

> "Revelation" is not a qualifier of the epistemic status of a kind of knowledge, but rather points to the *content* of a certain kind of knowledge. We call knowledge about God "revelation", not because of the rationality or irrationality of such knowledge, but because of what that knowledge is about.[54]

Interestingly, Hauerwas can agree (sort of) with both sides in the ancient dispute, with both Justin Martyr and (to use a contemporary example) Karl Barth (in fact, Hauerwas shows quite a bit of Barth's influence). He can do this because, in a sense, both sides are right, and, in a sense, both sides are wrong. In other words, they got the *problem* wrong: "all knowledge of God is at once natural and revelatory."[55] Hauerwas can have it both ways because he does not find it necessary to separate knowledge derived from "reason" (and therefore, in some eyes, at least, "certain") from knowledge derived from revelation (which is derived from testimony, and, in some eyes at least, even more "certain" than the former). The reason he does not find it necessary so to separate knowledge from faith is that he uses the word "knowledge" in a way somewhat congenial to the way in which we have come to use it in this project. He sees it, in other words, as contextual, and the word "story" in the quoted phrase "story of Christ" more or less gives this away.

Thus, while Hauerwas never explicitly mentions Heidegger, for example, he would by no means be unsympathetic to the distinction between "present-at-hand" and "ready-to-hand" knowledge, where the latter is the primordial, the former, the derived, category. Nor, presumably, would he find cause to disagree with the general thrust, as interpreted by us, of Stephen Toulmin, Michael Polanyi, and Hubert Dreyfus. But the philospher who is quoted on page after page by Hauerwas is none of these but rather is Alasdair MacIntyre, with whom we are quite familiar and with whom we are quite sympathetic.

Against such a background, Hauerwas can see the ancient problem of reason and revelation as the problem of Christianity's relationship to the non- Christian world: how does our story relate to those strangers outside our gates? How does it account for them? It is an intellectual problem, to be sure, but it is an intellectual problem because it is first of all a problem for a group of people trying to understand who they are and what they should do.

Thus the *first question* which we wanted to put to Hauerwas--is it possible to do theology without resting it ulitmately on philosophy--is shown to be phrased in an unacceptable way. If we have learned anything in this project, it is that the phrasing of the question determines in some way the answer to that question. And this question displays in its phrasing the belief that philosophy and theology need to be related to each other as foundation is related to dwelling. But for Hauerwas, the "foundation", as he said quite clearly, is simply the story, and this is as true for philosophy as it is for theology. Both these enterprises are carried on within the context of a set of goals, methods and criteria which dwell in a particular group of people. That these groups are not sealed off from each other, that they have permeable boundaries, is precisely the problem: how do we reconcile our various communities of interpretation?

Thus Hauerwas' attitude to Tracy's concern with foundations would not be that Tracy should not be so concerned. But he would not see Tracy's enterprise as providing a firm rational foundation for Christian theology, but rather as a theologian's dialogue with his philosophical colleagues, some of whom share his theological commitments, some of whom do not. In a sense, of course, Tracy's enterprise is, even in its "foundational" phase, still strictly inner-theological. That is, when a Christian theologian reflects on the "philosophical" corrolaries of the faith, he does not cease to be a theologian, but is still motivated by the basic desire to find his faith illuminated. Perhaps it's impossible to separate these two aspects. As Karl Barth has helped us see, when a Christian theologian (like Anselm) seems to be operating on "purely philosophical" grounds, things may not be what they seem.

What then is theology for Stanley Hauerwas? As one might expect from what we have said so far, Hauerwas is not particularly interested in Tracy's distinction between foundational, systematic and practical theology. There is simply theology, all of which is practical, or it is not theology. The fact that Hauerwas' special interest is theological ethics makes this point even clearer, for ethics for Hauerwas is not a separate field within theology; all theology is "ethical", though some theologies are more obviously concerned with what the community of the day regards as pressing moral issues. Strict distinctions within theology tend to ignore the fact that "theology has no essence, but rather is the imaginative endeavor to explicate the stories of God by showing how one claim illuminates another."[56]

The surprising claim that "theology has no essence" points to the fact that "we must begin in the middle, that is, we must begin with a narrative."[57] Or, again: "Christian ethics does not, methodologically, have a starting point."[58] Of course, theology is not unique in being without an essence; in Hauerwas' use of the term, philosophy would also be so described. The difference between the two enterprises is not that one has a foundation and the other doesn't, or that one bases itself on reason and the other on a story, but that while both of them are "rational" and both of them depend on narrative, theology reflects on the story of Jesus, and philosophy reflects on the story of Plato and Socrates and Aristotle (and their successors in the Western intellectual tradition).

That these two traditions have enriched (and at times enraged) each other over the last two thousand years almost goes without saying. In some ways the *two traditions* have become so intertwined that it is hard to tell where one begins and the other leaves off. (Still another reason to be suspicious of Tracy's attempt to found theology on "universal reason"). But surely the key point is that we are dealing here with two traditions and not with "universal reason" and "special revelation". (To be sure, to speak of two traditions is a gross simplification: there are numerous traditions and traditions within traditions which we are here describing. But to recognize this fact does not damage, but actually strengthens, our point.)

If, as Hauerwas claims, theology has no essence, no foundation other than the story which it explicates, then we must give up the search for absolute certainty which has been at the heart of the foundationalist enterprise. We are never going to be relieved of ambiguity. But this is no cause for despair, nor does it mean that we cannot know the truth which makes us free. In fact, for Hauerwas, "we should not want to know if religious truths or convictions are functional; we should want to know if they are true."[59] This sentence could easily be misunderstood. What Hauerwas is saying is that religious truths or convictions are inauthentically used if they are supports for a morality arrived at *by other means*. This was the Enlightenment hermeneutic of religious convictions, or at least the familiar vulgarization of it: religion is valuable because it shores up morality. For this position Hauerwas has no patience, because it unhistorically assumes that there is such a thing as universal morality (arrived at--how else?--by universal reason) which all people can recognize, no matter what their cultural background. Drawing on the arguments advanced by Alasdair MacIntyre in After Virtue and already familiar to us, Hauerwas rejects such a universal morality. It denies human diversity and, not incidentally, opens the door to imperialism. But if a religious conviction is not simply a prop to morality, neither is it separable from the way we live our lives. Indeed, "learning how *Christian convictions are a morality* is crucial for understanding what it means to claim these convictions are true."[60] And so we may appear to be in a state of confusion. On the one hand, religious convictions are not merely functional, they are *true*; on the other hand, the fact that they are true is intimately bound up with the effect they have on our moral lives. Is Hauerwas in a muddle?

Hauerwas is by no means in a muddle. He is merely reflecting an ancient Christian conviction that before we can see rightly we must be transformed in our hearts. (And, of course, before we can be transformed we must see rightly.) Christian convictions, alive in a community of language and practice, *form* people who see the world in a particular way--*the true way:*

> Christian convictions do not poetically soothe the anxieties of the contemporary self. Rather, they transform the self to true faith by creating a community that lives faithful to the one true God of the universe. When self and nature are thus put in right relation we perceive the truth of our existence. But because truth is unattainable without a corresponding transformation of self, "ethics," as the investigation of that transformation, does not follow after a prior systematic presentation of the Christian faith, but is *at the beginning* of Christian theological reflection.[61]

St. Paul began a long Christian tradition when he connected the immorality of the pagans with their idolatry, i.e., their refusal to see rightly: "For although they knew God they did not honor him as God or give thanks to him, but they became futile in their thinking and their senseless minds were darkened...Therefore God gave them up in the lusts of their hearts to impurity, to the dishonoring of their bodies among themselves."(Romans 1:21, 22, 24) Only through God's grace could they now begin to see themselves as what they were, sinners. Only through God's grace could they begin to live an entirely new life. Paul gives the old Jewish anti-idolatry polemic a new twist when he uses it to explain his gospel of grace: since both the minds *and* the wills of the gentiles are dark there must be a transformation of both, a transformation which can only occur through the free gift of God.

Not so coincidentally, this brings us back to the central point of our discussion about Hans-Georg Gadamer: prudence. Prudence as the accumulated practical wisdom of the *polis*, embodied in the person of experience, is absolutely primary to everything else. Without that intellectual virtue, one can neither see nor do, neither know nor act. Thus the Christian community is by no means unique in the fact that its members must be transformed (whether in their primary formation, as children, or late, through conversion) before they can understand what is going on. "Ethics" in this sense is indeed primary in every community, because each community's customs and mores are logically prior to, and form the background for, whatever it does.

Prudence, then, is at the heart of the Christian community. But we must be careful here. We wish to avoid the facile and incorrect assumption that the Christian vocabulary merely particularizes the vocabulary we derived from Aristotle. The point is not that every community has its wisdom, and the Christian community calls *its* wisdom by this name or that name. For better or worse, the Christian community has always made a stronger claim than this. As Hauerwas insists, Christian convictions are *true*, and, in many cases, Christian convictions explicitly contradict the convictions of other communities, communities which we could join.

We now come again, to a problem that continues to vex us. If "truth" simply means that which is disclosed in this particular community, then we seem to be faced with a narrow relativism. Outside of this conversation, nothing can even begin to count as true. All that we can do is affirm the (admittedly) rich and subtle truth which is disclosed in our particular traditon, and, if possible, develop and advance it. To talk with those who have not been "transformed", as Paul discovered in his abortive attempt to talk philosophy with the Greeks, is useless. All we can do is to proclaim the word, and, if by the mysterious grace of God some are moved to join us, then our response is gratitude, not self-satisfaction.

What we have done, then, is to reach the *second question* which we wanted to ask: Is it possible to see knowledge as communal without creating problems with other communities? Ultimately, in such a perspective as we have been adopting, different human communities seem to be simply *barbaroi* to each other, those who utter nonsense syllables, those who are not human. When one encounters such people, one unsheathes one's sword. One of the professed merits of the notion of universal reason is that it enables us to see each other, not as strangers, but as sharers in the common *logos*. We can agree with each other because we are all rational creatures. We have seen that this notion has its dangers. Hauerwas alerts us to the fact that the very notion which seems to bind us together--universal reason--can be and has been used to justify the imposition of one culture's view of reality upon another. The trouble with universal reason seems to be that what looks like universal reason to us is not all that universal. So once again, we are trapped in the seemingly hopeless choice of relativism in which nothing genuinely new can penetrate, or an objectivism which eventuates in a sterile will-to-power.

We recall at this point the Habermas-Gadamer debate, and the position we took with regard to that arguement, that ultimately we have no choice but to trust the tradition, the prudence imbedded in its words and practices, and thus imbedded in us, to be sufficiently self-correcting to allow truth to disclose itself. We spoke of the openness which characterizes the person of experience as opposed to the person captivated by dogma, an openness which is really the willingness to suffer.

Gadamer suggests that the discovery that truth requires an openness must be paid for in the coin of suffering--and that discovery is a religious one. It is important that Gadamer says this, for he is open to the charge that he is, in his own way, developing a transcendental analysis of human conversation, disclosing the conditions for the possibility of communication. What Gadamer does *not* admit is that his insight into the religious character of suffering and openness is not unrelated-- could hardly be unrelated--to the fact that Gadamer is a Christian.

It is at this most delicate point that Hauerwas is able to come to our aid. For Hauerwas it couldn't be clearer that "violence and coercion become conceptually intelligible from a natural law standpoint...The universal presumptions of natural law make it more difficult to accept the very existence of those who disagree with us."[62] How then do we relate to the rest of the world if we cannot assume on philosophical grounds that we can have a point of agreement with them? Once again: how can we escape relativism and fidesim? The answer is surely obvious. *What if there is a community in whose very language and practices, in whose very tradition, is an attitude of suffering love toward the stranger?*

Every community must have some sort of account of the "others"--the dark strangers who do not speak our language. For most communities that account is essentially secondary and defensive. But the Christian community not only has an account of the rest of the world, it is in some way constituted by its mission to them; it is a missionary movement. For Hauerwas, to say that Christian convictions are "true" is, in part, to say that they are not simply true "for us" but for others as well:

> The less sure we are of the truth of our religious convictions the more we consider them immune from public scrutiny. But in the process we lose what seems essential to their being true, namely that we be willing to commend them to others. For the necessity of witness is not accidental to Christian convictions; it is at the heart of the Christian life.[63]

Here Hauerwas gives nothing to Tracy in his concern for the "public" character of Christian convicitons. But notice that the source of this publicness is not universal reason, but the command of Jesus to go forth and preach the gospel, the "good news" which by definition must be told to others if it is to be still regarded as "news." The "others" to whom that news must be preached are central to the community:

> Jesus' openness to the "unclean", for example, is but one of the ways we see how his understanding of God's sovereignty was a challenge to that of the Pharisees. Such openness denotes that the

community created by that kingdom cannot shield
itself from the outsider. It must have confidence that
God is present even in the unclean--a confidence
made possible only because the community itself was
formed by the presence of the ultimate stranger,
Jesus Christ.[64]

What the openness to the stranger means is that one must love
even that stranger who makes himself our enemy, a love which
must extend to the acceptance of violence from that stranger.
The Christian analogue for the concern for universal reason as
the basis for universal human community is simply the love for
the stranger whose exemplification is the cross of Jesus.

To those who believe that, through technique or coercion
or education we can come, finally, to universal agreement,
Christianity preaches the cross. The cross here is not simply a
symbol of the inadequacy of all human notions of God, as in
Tillich; still less is it the event of the atonement whereby
a distant Father-God is appeased by the sacrifice of His son.
Rather, the cross is the revelation that the reign of God will
only come through the suffering love of the people of God as
they open themselves to the stranger outside the gates:

Jesus' cross, however, is not merely a general symbol
of the moral significance of self-sacrifice. The cross
is not the confirmation of the facile assumption that it
is better to give than to receive. Rather the cross is
Jesus' ultimate dispossession through which God has
conquered the powers of this world. The cross is not
just a symbol of God's kingdom; it is that kingdom
come. It is only by God's grace that we are enabled
to accept the invitaion to be part of that kingdom.
Because we have confidence that God has raised this
crucified man, we believe that forgiveness and love
are alternatives to the coercion the world thinks
necessary for existence. Thus, our true nature, our
true end, is revealed in the story of this man in whose
life, we believe, is to be found the truth.[65]

Thus the question whether it is possible to conceive of knowledge as basically communal without lapsing into a barbaric narrowness is answered by imagining a special kind of community, a community whose very language and practices point it to heroic openness to the rest of the human race. This is a community whose self-definition sets it apart from all others, precisely and paradoxically because it wishes to be open to them. A strange community is this, for it does not regard its own continuation as a goal; a realistic community is this, for it sees clearly that the price to be paid for truly universal community is a bloody one; but, says Hauerwas, finally a joyful community is this, for in living out the story of the suffering love of God-in-Jesus, the community experiences the freeing truth that in order to save one's life one must lose it. The community experiences the peace of the resurrection.

Resurrection peace, says Hauerwas, is the peace which comes when one has given up the need to control everything, to possess everything, including the self, including even the truth. Through the passage of crucifixion-resurrection, Christians understand that "unless we learn to relinquish our presumption that we can ensure the significance of our lives, we are not capable of the peace of God's kingdom."[66] Hauerwas employs the familiar concept of sabbath, the day of rest, to describe the special character of the Christian community:

> In effect Jesus is nothing less than the embodiment of God's sabbath as a reality for all people. Jesus proclaims peace as a real alternative, because he has made it possible to rest--to have confidence that our lives are in God's hands. No longer is the sabbath one day, but the *form of life* of a people on the move. God's kingdom, God's peace, is a movement of those who have found the confidence through the life of Jesus to make their lives a constant worship of God. We can rest in God because we are no longer driven by the assumption that we must be in control of history, that it is up to us to make things come out right.[67] (Italics mine.)

Odd as it may seem, the philosophical problem of truth, the epistemological question, is inseparably linked with the notion of a non- violent community, a community which is willing to risk death rather than coerce anyone. To say that knowledge is basically communal, as we have asserted, is also to say that the non-violent character of the community is the chief determinant of the dependibility of its knowledge. Only a community which is confident of its own fallibility, which has been freed of the need to coerce, can know the truth. (This line of thinking can function as an examination of conscience for those, like the author, in the Catholic tradition: is the notion of the infallibility of the pope, for example, a barrier to error or is it a panicked reaction to the fact that the people are refusing to listen to us?) Only a community which knows how to deal with its own mistakes--which can, in other words, accept forgiveness--can continue to be open to the novelties which the future continually discloses:

> To be forgiven means that I must face the fact that my life actually lies in the hands of others. I must learn to trust them as I have learned to trust God. Thus it is not accidental that Jesus teaches us to pray for our daily bread. We cannot live to insure our ultimate security, but must learn to live on a day-to-day basis. Or, perhaps better, we must be a people who have learned not to fear surprises as a necessary means to sustain our lives. For, ironically, when we try to exclude surprise from our life, we are only more subject to the demonic.[68]

Every tradition can point with sorrow to the times in its history when the fear of "surprise" led to vicious repression.

To see non-violence as truly central to the Christian community is to come upon a host of difficulties. Is this non-violence absolute? Is self- defense or the defense of the innocent to be denied to Christians? This is a question as old as Jesus' command to turn the other cheek. It is clear that Hauerwas' heart is indeed with those, like John Howard Yoder, who argue that pacifism is integral to the Christian message, rather than with those who, like Reinhold Niebuhr, regard violence as a regrettable but sometimes necessary demand of the Christian life in an evil world.

It is clear that Christians today have an uneasy conscience about the whole question, unable to reconcile the teaching they carry in their very bones about meekness, humility and gentleness, with what they regard as the absolute necessity to defend the innocent from the powerful, or (hard as this may be to admit) with the demonstrated need of human beings to feel the exhilaration of the *agon*, the contest. (We could do worse here than recall William James' discussion of the need to find a "moral equivalent to war".)

The conversation goes on within the Christian household, which is as it should be. And Hauerwas has no desire to turn "non-violence" into an absolute above the Christian conversation by which the conversation might be judged. This would be the opposite of a true openness to the Other which the doctrine of non-violence expresses. And surely a nation which feels compelled to call its missiles "peacemakers" is trying (perhaps hypocritically) to stay within that Christian conversation, a conversation where the best thing to do to the enemy is to love him, rather than conquer him.

Thus Christians are the people whose very existence as a people is determined by their mission to spread peace in the world, "to all nations". (Mt 28:19) This is universality of a sort, though that word has too Greek a provenance. "All nations" gives Christianity a *direction* rather than a *terminus*, a mission rather than a clear picture of a goal. It gives Christians, to sum up, a way of life, the way of peace, which is at once the way and the end.

But there were three questions which we wanted to explore with Hauerwas, and the third question was the one which began this entire work, namely, *what is faith*? And so the question that Hauerwas himself asks in his book is remarkably apt: "What does our having 'faith' have to do with the way of life?"[69] Hauerwas' question suggests that there is a link between our second question and the third, between the way of life of a non-violent people and the question of faith. Actually, this link was fairly obvious even in our discussion of that second question, but it can now be made even more explicit.

And so, what, after all, is *faith*? We have seen, in our discussion of the scriptural record and the tradition, that it is not an univocal concept, meaning only one thing, but is rich and many-sided. Efforts to restrict faith purely to the intellectual or purely to the volitional fall prey to the obvious fact that the word has always been used in a sense which includes both, even by those who would, in theory, restrict its primary meaning to one or the other. For Hauerwas,

> Faith is our appropriate response to salvation, and it is fundamentally a moral response and transformation. Faith for Paul is not some mystical transformation of the individual; rather it is to be initiated into a kingdom. Faith is not belief in certain propositions, though it involves the attitude and passion of trust. Faith is not so much a combination of belief and trust, as simply fidelity to Jesus, the initiator of God's kingdom of peace...Faith is, in effect, finding our true life within the life of Christ...But notice that this life is fundamentally a social life. We are "in Christ" insofar as we are part of that community pledged to be faithful to this life as the initiator of the kingdom of peace.[70]

This may seem to be thin gruel after all we have been through. But note that Hauerwas is saying something very similar to what we suggested in chapter one was going to be our own view of faith. We suggested there that faith was the *fact* and *style* of a community, and as such fundamentally *social*. Christian faith, as Hauerwas says here, is finding ourselves as members of a particular community and living out our lives as authentic members of that community. As we have also suggested before, it is not so helpful to focus on the "initiation" aspect of faith. If faith is seen as the initiation into the kingdom, then what do we call the continuing attitude of openness and fidelity? Our whole approach tends to be suspicious of attempts to find an isolated moment when faith begins. Rather, faith is the continuing and ever- widening life of this community.

Note that "faith" here seems to be contentless. It can only be specified as the community goes along, applying its accumulated wisdom and prudence in each new moment, discovering what the Christian way of life is only as it lives it and not before. As such, perhaps we can say that"faith" is not necessarily Christian, for there are many communities, many kinds of fidelity. But there is something peculiarly Christian about faith, after all, as we already saw in our discussion of Tracy. *For Christianity is the community where faith is an issue, where the obvious truth that faith is the foundation of all community is made explicit.* We might say that this is a *formal* characteristic of Christian faith. *Materially*, of course, Christian faith is the fidelity of this particular community which follows this man Jesus and which carries on in its language and practices his very life. But the material and the formal are not separate: *Christianity is the community in whose material practices is revealed a formal truth about faith, namely, that to know anything is to be faithful, that to do anything is to be faithful, that to be human is to be faithful.*

There is something more, of course. The Christian community does not simply reveal that faith is necessary, that faith is both *that* and *how* we live; it goes further. It proclaims that faith is worthwhile, or, better, that in the very fact that in each community there is a giving-over-of-ourselves to each other lies hidden the deeper fact that this giving-over is justified. Resurrection faith finally allows us to give ourselves because God can be trusted. The Christian tradition is not wrong in its constant teaching that, ultimately, the ground of faith is God, and not simply this community, and that God cannot be grasped.

Notes

1. David Tracy, <u>The Analogical Imagination</u>, (New York: Crossroads, 1981), p.xi.

2. Tracy p. 6.

3. David Tracy, <u>Blessed Rage for Order</u> (New York: Seabury, 1979), p. 7.

4. Tracy, BRO, p. 7.

5. Tracy, BRO, p. 8.

6. Tracy, BRO, p. 8.

7. Tracy, <u>The Analogical Imagination</u>, p. 9.

8. See: Bernard Lonergan, <u>Method in Theology</u>, (New York: Herder and Herder, 1972), p. 53.

9. Tracy, AI, p. 13.

10. Tracy, AI, p. 13.

11. Tracy, AI, p. 12.

12. Though all specialties relate, ultimately, to all three publics. Cf., p. 29.

13. Tracy, p. 21.

14. Tracy, p. 24.

15. Tracy, p. 22.

16. Tracy, p. 24.

17. Tracy, p. 25.

18. Tracy, p. 63.

19. Tracy, p. 57.

20. Tracy, p. 68.

21. Tracy, p. 130.

22. Tracy, p. 131.

23. Tracy, p. 132.

24. Tracy, p. 132.

25. Tracy, AI, p. 200.

26. Tracy, AI, p. 200.

27. Tracy, AI, p. 237.

28. Tracy, AI, p. 238.

29. Tracy, AI, pp. 264-265.

30. Tracy, AI, p. 266.

31. Tracy, AI, p. 267.

32. Tracy, AI, p. 274.

33. Tracy, AI, p. 269.

34. Tracy, AI, p. 272.

35. Tracy, AI, p. 272.

36. Charles M. Wood, <u>The Formation of Christian Understanding</u> (Philadelphia: Westminster, 1981), p. 103.

37. Tracy, p. 274.

38. Tracy, p. 275.

39. Tracy, p. 275.

40. Tracy, p. 278.

41. Tracy, p. 326.

42. Tracy, p. 282.

43. Tracy, p. 284.

44. Tracy, p. 312.

45. Tracy, p. 313.

46. Tracy, p. 323.

47. Tracy, p. 323.

48. Tracy, p. 324.

49. Tracy, p. 324.

50. Tracy, p. 324.

51. Tracy, p. 330.

52. Tracy, p. 332.

53. Stanley Hauerwas, <u>The Peacable Kingdom</u>, (Notre Dame: University of Notre Dame Press, 1983), p. 67.

54. Hauerwas, p. 66.

55. Hauerwas, p. 66.

56. Hauerwas, p. 62.

57. Hauerwas, p. 62.

58. Hauerwas, p. 62.

59. Hauerwas, p. 15.

60. Hauerwas, p. 16.

61. Hauerwas, p. 16.

62. Hauerwas, p. 61.

63. Hauerwas, p. 14.

64. Hauerwas, p. 85.

65. Hauerwas, p. 87.

66. Hauerwas, p. 86.

67. Hauerwas, p. 87.

68. Hauerwas, p. 89.

69. Hauerwas, p. 93.

70. Hauerwas, p. 93.

Conclusion

At the end of a project like this, it is customary to look back and sum up what has been learned. In retrospect, the central message turns out to be extremely simple, even obvious: when humans know anything, they seem to do so against a rich background of which they are necessarily unaware. Humans are, in other words, historical, communal, bodily creatures. Thus, faith turns out to be the underside of any act of knowing. Unless some things can be taken for granted, nothing can be taken at all. Unless some things are allowed to remain unquestioned, nothing can be doubted. Unless some things are believed, nothing can be known.

Reflection uncovers a tragic dimension to human knowing and believing. If knowledge and faith go together, then knowledge is as precarious as faith. Gadamer tells us that the search for truth requires an openness which must be painful to be authentic. If it were not painful to be wrong and confused, human beings would not have spent lifetimes searching for certainty. Openness to the truth requires us to be willing to admit we were wrong, and this willingness has no logical place to stop until it reaches what we might call, with Yeats, "the rag-and-bone shop of the heart."

The Christian cross is not really the translation into religious language of this philosophical insight of Gadamer; it's the other way around. Gadamer's insight shows how a Christian might speak about truth when he is not talking to other Christians.

To conclude a discussion of faith with the cross and suffering may seem to end sadly. There does seem no way to get around the fact that faith is a sign of human limitation. We see, if at all, "in a glass, darkly." But Christians have always made the startling claim that acceptance of the cross leads to resurrection joy. Faith is not alone, but arrives with hope and love. But that is matter for another investigation.

Bibliography

Achtemeier, Paul. *An Introduction to the New Hermeneutic.* Philadelphia: Westminster Press, 1964.

Aristotle. *The Nichomacheann Ethics.* Translated by J. A. K. Thompson. New York: Penguin Books, 1955.

Bellah, Robert N. *Beyond Belief.* New York: Harper and Row, 1970.

Berger, Peter L. and Luckman, Thomas. *The Social Construction of Reality.* Gardner City, New Jersey: Doubleday, 1966.

Bernstein, Richard J. *Beyond Objectivism and Relativism.* Philadelphia: University of Pennsylvania Press, 1983.

Bleicher, Joseph. *Contemporary Hermeneutics.* London: Toutledge and Kegan Paul, 1980.

Brown, Robert McAfee. "My Story and 'The Story.'" *Theology Today* 32 (July1975): 166-73.

Congar, Yves. "Norms of Christian Allegiance and Identity in the History of theChurch." Translated by John Griffiths. in *Truth and Certainty,* pp. 11-26. (*Concilium* 83) Edited by Edward Schillebeeckx and Bas van Iersel. New York: Herder and Herder, 1973.

Crites, Stephen. "The Narrative Quality of Experience." *Journal of the American Academy of Religion* 39 (September 1971): 291.

_____. "Myth, Story, History." In *Parable, Myth and Language.* Edited by Tony Stoneburner. Cambridge: Church Society for CollegeWork, 1968.

Davis, Charles. *Body as Spirit.* New York: Seabury, 1976.

_____. "The Theological Career of Historical Criticism of the Bible."*Cross Currents* 32 (Fall 1982): 267-284.

Dreyfus, Herbert. *What Computers Can't Do*. New York: Doubleday, 1978.

Dulles, Avery. *Models of the Church*. New York: Doubleday, 1978.

_____. *The Survival of Dogma*. New York: Crossroad, 1982.

Dilthey, Wilhelm. *Selected Writings*. Edited and Translated by H. P. Rickman.Cambridge: Cambridge University Press, 1976.

Ebeling, Gerhard. *The Nature of Faith*. Philadelphia: Fortress, 1987.

Farley, Edward. *Ecclesial Man*. Philadelphia: Fortress, 1975.

_____. "Theology and Practice Outside the Clerical Paradigm." In *Practical Theology*, pp. 21-41. Edited by Don S. Browning. San Francisco: Harper and Row, 1983.

Farrar, Frederick W. *A History of Interpretation*. New York: E. P. Dutton, 1886.

Frei, Hans. *The Eclipse of Biblical Narrative*. New Haven, Connecticut: Yale University Press, 1974.

Funk, Robert W. *Language, Hermeneutic and the Word of God*. New York: Harper and Row, 1966.

Gadamer, Hans-Georg. "The Historicity of Understanding as Hermeneutic Principle." In *Heidegger and Modern Philosophy*. Edited by Michael Murray. New Haven, Connecticut: Yale University Press, 1978.

_____. *Philosophical Hermeneutics*. Translated and Edited by David E. Linge. Berkely: University of California Press, 1976.

. "Practical Philosophy as a Model for the Social Sciences." *Research in Phenomenology* 9 (1980): 74-85.

_____. *Reason in the Age of Science.* Translated by Frederick G.Lawrence. Cambridge, Massachusetts: MIT Press, 1975.

_____. *Truth and Method.* Translated and Edited by Garret Barden andJohn Cumming. New York: Seabury Press, 1975.

_____. *Wahrheit und Methode.* Tubingen: J. C. B. Mohr, 1975.

Giblet, Jean. "Aspects of the Truth in the New Testament." Translated by Dinah Livingstone. In *Truth and Certainty*, pp. 35-42. (*Concilium* 83)Edited by Edward Schillebeeckx and Bas van Iersel. New York: Herder and Herder, 1973.

Grant, Robert M. *A Short History of the Interpretation of the Bible.* New York: Macmillan, 1963.

Gustafson, James. "A Theology of Christian Community." In *The Church as Moral Decision Maker*, pp. 63-80. Philadelphia: Pilgrim Press, 1970.

Haan, Norma; Bellah, Robert N., et. al.. *Social Science as Moral Inquiry.* NewYork: Columbia University Press, 1983.

Habermas, Juergen. *Knowledge and Human Interests.* Translated by Jeremy J.Shapiro. Boston: Beacon Press, 1971.

_____. "A Review of Gadamer's Truth and Method." *In Understanding and Social Inquiry,* pp. 353-363. Edited by Fred R. Ballmayr and Thomas McCarthy. Notre Dame, Indiana: Notre Dame University Press, 1977.

_____. "Summation and Response." *Continuum* 8 (1970), pp. 123-133.

Haroutunion, Joseph. *God Is with Us.* Philadelphia: Westminster Press, 1965.

Hart, Ray L. *Unfinished Man and the Imagination: Toward an Ontology and a Rhetoric of Revelation.* New York: Seabury Press, 1979.

Hauerwas, Stanley. "Casuistry as a Narrative Art." *Interpretation* 37 (October,1983): 377-388.

_____. *Character and the Christian Life.* San Antonio: Trinity University Press, 1975.

_____. *A Community of Character.* Notre Dame, Indiana: University of Notre Dame Press, 1981.

_____. *The Peaceable Kingdom* . Notre Dame, Indiana: University of Notre Dame Press, 1983.

_____. *Vision and Virtue.* Notre Dame, Indiana: University of Notre Dame Press, 1974.

Hauerwas, Stanley, with Bondi, Richard, and Burrell,David B. *Truthfulness and Tragedy.* Notre Dame, Indiana: University of Notre Dame Press, 1977.

Heidegger, Martin. *Being and Time.* Translated by John Macquarrie and EdwardRobinson. New York: Harper and Row, 1962.

_____. *Discourse on Thinking* . Translated by John M. Anderson and Hans Freund. New York: Harper and Row, 1966.

_____. *Identity and Difference.* Translated by Kurt F. Leidecker. New York: Philosophical Library, 1960.

_____. "Only a God Can Save Us." (The Spiegel Interview) In *Heidegger: The Man and the Thinker.* Edited by Thomas Sheehan.Chicago: Precedent Publishing Company, 1981.

_____. *On Time and Being.* Translated by Joan Stambaugh. New York:Harper and Row, 1972.

_____. *Poetry, Language and Thought.* Translated by Albert Hofstadter. New York: Harper and Row, 1971. .e Hermann, Ingo. The Experience of Faith. Translated by Daniel Coogan. New York: P.J. Kennedy & Sons, 1966.

Johann, Robert O. *The Pragmatic Meaning of God.* Milwaukee: Marquette University Press, 1966.

Kelsey, David. *The Uses of Scripture in Recent Theology.* Philadelphia: Fortress Press, 1975.

Knox, John. *The Early Church and the Coming Great Church.* New York: Abingdon, 1955.

Kockelmans, Joseph, editor and translator. *On Heidegger and Language.* Evanston: Northwestern University Press, 1972.

Kuhn, Thomas S. *The Structure of Scientific revolutions.* 2d. ed. enl. Chicago: The University of Chicago Press, 1972.

Lakatos, Imre, and Musgrave, Alan, eds. *Criticism and the Growth of Knowledge.* Cambridge: Cambridge University Press, 1970.

Lehmann, Paul. *Ethics in a Christian Context.* New York: Harper and Row, 1963.

Lynch, William F. *Images of Faith.* Notre Dame, Indiana: University of Notre Dame Press, 1973.

McClendon, James Wm., Jr., and Smith, James M. *Understanding Religious Convictions.* Nashville: Abingdon Press, 1974.

McCarthy, Thomas. *The Critical Theory of Juergen Habermas.* Cambridge, Massachusetts: MIT Press, 1978.

MacIntyre, Alasdair. After Virtue: *A Study in Moral Theory*.
     Notre Dame, Indiana: University of Notre
     Dame Press, 1981.

_____. *Against the Self-Images of the Age*. New York:
     Schocken Books, 1971.

_____. "Epistemological Crises, Dramatic Narrative and
     the Philosophy of Science." *Monist* 60 (1977):
     453-72.

_____. *A Short History of Ethics*. New York:
     Macmillam, 1966.

Misgeld, Dieter. "Critical Theory and Hermeneutics: The
     Debate BetweenHabermas and Gadamer." In
     On Critical Theory, edited by John
     O'Neill. New York: Seabury Press, 1976.

Mooney, Michael, Joseph Koechler, John Dinges, and Michael
     C. Scheible, eds., *Toward a Theology of
     Christian Faith*. New York: P.J. Kennedy &
     Sons, 1968.

Moltmann, Jurgen. *The Church in the Power of the Spirit*.
     Translated by Margaret Kohl. New York:
     Harper & Row, 1977.

_____. *The Crucified God*. Translated by R.A. Wilson
     and John Bowden.New York: Harper & Row,
     1974.

Moran, Gabriel. *Religious Education Development*. New
     York: Winston Press, 1983.

Murphy-O'Connor, Jerome. *Becoming Human Together*.
     Wilmington, Delaware: Michael Glazier, Inc.,
     1977.

Newman, John Henry. *An Essay on the Development of
     Christian Doctrine*. Harmondsworth,
     - Middlesex, England: Penguin Books, 1974.

Niebuhr, H. Richard. *The Meaning of Revelation*. New York:
     Macmillan, 1941.

_____. *The Responsible Self: An Essay in Christian Moral Philosophy.* New York: Harper and row, 1978.

_____. Ommen, Thomas B. *The Hermeneutics of Dogma.* Missoula, Montana: Scholars Press, 1975.

Owens, Joseph. "Aristotle's Contribution on the Nature of Ethical Norms." *Listening* 18 (Fall 1983): 225-234.

Palmer, Richard E. *Hermeneutics: Interpretation Theory in Schleiermacher, Dilthey, Heidegger, and Gadamer.* Evanston, Illinois: Northwestern University Press, 1969.

Polanyi, Michael. *Knowing and Being.* Edited by Marjorie Greene. Chicago: University of chicago Press, 1969.

_____. *Personal Knowledge.* Chicago: University of Chicago Press, 1962.

_____. *Science, Faith, and Society.* Chicago: University of Chicago Press, 1946.

_____. *The Study of Man.* Chicago: University of Chicago Press,1959.

Polanyi, Michael, and Harry Prosch. *Meaning.* Chicago: University of Chicago Press, 1975.

Rabinow, Paul, and Sullivan, William M., eds. *Interpretive Social Science: A Reader.* Berkeley: University of California Press, 1979.

Rahner, Karl. *Do You Believe In God?.* Translated by Richard Strachan. New York: Newman, 1969.

_____. *Kerygma and Dogma.* Translated by William Glen-Doepel. New York: Herder and Herder, 1969.

_____. *Revelation and Tradition.* Translated W. J. O'Hara. New York: Herder and Herder, 1966.

Ramsey, Ian T. *Models and Mystery.* London: Oxford University Press, 1964.

Ricoeur, Paul. *The Conflict of Interpretations: Essays in Hermeneutics.* Edited by Don Ihde. Evanston: Northwestern University Press, 1974.

_____. *Interpretation Theory: Discourse and the Surplus of Meaning.* Fort Worth: Texas christ University Press, 1976.

_____. *The Philosophy of Paul Ricoeur.* Edited by Charles Reagan and David Stewart. Boston: Beacon Press, 1974.

_____. "The Task of Hermeneutics." In *Heidegger and Modern Philosophy.* Edited by Michael Murray. New Haven: Yale University Press, 1978.

Robinson, James M. and Cobb, John B. Jr., eds. *The Later Heidegger and Theology.* New York: Harper and Row, 1963.

Rorty, Richard. "Method and Morality." In *Social Science as Moral Inquiry*, pp. 155-176. Edited by Norma Haan, Robert Bellah et.al. New York: Columbia University Press, 1983.

Schillebeeckx, Edward. "The Crisis in the Language of Faith as a Hermeneutical Problem." Translated by David Smith. In *The Crisis of Religious Language*, pp. 31-45. (*Concilium* 85) Edited by Johann Baptist Metz and Jean-Pierre Jossua. New York: Herder and Herder, 1973.

_____. *Christ: The Experience of Jesus as Lord.* Translated by John Bowden. New York: Crossroads, 1983.

Schleiermacher, Friedrich. *Hermeneutics: The Handwritten Manuscripts*. Edited by Heinz Kimmerle. Translated by James Duke and Jack Forstman.Missoula, Montana: Scholars Press, 1977.

Schneiders, Sandra. "The Foot Washing (John 13: 1-20): An Experiment in Hermeneutics." *Cathlic Biblical Quarterly* 43 (January 1981).

Shils, Edward. *Tradition*. Chicago: University of Chicago Press, 1981.

Tillich, Paul. *The Dynamics of Faith* . new York: Harper and Row, 1957.

_____. *Systematic Theology,* Volume One. Chicago: University of Chicago Press, 1951.

Tracy, David. *The Analogical Imagination:* Christian Theology and the Culture of Pluralism. New York: Crossroad, 1981.

_____. *Blessed Rage for Order: The New Pluralism in Theology*. New York: Seabury, 1975.

_____. "The Foundations of Practical Theology." In *Practical Theology,* pp. 61-82. Edited by Don S. Browning. San Francisco: Harper and Row, 1983.

Troeltsch, Ernst. *The Absoluteness of Christianity and the History of Religions*. Translated by David Reid. Richmond, Virginia: John Knox Press, 1971.

Wheelwright, Philip. *Metaphor and Reality*. Bloomington, Indiana: Indiana University Press, 1962.

Wilder, Amos Niven. *Theopoetic: Theology and the Religious Imagination*. Philadelphia: Fortress Press, 1976.

Williams, Bernard. *Morality: An Introduction to Ethics*. New York: Harper Torchbooks, 1972.

Yoder, John Howard. *The Politics of Jesus.* Grand Rapids: Eerdmans, 1973.

_____. "Radical Reformation Ethics in Ecumenical Perspective." *Journal of Ecumenical Studies*, Fall, 1978.